UNDER A
SICKLE MOON

A JOURNEY THROUGH
AFGHANISTAN

PEREGRINE HODSON

THE ATLANTIC MONTHLY PRESS
NEW YORK

◆

First published in Great Britain in 1986 by Hutchinson, London, England.

First American edition, 1987.

Library of Congress Cataloging-in-Publication Data

Hodson, Peregrine.
   Under a sickle moon.

   "Traveler."
   1. Afghanistan—Description and travel.
2. Hodson, Peregrine—Journeys—Afghanistan. I. Title.
DS352.H58   1987   915.8'10444   87-14386
ISBN 0-87113-161-7

Printed in the United States of America

First printing

Contents

Acknowledgements

I owe my thanks to many people, especially those inside Afghanistan who gave to me generously when they had almost nothing, who offered me shelter often at great risk to themselves and their families, and who trusted me to share their lives. I am also indebted to Peter Jouvenal and Julian Gearing for their companionship on the journey out of Afghanistan and for their kindness in providing photographs and information.

Kate Mosse and Reginald Boyle have patiently helped me correct a number of inaccuracies and inconsistencies in the text, as have Yaqub Kakar, Dr Sa'id Goodarznia, Dr Khan, Dr John Gurney and Richard Coltart, who have also given me invaluable specialist advice.

Peter and Cynthia Rockwell and their family, and Felix Pearson, have helped me with their friendship, humour and hospitality.

Richard Cohen, my editor, has managed a difficult manuscript with patience and nerves of steel, and has made many excellent suggestions.

Finally, the book might still be unfinished if it were not for Tara Howard, who took a mass of pages of near-illegible scrawl and produced a clear script. In time and energy, much of this book is hers.

Tokyo
June, 1986

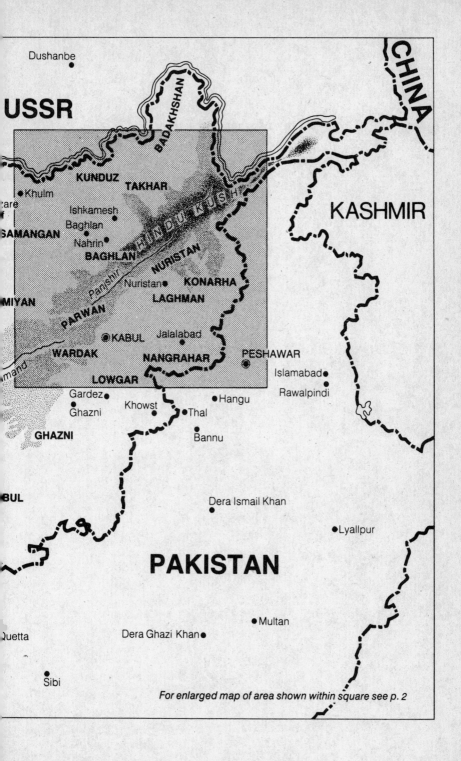

Dushanbe

CHINA

USSR

KASHMIR

BADAKHSHAN

KUNDUZ   TAKHAR

Khulm

are

Ishkamesh   HINDU KUSH

SAMANGAN   Baghlan

Nahrin   NURISTAN

BAGHLAN

MIYAN   Panjshir   Nuristan   KONARHA

PARWAN   LAGHMAN

KABUL   Jalalabad

WARDAK   PESHAWAR

NANGRAHAR

LOWGAR   Islamabad

mand   Gardez   Hangu   Rawalpindi

Ghazni   Khowst   Thal

GHAZNI   Bannu

BUL

Dera Ismail Khan

Lyallpur

PAKISTAN

Quetta   Multan

Dera Ghazi Khan

Sibi

For enlarged map of area shown within square see p. 2

To my Mother and Father

IN THE NAME OF GOD THE MERCIFUL THE COMPASSIONATE

Listen to the reed how it tells a tale complaining of separations

> The opening words of The Mathnawi
> of Jalal Uddin Balkhi Rumi,
> translated by R. A. Nicholson

For we wrestle not against flesh and blood, but against principalities, against powers, against the rulers of the darkness of this world, against spiritual wickedness in high places.

> Ephesians, Chapter VI verse 12

Introduction

This book is the account of a journey which I made through Afghanistan during the summer and autumn of 1984: it is not an analysis of the war or the politics of the region.

I travelled through the north-eastern part of Afghanistan, through the provinces of Lowgar, Wardak, Bamiyan, Samangan, Baghlan, Takhar, Kunar and Nuristan. On the way I talked with people about many things: the price of corn and Persian poetry, the swiftness of horses and the thousand names of God. Sometimes we talked of the war.

I kept a diary and made tape recordings of a number of these conversations. A substantial part of this book is drawn from passages in my diary and transcripts of the recordings: the rest is drawn from memory.

In the last days of 1979 the Afghanistan government, according to the December 31st edition of *Pravda*, 'made a request to the Soviet Union for the provision of immediate aid and support in the struggle against outside intervention. The Soviet Union decided to satisfy this request and to send to Afghanistan a limited Soviet military contingent which', the article continued, 'will be used exclusively to help repel armed interference from outside. The Soviet contingent will be completely withdrawn from Afghanistan when the factors that made this action necessary are no longer present.'

For a while the attention of the world was focused on Afghanistan. In January 1980, the U.N. General Assembly, by a 104–18 vote, passed a resolution calling for 'immediate, unconditional, and total withdrawal of foreign troops from Afghanistan'.

By February, there were 75,000 Soviet troops inside Afghanistan. At first, resistance to the Soviet presence was scattered and ineffective: although the mujahedin had the support of the greater part of the population, they lacked organisation and weapons. As a result, there were only minor skirmishes, and foreign journalists, who at that time, were still permitted to enter the country, saw little evidence of any fighting. Their reports were correspondingly un-

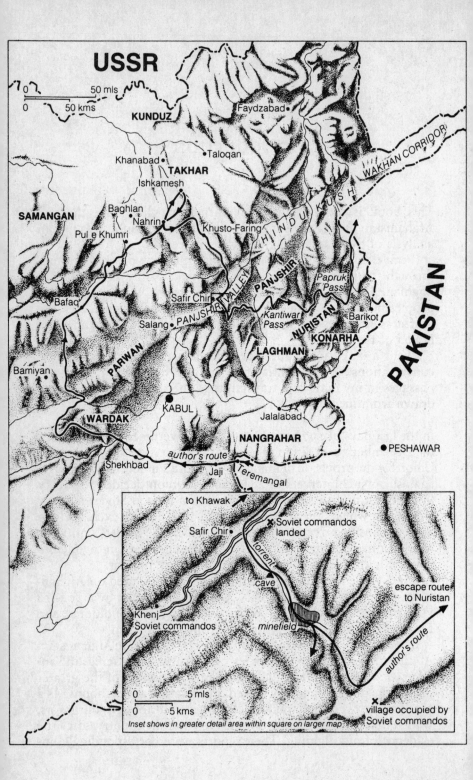

dramatic. Some doubted whether there was any real resistance at all, others considered opposition to the Soviet contingent was limited to a few bandits or so-called 'religious fanatics'.

By August, the number of Afghan refugees who had registered in Pakistan had reached one million. Meanwhile, the resistance was becoming better armed; either by capturing weapons from the Soviet forces or through widespread desertions on the part of native soldiers from the Afghan state army. Fighting intensified and the Soviet-backed government of Babrak Karmal banned all journalists from entering the country, except for those who could be relied on to give a favourable account.

Unlike Vietnam, difficulty of access made any sustained news coverage of the war almost impossible and, despite intermittent reports of heavy fighting and occasional television documentaries, Afghanistan gradually became known as a country whose war had been forgotten.

By the spring of 1984, the Soviet contingent had increased to some 120,000 troops, while over three million Afghans had fled their homes for the tented refugee camps in Pakistan and Iran. The number of those killed inside Afghanistan was unknown.

In March 1984, I approached the *Sunday Times* with my ideas for a report on the 'people's war'. They kindly provided me with letters of accreditation and said they would consider any article I wrote for publication.

The following month, I visited the Paris Information Office of representatives of the Afghan resistance, where I discussed my proposed journey with members of the Jamiat Islami. Together we decided that I should go to the north of Kabul, to a town called Nahrin. It seemed an appropriate destination for several reasons: I had studied Farsi at university and the language spoken in that part of Afghanistan was Dari, a form of Farsi; it was an ordinary Afghan town, which had been known for its pistachio industry before the war; and since the beginning of the year it had experienced aerial bombing.

Once I arrived there I would contact the regional mujahedin commander, Abdul Haq, who would look after me during my stay while I lived among the people of the town, recording impressions for an article to be written on my return to England.

Two months later I bought a ticket to Islamabad, telephoned my future employers to say that I would be back to start work at the beginning of September, and insured myself and my belongings with Lloyds of London.

I wanted my presence among the mujahedin to be as unobtrusive as possible, so I decided against taking equipment such as a tent or sleeping bags. Also, I dislike heavy luggage and, since I could only take what I was prepared to carry, I limited myself to a satchel and a small, frameless rucksack which contained the following:

3 pairs of cotton socks	1 pair of plimsolls
3 pairs of woollen socks	1 pair of boots
3 pairs of pants	1 jumper
3 shirts	1 handkerchief
needles and thread	imitation Swiss Army knife
assortment of pills	phial of iodine
2 rolls of bandages	glucose tablets
talcum powder	plasters
money belt	aluminium water bottle
camera and lenses	hand-held tape recorder
film	pens and pencils
Walkman	notepads
pocket Bible	Farsi grammar and dictionary
maps	comb
soap	toothbrush and toothpaste
spare pair of bootlaces	tapes (Bach, Vivaldi, The Doors, Bob Dylan)

I said goodbye to a few friends, my mother expressed the hope that I would not be a nuisance to the mujahedin and a week later I was in Peshawar, Pakistan.

Within a few days of my arrival I received a call from the Jamiat Islami political office, informing me that a party of mujahedin were about to set off towards Nahrin with supplies of arms and ammunition. I could accompany them if I liked, but they were already in the border town of Teremangal, and I would have to leave immediately.

I spent the night at the Jamiat Islami office. There I changed out of my Western clothes into a pair of loose-fitting trousers and a shirt of dark green cotton which I had bought in the bazaar earlier in the day.

My hosts found my name, unabbreviated, was difficult to pronounce, while in its shortened form it sounded like a word in Dari meaning 'fairy' or 'female angel': so I was given the name Abdul. I added the word 'baz', meaning falcon, and for the next few months I was Abdul Baz.

PART ONE

Teremangal

Early in the morning we arrived in Teremangal, a border town just inside Pakistan. It had rained the night before and the winding streets were thick in mud churned up by pack animals laden with supplies.

'Stay here, Abdul. Don't talk to anyone. Wait for a man called Mahmoud.' So said my guide, who promptly disappeared into the jostling crowds of men. With a sense of unease that was almost pleasurable I was on my own. Camel trains laden with great beams of rough-cut wood swayed past; small boys in ragged shirts threw stones at dogs that darted between the hooves of horses; chai sellers carrying trays of steaming tea stepped gingerly through the slush and horse-droppings; while beside me a couple of Pathans haggled over the price of a saddle. Everywhere there were men wrapped in dun-coloured petous and carrying guns.

I was squatting by the side of the road with the sun on my back and the smell of wood-smoke in the air but my thoughts were elsewhere: moving between images of Kipling and memories of charades. Three days before I had been lying on my bed at Green's Hotel in Peshawar, looking at the fan going round in the ceiling. At the time it had seemed faintly amusing that life could counterfeit cliché so realistically. Now I sensed, fleetingly, how a schoolboy dream could become a nightmare. I took refuge in the everyday: don't bother trying to understand what's going on, I told myself. Patience. Think of breakfast.

Two men were walking purposefully towards me. I turned away from them and stared at the hills on the other side of the valley. There was nothing to worry about, absolutely nothing to worry about. The two men were coming closer. Where on earth was Mahmoud? The men stopped in front of me. Damn. 'Abdul?' The taller of the two men was smiling. 'My name is Mahmoud.' I stood up and we shook hands.

Mahmoud was a broad-shouldered Tajik with a black beard and a bandolier of bullets hanging from his shoulder. He smiled too often and too easily for my liking. His companion was an Uzbeki with deep-set eyes and a sparse, wispy grey beard who seemed embarrassed to be in the company of the big, laughing Tajik. His name was Anwar. His clothes were of sunbleached grey cotton and there was a pistol in his belt.

'Come, Abdul,' said Mahmoud. 'Now we must meet the others, then you can have something to eat. Chai, kebabs, nan[1] – we have plenty of food here.'

I pulled my knapsack on to my back and followed them through the streets, watching the faces of the passers-by to see whether they noticed I was foreign. The few who glanced at me showed no surprise. It was reassuring. Mahmoud had a taste for the melodramatic and had warned me repeatedly with stage whispers and extravagantly secretive gestures to be on my guard – 'Whatever you do, don't look suspicious . . .' – until I had begun to feel like someone wearing a false nose and beard.

Eventually, at the end of a little lane, we came into a straw-littered courtyard. Some men were sitting on ammunition boxes drinking glasses of green tea and laughing; nearby a boy in a gold-embroidered cap was plucking a chicken.

Mahmoud called one of the men over and began talking to him in a dialect I couldn't understand. I watched the man's face carefully. It was middle-aged but heavily lined and difficult to interpret. At first his eyes were guarded and several times he looked at me as if to check what Mahmoud was saying. Gradually his face relaxed and at intervals he nodded in agreement. Then he stretched out, shook my hand and smiled. His companions, who had been silently gazing in our direction, turned to each other and began talking in lowered voices.

'He says you are *mehman*, his guest, and you are welcome for as long as you like.'

Mahmoud pointed to the second floor of a building where a ramshackle ladder was leaning against a wooden veranda. Several pairs of wide cotton trousers and socks hung limply from the railing, and at one end of the veranda coils of smoke billowed from a primitive stove. Mahmoud stepped heavily on to the first rung of the ladder.

Seeing Mahmoud's ample backside swaying up the ladder and hearing the protesting squeaks and cracks as he placed his feet on its fragile rungs, I waited until he was safely at the top before following him up.

'What's the matter, Abdul? You're not afraid?'

'You're a big man, Mahmoud.'

---

[1] A glossary appears on p. 216

'That's the truth!' He slapped his thigh and laughed extravagantly.

As I started to climb the ladder Anwar insisted on taking my pack
for me. Somewhat unsteadily I reached the top of the ladder and
stepped on to the veranda.

'Here you will eat and sleep until it is time to go,' said Mahmoud,
gesturing through a cloud of flies into the shadow of the doorway.
'Anwar and I have many things to do before the journey starts. We
must buy horses and provisions and check the weapons; and
everything costs money, doesn't it, Anwar? Wait for us. We will see
you later today or tomorrow, *Insha'allah*. Don't go anywhere else.
Otherwise the Pakistan police may see you, and then . . .' He
clenched his pudgy fists, one on top of the other, as if they were
handcuffed, 'Who knows? Pakistan prison isn't a good place,
Abdul. Be careful.'

I waved farewell to Mahmoud and the quiet Uzbeki, then kicked
off my muddied shoes and stepped into the shadows of the room
which was to be my home for the next few days. It was large, with a
high ceiling. At one end there was a window with a makeshift
curtain drawn against the heat: the ragged material was pierced by a
thin beam of sunlight which shone on to a patch of worn carpet. The
flaking plaster walls were hung with posters of Jamiat Islami
commanders and crudely drawn pictures of Karmal suffering in-
dignities at the points of assorted bayonets and swords. Next to the
door was a couch spread with grimy cushions; above it the phrase
'*La ilaha illa lahu*' had been painted in bold calligraphic script, and
there was a garishly coloured photograph of the Ka'aba.

I laid my pack in a corner and sat down beside it. My mind was
still thrumming with unfamiliar sights and sounds and, for the
moment at least, I was glad to be alone. I watched the particles of
dust moving in the sunlight, smelt the warm, sweet smell of boiling
rice and meat and listened to the sound of twigs being snapped for
kindling and of pots being scoured with sand.

A boy's figure appeared in the brightly lit doorway, paused, then
came towards me through the half shadows. I got up to greet him.
As we shook hands I tried to see his face but its details were lost
against the light. Releasing my fingers, he placed his hand over his
heart in a gesture that I learned to love and practise as my own.

'My name is Ali. I will bring you chai and nan,' he said, and went
out of the room.

A few minutes later he returned with a little aluminium tea pot
and a glass, which he placed in the band of light which stretched
across the threadbare red and orange carpet. He then sat down in
silence beside me.

He was young, no more than seventeen or eighteen, but his brown eyes held the gentle certainty of someone older. His features were clear and even: a softly aquiline nose, and lips that rested in a half smile. His face reminded me of a line of Sa'adi's poetry: 'Now that ants have covered the face of the moon . . .' Years before, at Oxford, I had found it an over-contrived metaphor: the moon-like beauty of the Beloved's face and the beginnings of a beard. Now I understood the meaning of the words.

I unpacked my Persian grammar and studiously ignored him. Nevertheless, I could sense him scrutinising my appearance: the comparative newness of my clothes; the slight differences of style between Afghan and Pakistan shirts, the collar, the sleeves; my thick woollen socks and the strange disjointed letters of the book I was reading.

His parents had been killed in a raid and after burying them and saying goodbye to his remaining brothers and sisters he had made the journey to Pakistan with his uncle. That was three years ago and since then they had lost touch with each other. Yes, one day he would cross the border and find his elder brother, *Insha'allah*. Until then he had to stay here, cooking for the groups of mujahedin. It was hard work, but the master of the chaikhane was a good man; he had enough to eat and, little by little, he was saving some money. Later he would join the mujahedin, but machine guns were expensive and almost impossible to buy for someone who was not a member of a group. He told me all this in a matter-of-fact tone of voice without a trace of bitterness.

'My parents are *shahid*, but my brothers and sisters are still in Afghanistan. One day I will return. Now I must prepare the midday meal. The men will be coming soon and they will be hungry – they have been working since before sunrise.'

As I sipped the tepid remains of the tea and wrote another entry in my diary, I tried to imagine what life was like on the other side of the border. I had clues – films and newspaper articles, statistics and eyewitness reports – but I was beginning to realise that I knew almost nothing at all about the reality. Reassuring myself with the thought that preparing for the unknown is a waste of time, I lit a cigarette and settled down to wait for the members of the group to arrive.

They came in twos and threes. The younger ones had Lee-Enfields over their shoulders, and the way they carefully unslung them, placing them reverently by their sides, suggested that they had only just received them. The others had Kalashnikovs, and they too seemed only half-familiar with their weapons. The oldest couldn't have been more than twenty-five, and when they looked at me they nervously avoided meeting my eyes. Finally, one of them came up to me and offered a boiled sweet.

'Are you French?'

'No, I'm English.'

'Are you a doctor?'

I explained that I wanted to write about the people of Afghanistan. He paused as if my answer were somehow meaningless. Then his features lit with a sudden idea.

'And are you coming with us?'

'*Insha'allah*.' I said.

'Then you are a mujahed.'

They sat cross-legged around the three walls of the room facing the door while Ali hurried in and out in preparation for the meal. First a long strip of cotton was spread over the floor, and on it he placed small bowls and glasses, one for each man. Then he reappeared with a tall metal ewer and a basin for all to wash their hands. This had to be done in order of seniority. Ali seemed uncertain whether or not to approach me first. Sensing his indecision, I said that I was not hungry and watched while he went round the semi-circle of men, stopping in front of each of them in turn to pour a trickle of water to moisten their hands outstretched over the basin, waiting while they carefully rubbed their hands clean and then pouring another trickle of water to rinse the dirt away. It was a skilful business to measure out the water for the score or so of men present and still leave enough for latecomers, but Ali completed his task easily.

After these ablutions, a bundle of nan loaves was brought in, followed by half a dozen large plates of rice, which were set at intervals along the row. Finally, the little boy in the gold-embroidered cap staggered in carrying a huge cauldron of stew which he ladled into the bowls. Only one man questioned his share and the others laughingly shouted him down. After murmuring a brief prayer, the men gathered into groups around the plates of rice and began to eat.

There was little conversation during the meal, but when the men had finished they washed their hands to remove the grease, said a prayer of thanks and began to talk. They told me how they had been in Peshawar for several weeks – resting up after the outward journey, seeing members of their families who had fled to Pakistan and buying supplies and presents for those who remained in Afghanistan. For most of them it was the first time they had left their country, and they were garrulous with their impressions of

Pakistan: its people, their comparative wealth and unfamiliar customs. Underlying everything they said was the secret envy of a people at war for a country at peace.

'The police do not trust us,' said the man next to me. 'Once a policeman saw me carrying a tape recorder which I bought in the Khyber Bazaar. He told me I was a thief and took it away from me. I shouted at him but he said he would throw me in prison.'

'It is wrong to steal from a brother Muslim,' commented his neighbour.

'There are many unbelievers in Pakistan. Perhaps they speak the words of the nemaz with their lips, but in their hearts they can only think of money.'

'The weather is too hot and the water is dirty. I was always ill,' said another.

'Wait, Abdul. When you come to our towns and villages you will drink clean water. It is cold and comes from the snow in the mountains.'

'And the kebabs are no good in Peshawar. In our town the kebabs are *this* big.'

'And the fruits are sweeter.'

'The grapes will be ripening in my garden, Abdul. They are the sweetest grapes in the world.'

Some of the men covered themselves with their petous and settled down to sleep. Others began meticulously oiling their guns or took out boxes of naswar which, after tipping some into their hands, they deftly flicked under their tongues and continued talking.

Naswar is a preparation of finely ground tobacco and spices. It is like snuff except that it is placed under the tongue and spat out after ten minutes or so. It varies in strength and colour; the darker it is, the more potent. Prolonged use damages the gums, and the sign of an inveterate naswar-taker is the absence of his lower front teeth. It has a hot, bitter taste and some prefer to keep their mouths slightly open while they are taking it, giving themselves a distinctly moronic expression. The art of taking naswar is to make sure that once it is under the tongue it stays there. Otherwise, it mixes with one's saliva and tastes revolting. Once the stimulant has been sufficiently absorbed into the blood-stream one scoops the naswar on to the tip of the tongue and spits it out. It is best not to swallow it.

Naturally, the first time I was offered naswar I knew nothing about it. A filthy old man sitting next to me, with a low forehead and green, saliva-stained teeth, grasped my wrist and, before I could stop him, tipped a generous amount of the mixture into the palm of my hand. While the others watched, he pretended to pour the contents of his box into his gaping mouth; winking furiously, he nodded encouragement to follow his example. I did so – it tasted vile. My first reaction was to spit it out, but the manners of the nursery prevailed. I sat there with my tongue burning and an unconvincing grin of pleasure on my face while the old man studied my reactions. Eventually I could endure it no longer, but what was I meant to do with the wretched stuff?

I remembered a story, probably apocryphal, of a candidate for All Souls, Oxford, who was invited to dinner at high table. All was going well until it came to the cherry pie and he was faced with the awful dilemma of what to do with the cherry stones. Should he spit them into his hand or slip them out on his spoon? Deciding that discretion was the better part of valour, he swallowed them. It seemed a good precedent so I followed his example and gulped the naswar down.

It was a mistake. 'Thank you very much – it was delicious,' was all I could manage before a wave of nausea struck the pit of my stomach. I began to sweat furiously and, for a moment, thought I was about to faint.

'He's swallowed it!' someone exclaimed. 'Abdul has swallowed the naswar! Quick, Ali, get some water.'

Through a semi-conscious haze I could just make out a circle of faces; some laughing and some concerned. The old man leered at me companionably.

'Abdul, if you swallow it your head will turn like a wheel and your heart will beat like a drum. You should do like this . . .' Bending over a battered spittoon which had appeared from nowhere, he dropped into it a gob of dark green saliva, an expression of self-conscious delicacy on his face.

Later that afternoon I met Sa'id, one of the leaders of the group which had made the outward journey from Nahrin. He had a fine face with a prominent nose: his flowing black beard and deep-set eyes reminded me of an early Byzantine icon. He had spent some time in England and so, for the first time in several days, it was possible to talk in English.

'When I was in your country I stayed with Mr and Mrs Robinson in Battersea. Do you know them? They were very kind to me; every morning they gave me jams at breakfast. I liked the strawberry jam very much indeed. Sometimes, in the evening, Mr Robinson tried to persuade me to drink wine, but I refused because it is *haram* – forbidden by my religion.

'London is a big city. When I first arrived I couldn't believe the size of the buildings. And so many ladies. I think English ladies are very beautiful because you can see their faces, but the clothes they wear are very strange. Sometimes it was difficult for me not to look too closely.'

I asked him whether he had an English girlfriend.

'Oh no. I am a modest man and English women are very direct, but once . . .' he leaned closer to me, 'once the eldest son of Mr and Mrs Robinson asked me if I liked dancing. I said yes, so he took me to a place where there were many people, it was dark and there was loud music and red and blue and yellow lights. I waited for Paul while he talked to his friends; he was away for a long time and I thought perhaps he was gone. When he came back he was with a girl, she had long yellow hair and she laughed when she heard my name and then . . .' his voice dropped to a whisper, 'she kissed me on the lips.'

His eyes searched mine to see whether I had registered the full significance of what he said.

'She was called Susan. I remember her name because in Persian it is the name of a white flower which you call a lily.'

Ali brought some tea for us while Sa'id told me more about his time in London. I tried to picture his descriptions: of the tall red buses, the lights of Piccadilly Circus, the shops in Oxford Street and the clocktower of Big Ben. But they all seemed vague and indistinct, as if seen through a fine gauze.

Just then there was a dull rumble. At first I thought it was thunder but the sound grew in intensity. There was a sporadic rattle of small-arms fire and then, as the roar of jets swept over us, the sharp rhythmic sound of DSHKR guns echoed from the hills around the town. Sa'id leapt to his feet and ran outside on to the wooden veranda where he stared into the sky, shielding his eyes against the afternoon sun.

'Shuravi – Russians,' he shouted back into the room.

He was obviously frightened and had difficulty translating his thoughts into English.

'*Kojah*? Where are they, Abdul? Can you see them?' I did not associate the sound of jets with danger, and his alarm seemed curiously unreal to me.

By the time I joined him the planes had disappeared. Then, from the other side of the mountains, came the muffled sound of explosions.

'We are very close to the border, Abdul. The Shuravi know we are here so they bomb the villages on the other side to make it difficult for us to travel through the land. All the people leave, no one works the land and it is difficult to find food for us or our animals to eat.'

It was several minutes before the two of us left the verandah. After we sat down I noticed that he was still trembling.

'When the jets come, Abdul, everyone is frightened. The sound of the bombs is terrible. I have lost the hearing in my right ear. Immediately the people hear the Shuravi approach they hide among the rocks and under the trees, but the women have nowhere to go because, by our custom, they should not leave the walls around the house. Some of the houses have cellars but, because our families are large and the cellars are small, not everyone can fit inside. Then it is a difficult choice.

'The mujahedin have their training camps some distance from the town. We can see the jets dropping bombs on the town and each one of us thinks of our family. Since the spring the Shuravi have bombed us often. They come two or three times a week and each time ten or fifteen people are killed, sometimes more. The day before we left a bomb hit a building where many people had sheltered; twenty-three people were *shahid*. All this is difficult to believe, but you will see it with your own eyes, *Insha'allah*.' For several minutes Sa'id was silent. Then, after finishing the remains of his tea, he smiled and left me.

For the rest of the day I was alone and passed the time by writing my diary. Now and again the sound of gunfire was renewed but the jets did not return and I assumed it was merely the mujahedin in high spirits, practising with their newly acquired weapons. At some point I fell asleep.

When I awoke the room was in darkness and Ali was lighting a hurricane lamp beside me. As the flame grew and cast its light across the room I saw a small group of men sitting in a semi-circle towards the lamp. I recognised Mahmoud and Sa'id, but there were others whose faces were new to me. One man had clothes which seemed of a better quality than the others'. He was wearing a brown tweed waistcoat over a white cotton shirt and trousers. On his head was an embroidered white skull cap.

Mahmoud noticed I was awake and called me over to be introduced. First of all he turned to the man in the white skull cap. He seemed slightly older than the other mujahedin and unlike them he was clean-shaven except for a neatly-trimmed moustache. He seemed watchful and intelligent, and when he heard himself being described as a 'very learned man' and a 'university professor' the corners of his eyes wrinkled humorously. He was called Wakil.

'He speaks English too. Go on, Wakil, say something in English.'

The Professor hesitated. I sensed he was reluctant to reveal his ignorance in front of the others, but then he stretched out his hand in greeting. I had momentarily forgotten that my name was Abdul, and introduced myself as 'Peregrine'.

'Hallo, Mr Pelican, and how is your health?'

As we solemnly shook hands I knew we would be friends. Before I could say anything in reply, Mahmoud was introducing me to the next man.

'And this, Abdul, is a very important man. He is the nephew of Abdul Haq and the leader of the group – Nazim Khan.'

Mahmoud adopted an expression of false gravity and, as he gestured to the man sitting opposite, I thought I detected the flicker of a smile pass between them.

It was a weak face. The eyes were evasive and almost feminine, with unnaturally long eyelashes, the mouth small, with a sensual lower lip, and his moustache the sort that sixteen-year-olds grow to prove their manhood. I had an instant sense of foreboding which increased when he smiled and his upper lip drew back slightly like that of an animal at bay.

Meanwhile, the room had been arranged for the evening meal and by now I was looking forward to eating. I sat next to the Professor who was most attentive, carefully placing the choicest pieces of meat within my reach and even insisting that I should have some of his share. Mahmoud was mercifully silent, his energies occupied with a large mutton bone which was coating his beard with grease. When the others had finished eating he scooped up the remains of rice from the central plate, squeezed it into a glutinous ball and crammed it into his mouth.

Once the plates and dishes had been cleared away Nazim Khan produced a radio and tried to locate the BBC World Service. He refused the Professor's attempts to help him and so, for twenty minutes, we were subjected to a random selection of religious chanting and Pakistani music punctuated by prolonged bursts of hissing and spluttering from the cosmos.

Eventually Sa'id stood up and placed his petou on the ground in preparation for nemaz. One by one the other men followed his example until everyone, including Nazim, was standing, turned towards Mecca. Not wishing to obtrude, I moved to one side with my back to the wall and watched.

The scene reminded me of House Prayers at school, except that among the mujahedin there was a more immediate sense of belief. Most of them prayed with devotion, but there were some who performed the ritual without any obvious enthusiasm and a few whose concentration wandered, particularly the younger men, who glanced surreptitiously in my direction and, when they caught my eye, adopted attitudes of irreproachable piety. The prayers seemed to go on for a long while; perhaps they felt a certain duty to set a good example for the Christian among them. At last the Professor, who seemed to be the unofficial leader of the prayer, murmured an especially audible '*Bismillah*' and the men began to settle down to sleep. Ali put one of the grimy cushions beside me and, after motioning to me to use it as a pillow, pulled a dusty petou from under the couch and pressed it into my hands.

'The night is cold – tomorrow I will show you where to buy your own petou.'

The lamps were blown out and a cool breeze soon cleared the air. Through the open door the stars glittered and somewhere a dog was barking.

It was still dark when the chanting of the *muezzin* woke me with the early morning call to prayer. After a momentary twinge of annoyance, I lay back and listened to the long-drawn-out cadences, rising and falling, while around me the shadows of my companions stirred from sleep and murmured to one another in the darkness.

To hear the call to prayer chanted by a true believer is to be touched by the spirit of Islam. The sound is of another world, much as I imagine the voice that cried in the wilderness, calling across an abyss of time – the revelation of the unchanging word of God.

A mujahedin's foot stumbling against my shoulder returned me to the present. The air was cold and as the men filed out of the door I pulled the petou over my head and closed my eyes.

When I opened them again the room was full of light. Beside me there was a glass and a teapot with an iridescent thread of steam curling from its spout.

'Abdul? You are the laziest of all of us.'

Sa'id emerged from the light of the doorway and sat down.

'Unfortunately we have no jam – and it is so late that all the bread is cold – but it is still fresh,' he said and took a nan from a little cloth bundle. Between mouthfuls of bread and sips of hot sweet chai, I asked him when we were going to start the journey and what our route would be.

'Tomorrow, in the evening, you will cross the border, *Insha'allah*. The country on the other side is dangerous. "*Khatarnak*" – that is a word you must remember. The Shuravi know many of the crossing points and sometimes they are waiting. You are not afraid?'

I shook my head and tried to look unconcerned. He grinned mischievously.

'Don't worry, everyone is afraid sometimes. But trust in God. He will be with you.'

I took out a map and asked him to trace the approximate course of our journey to Nahrin. He leaned over the rectangle of paper and appeared to be studying it, but after a minute or so his finger was still wandering erratically over the south of Afghanistan, hundreds of miles from where we were. I was surprised, since some of the place names were clearly marked in Persian as well as English. Eventually he raised his head and looked into my face.

'It is difficult for me because my eyes are losing their sight. I have cataracts, and if I don't receive treatment for them soon I will be blind. Reading is nearly impossible, although I can still write. For battle I am useless.'

He smiled awkwardly.

'Some people said that I could not bear the bombing and that I was a coward, but they are fools. Only Allah knows what is in a man's heart.'

He unclipped the holster at his belt and, after checking the magazine, handed me a pistol. It was heavy but well balanced.

'I took this from a dead Shuravi two years ago. It is the only thing of value I possess. Soon I will sell it and the money will pay for my sight to be healed. *Insha'allah.*'

He asked me about the cost of such an operation in England, and whether I knew someone who might be able to help him. How much was a ticket to England? Could I persuade anyone to pay for his journey? But he knew as well as I that his hopes were far-fetched.

We talked more about the coming journey. It was going to be difficult.

'You will cross mountains and rivers and places where there is no water. In some parts the Shuravi have put mines in the road. Be careful where you place your feet. The Shuravi try to stop mujahedin bringing weapons into the country. They have machines with which they can see in the dark and sometimes they attack at night. During the day they look for the mujahedin with helicopters and if they see anyone they shoot them with rockets.'

I asked him how long it would take to reach Nahrin. 'Ten days, perhaps two weeks. For the first two or three days you will travel eighteen to twenty hours a day. Between here and the other side of Lowgar the road is very dangerous. But after you have crossed the plain of Lowgar it is not so dangerous – the land is in the control of the mujahedin and the Shuravi are afraid to enter it. From there you will go towards Bamiyan and then, after four or five days, you will come to Pul e Khumri. The Shuravi have a base there and there are many tanks guarding the road. You must cross the road. From there it is only one or two days before you arrive in Nahrin.'

He hoped that I would be able to manage the journey and advised me to buy supplies of sweets for energy and painkillers in case my legs suffered from cramp.

'Even if you are very tired you must go on. No one will be able to wait for you. The food will be very simple – rice, bread and tea – not like the food you eat here, which is good. While you are here you must eat as much as you can because you will need your strength later.'

Sa'id explained how the men were fed on the journey. Each man was allotted a certain sum of money for food; this was held in a fund controlled by Nazim, out of which money was paid as and when required. Sa'id suggested that I give Nazim enough to cover the cost of my food during the journey, any remainder to be returned to me when we arrived in Nahrin. I saw that I would need some more Afghan money. Ali kindly offered to go with me to the bazaar to help me bargain my rupees for afghanis and buy some clothing. I agreed to his suggestion and we set off together.

Staying in the chaikhane had begun to strain my patience and I felt a sense of relief to be walking through the streets of the town. Although by now my clothes had acquired a layer of dust and my beard was beginning to thicken, I still felt awkward and self-conscious. In the first shop we entered the man addressed me in Dari and seemed genuinely surprised to learn that I was not an Afghan. Inwardly I was reassured; Mahmoud's dire warnings seemed unnecessarily extreme.

Ali was concerned that I should get the best rate for my rupees and he was soon bargaining so vigorously that it was impossible to find anyone prepared to exchange my money at a price he considered acceptable.

We left one money-changer after another, each grimly shaking his head while Ali cursed them all for their meanness and I began to despair of ever changing the money at all. Guessing that my company was making the business more difficult, I told him I would give him the rupees and meet him later at the chaikhane. At first he was reluctant. What if he failed to get a good price, and how was I know that he wouldn't cheat me? I quickly put his mind at rest and was about to give him the rupees when he gripped my arm.

'Wait. Not now. Don't let people see your money. Most of us here are good men, but you must always be careful.'

Of course, he was right. Even so, it was hard not to feel comically

furtive as I passed a wad of notes to him in the shade of a nearby fig
tree.

The streets were dry and it was pleasant to walk aimlessly
through the town, letting my Occidental sense of time and purpose
dissolve in the hubbub around me. Kebab sellers fanned their
glowing charcoal under grills of sizzling meat, sending showers of
crackling sparks and wafts of delicious-smelling smoke among the
passers-by. Old men squatted on the ground beside carefully balanced pyramids of fruit, tapping their naswar boxes and critically
eyeing the horses going by. There were shops selling second-hand
clothes and pedlars with trays of flashy-looking watch straps, Day-
glo plastic combs and skeins of brightly coloured wool. The sound
of bones splitting came from a butcher's shop where sides of meat
and glistening rib-cages hung in a blur of flies. On a stretch of waste
ground a group of men were pounding empty oil cans with rocks
into flat squares of metal and nearby a youth of fifteen with
blackened clothes sorted through a mound of assorted gears that
looked like a mechanic's nightmare. Beside the mosque, builders
were busy repairing the walls of a house; one tirelessly mixed earth
and mortar together with buckets of water, while a workmate
passed baskets full of dripping mud to a third man on the wall who
patted the material into shape. Music blared from shops selling
cassette tapes: it was wilder and fiercer than the sugared songs of
Pakistan, and I thought of Kubla Khan and of ancestral voices
prophesying war.

When I got back to the chaikhane Ali was already waiting for me.
He had changed the money satisfactorily, and had also bought me a
petou and one of the floppy woollen hats worn by many of the
mujahedin. But when I examined the petou I was disappointed. In
his zeal to save me money he had bought the cheapest kind: a thin
wool and nylon affair with unpleasantly sharp colours at the
borders, unlike the softer, naturally dyed petous of closely woven
wool which I so admired. Sa'id had recommended me to buy a
mujahedin hat, for camouflage and protection against the sun.
Personally I disliked them. I found the wool hot and scratchy and
when I glanced in the mirrored lid of a naswar box it looked like a
collapsed soufflé perched on the top of my head. I thanked Ali and
inwardly resolved to lose the thing as quickly as possible.

That evening, Sa'id tried to sell his gun to Mahmoud. To begin
with the discussion seemed quite amicable but soon the tempo
quickened and it became clear that the price Mahmoud was offering
was far less than Sa'id had hoped for. The others were silent while
the two men argued, the one quivering with nervous energy, the

other stolidly shaking his head or laughing scornfully. Was this the way to treat a brother Muslim? Sa'id appealed to the circle of men; in Nahrin such a gun would fetch double the price he was asking!

'Not here, brother. Everyone has guns here, and who wants a little pistol like that? Now if it were an anti-tank rocket . . .' Mahmoud rubbed his nose and smiled at Nazim. 'Then I could pay you a very good price indeed.'

'We all know what you're talking about,' replied Sa'id, scanning the members of the group, some of whom shifted their positions and looked uncomfortably away from him. 'Yes, we all know, but I am talking about this gun, my gun and a fair price.'

He turned to the Professor.

'Do you think I am greedy, Wakil?'

The Professor took a cigarette from his waistcoat pocket and lit it before replying:

'No, brother, you are not greedy. But remember, we are not in Nahrin now and the prices are different. And you, Mahmoud, should remember that this brother is not like you. He is not a trader in weapons, he is a mujahed.'

At this, several men nodded in agreement.

'One more thing, the most important of all; this brother will lose his sight unless he can pay for a doctor. That is all.'

No one spoke and everyone's attention was focused on Mahmoud, who grunted and began picking his teeth with his little finger.

'Well spoken, Wakil,' he said at last. 'The words of a wise man. But now I am hungry, and when I am hungry I cannot think. Sa'id, let us eat together like brothers and we can talk about this little difficulty in the morning.'

Sa'id was silent; the bitter shadow in his face was sufficient reply.

During the night there was a heavy thunderstorm; flashes of yellow lightning crashed outside the door, casting an instant of light into the rain pouring out of the darkness. I sat on the balcony sharing a cigarette with one of the mujahedin, listening to the thunder echoing in the hills. The buildings on the other side of the yard were lost in a hissing mist of water. We said nothing, but when a flash of lightning lit his face and I saw that his eyes were wide with excitement I knew we shared the same pleasure.

I woke before the muezzin's call with ominous rumblings below my navel and fumbled towards the door, doing my best to avoid the blanketed forms at my feet. A voice hissed out of the darkness.

'Abdul, Abdul, where are you going?'

'Very necessary, very quick.'

There was a puzzled silence.

'My stomach is bad.'

'Don't worry. I will show you where.'

We scrambled down the ladder and squelched through the mud to the pebbly banks of the river where a strong smell of faeces revealed we had come to the right place. Squatting down and grabbing hold of a small branch for balance, I wished I was in England. I had no paper and followed native custom, but as I reached blindly for a smooth enough stone, the disquieting thought passed through my mind: had it been used already?

My sombre considerations were interrupted by the Uzbeki who gave a few companionable honks and then shouted, 'Afghanistan – is it good?'

'Yes, very good.'

We washed in the river and retraced our footsteps under a grey, starless sky. There was a hoarse, rhythmic gasping in the half light and we passed two men kneeling beside an ox, one holding its head while the other cut its throat: I wondered whether we would be having it for supper. Back at the chaikhane I huddled under my petou and was asleep when the call to morning prayer rang out across the valley.

By now I had settled into the routine of the chaikhane and begun to get to know the people who worked there. There was the boy with the gold-embroidered cap whom I had seen when I first arrived. He had the wide fleshy hips and soft features of a natural eunuch and looked no more than eleven or twelve although he told me he was eighteen. He cooked the meals, washed the plates and gathered kindling. Several times a day he hauled the jerrycans full of water from the river to the chaikhane with the sinews standing out from his delicate wrists and his narrow shoulders bowed under the weight. After the mujahedin had finished eating he would sweep the floor, singing to himself. Several times, when the others were away, I saw him pick up empty glasses of tea and dance a pirouette before taking them out on to the veranda to rinse them in a bowl of greasy water. He was never still; only once, when the men were cleaning and oiling their guns, I noticed him sitting motionless in the corner watching them with the expression of a child listening to a wonderful story, until one of the men caught his eye.

'Hey, you! What are you doing? Bring some more tea and some sweets for Abdul!'

The look of wonder vanished from his face and without a word he jumped to his feet and scampered out of the door.

He had a quick intelligence and, on one of the few occasions when he was not busy, he tried to teach me some words of Pushtu, his native language. First, he solemnly pointed to a glass of water and a fragment of bread and pronounced the words very carefully. I repeated them as best I could. Encouraged by my efforts, he hurried out and came back with a handful of vegetables, an egg and a knife, but my pronunciation soon had him clapping his hands in glee and rolling on the floor with laughter.

The master of the chaikhane was called Haji, the name given to those who have made the haj pilgrimage to Mecca, which he had visited ten years before. After the mujahedin had wrapped themselves in their petous for the night, Haji would remain in prayer, by the shifting light of a hurricane lamp, with an aura of self conscious sanctity draped around him; but the men trusted him and paid him well for the risks he was taking.

And there was Ali. When we first met there had been an immediate and instinctive understanding between us and, during the few days that I spent at the chaikhane, this grew into an unspoken friendship. More than anyone else, Ali welcomed me and looked after me with affection.

I am sitting by the window watching a group of men loading mines on to a tractor-trailer and the man on the tractor-seat is smoking a cigarette. Ali takes an apricot from the side of the windowsill that is still in shadow and offers it to me, saying, 'Here, eat it before it becomes warm.'

There are four or five mujahedin sitting around me, tapping my shoulder and asking questions until my head begins to spin with the effort of speaking in Dari. Ali silently fills my glass with tea.

Thinking of a girl and the lines of the poem by Donne which begins, 'Sweetest love, I do not go, for weariness of thee . . .' I hear a voice calling a name which I suddenly recognise as my own.

'Abdul, Abdul.' Ali's face is puzzled and concerned. 'Why are you sad, Abdul? Be happy, be happy!' His forehead clears and his eyes twinkle with humour. 'Life is short but God is great.'

The afternoon before we were to set off I wandered over to the dusty field where last-minute preparations for the journey were being made. Boxes of ammunition, guns, sacks of oats and harnesses were strewn everywhere. The horses and mules were hanging their heads in the heat while, nearby, Nazim Khan and the older members of the group sat and talked in the stifling shade of a tent.

I joined them but found it difficult to follow their conversation. However, it was obvious that Nazim and Mahmoud were being criticised by the others. Wakil beckoned me over and whispered, 'These words are not good. Guns and money. Very difficult.'

I nodded as sagely as I could and propped myself against a saddle to piece together what was going on, but they were talking too fast and my concentration began to wander. Mahmoud and Sa'id were sitting opposite me and, as I looked from one to the other, I imagined that I saw different aspects of the war reflected in their faces.

Mahmoud's features had a slow, calculating intelligence, particularly his eyes which were almost concealed behind fleshy lids. I remembered the advice of a long-haired traveller, years ago in India: 'Don't trust fat people in thin countries.'

The genial plumpness seemed faintly obscene, almost dishonest, as if it had been acquired by some trick from the gaunt physique of Sa'id whose face, by comparison, had the strength and intensity of an ascetic. I thought of the casual and unpredictable way in which war redistributes wealth, and wondered who would finally possess the dead Russian's pistol.

At last the argument resolved itself and Nazim Khan asked me to take a photograph of the men standing beside the piles of ammunition. A dozen men grabbed the nearest gun or anti-tank rocket they could find and posed with suitably grim expressions. Nazim Khan was in the middle, blithely unaware of the barrel of a Kalashnikov cradled comfortably in his neighbour's arms and pointing directly at his temple. After I had taken a couple of photographs and ostentatiously put the camera away, the men began to load the horses. I went back to the chaikhane to collect my things.

Ali stood beside me while I packed. At first he tried to help by passing me books or clothes which I had laid out on the floor, but he quickly realised it only complicated things. Just as I had finished, the boy with the gold-embroidered hat appeared and pointed at my camera. For a moment I thought he wanted me to give it to him but, like Nazim Khan, he only wanted his photograph taken. I had planned to take a photograph of Ali alone, but it seemed unfair to resist. So they stood together, arms stiffly by their sides, with the rays of the setting sun rendering them quizzical and expressive, while I fumbled with the light meter. Click. It was time to go.

Ali said goodbye in a carefully controlled voice and hurriedly started peeling some potatoes. Walking away from the chaikhane I asked myself what right I had to enter and leave another person's life so easily.

In the dusty field, there was a crowd of forty or fifty men gathered together, most of whom I recognised. These were the men with whom I would be travelling to Nahrin. In addition, there was a score of mules and horses already loaded with boxes of ammunition and guns. The men were armed with Kalashnikovs, carbines or rocket-launchers.

Nazim Khan clapped his hands together in an ineffectual attempt to attract the men's attention, then briefly set out the night's itinerary, warning us of the dangerous areas and reminding us not to show any lights nor to talk except when it was absolutely necessary. Then he led the men in prayer. The sun had just set over the tops of the mountains but the sky was still light. I watched the men's faces as they murmured their prayers. Some, perhaps, were thinking of the difficulties and dangers of the journey or dedicating themselves to the service of God in the fight to cleanse their land of unbelievers while others may merely have been repeating the nemaz unthinkingly, through force of habit.

It was time to make our farewells; Mahmoud embraced me fondly. I should contact him without fail when I returned to Peshawar, when he would be able to offer me a good price for my tape recorder. Only when the quiet Uzbeki shook my hand did I realise that he was remaining in Pakistan. Sa'id embraced me, then looked into my face and said:

'Do not be afraid, Allah is with us. *Khoda hafiz* – may God protect you.'

The path sloped gently upwards but the younger mujahedin pushed ahead at such a pace that I was soon lagging behind. My boots seemed to get heavier and heavier, my pack began to bite into my shoulders and I cursed myself for being so unfit.

On the way we passed an old woman begging by the side of the road but only the Professor paused to give her any money; the rest of us continued, unwilling to break our rhythm. Ragged children driving a goat along the road stopped and watched us go by in silence; some women carrying jars of water on their heads carefully pulled their *chador* over their faces; a couple of dogs loped up from a huddle of refugee tents and barked at us until the mujahed in front of me picked up a fist-sized stone and hurled it with all his strength in their direction, hitting one of them with a thud in the ribs. The dog yelped and there was a burst of appreciative laughter from my companions. Then we left the last of the encampments behind us and began the steep climb to the top of the hills. We rested a few minutes a little before the highest point and I rewarded myself with a final cigarette as I looked back down over the town of Teremangal.

2

Lowgar

The land was sinking into the shadow of the night. Here and there were the tiny orange glimmerings of camp-fires and I caught a trace of woodsmoke in the cool air on my face. A distant voice was calling in the twilight, then the wind shifted, carrying the sound away. There was no turning back. I stubbed out my cigarette, shouldered my pack and in another couple of minutes the path was sloping downhill. I was in Afghanistan.

It reminded me of illicit expeditions at school: walking off into the twilight with a bottle of cheap sherry and a packet of cigarettes, the warm night air full of hidden promise and one's heart beating with the exhilaration of being out of bounds. But there was no sherry and, instead of another fifteen-year-old companion-in-drunkenness, I was with a group of men prepared to sacrifice their lives for their beliefs. It was a humbling thought, emphasised when the mujahed beside me pointed to the shattered stumps of trees on either side of the road and whispered, 'Shuravi.'

The sky turned from deep green to dark blue, scintillating with summer stars. The track was a soft grey in the darkness and our footsteps were absorbed in fine dust.

We settled into a fast silent rhythm, only interrupted when we came to a river and there was the sound of horses crossing the water in the dark. Thereafter, the path became uneven and occasionally the horses stumbled, their hooves throwing off sparks against the rocks. The group had subtly assumed another identity in the darkness, as if we were the eyes and ears of a single, instinctive body, and when someone detected a movement in the night before us the men cocked their rifles as one and spread out on either side of the road. With a faint tinkle of bells, the shapes of camels, loaded with timber, appeared silhouetted against the stars. The men gathered around the driver and, after exchanging whispered greetings, questioned him briefly about the situation further along the trail. Then, with a resounding thwack on the flank of the leading animal, the camel train set off and once more disappeared into the darkness.

We came to the remains of a town called Jaji. The air was sharp with the smell of ash. At one time several thousand people had lived there, now it was deserted and the only sign of life was the hesitant glow of fireflies among the dark ruins. The sorrow of the place fell on us and we walked more slowly.

At the farther side of the town we stopped for a rest in the shelter of a bombed-out chaikhane and waited for the pack animals to catch up with us. When they arrived I noticed that Nazim Khan was riding on horseback, well at the rear of the group. I passed my water bottle round the circle of faceless shadows and it came back to me empty. Several of the men asked whether I was tired. I denied it as strongly as I could, but my replies must have sounded unconvincing, for one of them insisted on taking my pack and lashing it on to his own tiny donkey, which was already laden with baggage and mortars.

I had no watch, but at a guess we had already been marching for five or six hours. I asked the man next to me how long it would be before we reached our halt for the night. He did not know, nor did the next man I asked and eventually I abandoned hope of finding out. Slowly and painfully I was learning to think like a mujahed.

We set off again; there were explosions in the distance and the horizon was flickering like a candlelit room. The path was very difficult and most of my attention was taken up with keeping my balance and following the pale gleam of the white-turbanned head of the man in front of me. I had no more thoughts, only walking, moving my knees; first one, then the other. I surrendered to the movement of my body. Stones, roads and pathways disintegrated into a jumble of invisible thorns and boulders. At some point I stopped to drink from an evil-looking shadow beside the path and took the opportunity to wash the sweat and dust from my face. Several times groups of mujahedin passed us from the opposite direction murmuring the words: '*Manda nabashi* – may you not be tired', to which the reply was: '*Zenda bashi* – may you live.'

Events began to assume a dream-like quality: hundreds of men moving silently through the summer night with the graceful wandering fire of tracer winging through the darkness; bursts of machine gun fire and a spray of stars suspended over the black mass of hills; the word '*Dushman* – enemy' hissed in my ear and the man beside me pulling my wrist and crouching in silence by the side of the path; the smell of cordite in the dark and the oddly comforting sound of a horse champing its bridle and drumming the dry earth with its hoof.

Once more we continued. Dust entered my nose and mouth and

when I heard the rippling of an unseen stream it drew me like a magnet. A shadow knelt beside me and murmured '*Bismillah*' before bending his head to drink.

At last we came to the light of a kerosene lamp under a roof of branches and dry, withered leaves, and threw ourselves down on an earth floor covered with straw. Two boys of seventeen or eighteen prepared chai and nan for us. Their faces were masks of tension, their eyes fractured and unseeing. I could only guess at the strain of providing for parties of mujahedin like ourselves, night after night, under the constant fear of reprisals. That day, helicopter gunships had attacked the surrounding area and every hour we stayed there increased their risk, but the rest of the group seemed oblivious to such thoughts. Instead they shouted impatiently for chai and complained at the quality of the rice. The boys took refuge in silence and, for the first time, I saw how the mujahedin sometimes considered themselves superior to the people who fed them and gave them shelter. It was an uncomfortable revelation.

Taking off my boots I arranged them as a makeshift pillow for my head and lay back, my stomach swollen with rice and tea. For a few minutes I listened to the snores of the man next to me and then, nothing.

Two hours later the Professor woke me. The pack animals were already loaded up and it was time to set off. I stamped my feet to get rid of the stiffness in my legs and, in a somnambulistic daze, tumbled out of the lamplight into the darkness. Gradually the sky paled and the stars faded. In mid-stride I felt a sharp pain in my stomach and just had time to reach the sparse cover of a bush at the side of the track before being gripped by a violent attack of diarrhoea. Ten minutes later, as I got unsteadily to my feet and fumbled with the cord of my trousers, the prospect of another day's walking, let alone two or three weeks, filled me with blank despair. Only for a moment: then I remembered the helicopters. Fear is a wonderful stimulant, and in half an hour I had caught up with the others and once more settled into the pace of the group.

We made our way through a valley watered by little streams with bushes of wild lavender on either side, like clouds of blue smoke. The sun had just risen and I glimpsed a solitary figure moving through a field of green maize. We passed through several tiny villages – a few houses scattered on either side of the path – but most of them were deserted and the fields surrounding them were overgrown with weeds.

The track climbed steadily upward and the landscape became more rocky; we left the fertile valley and entered a more mountainous region. The sun grew hot. The man in front of me shifted the anti-tank rocket from one arm to the other and a shadow of sweat spread slowly across his shoulders. The track narrowed to a path, which in turn became a furrow of dust that meandered perversely up and down the sides of a wide river gorge, always taking what seemed to be the most inconvenient direction. Several times it disappeared in a treacherous slope of loose sand and gravel which we had to edge across, using the dried stalks of flowers to steady ourselves. At other times it dipped down to the water's edge, where we splashed the dust and sweat from our faces. The pack animals, meanwhile, followed a different route that took them through the slow-moving shallows of the river.

The gorge broadened out and we came to a village overlooking the river. Some of the group went off to find a chaikhane while the rest of us unsaddled the animals and sat in the shade of some poplar trees by the water.

A Badakhshani who had been my walking companion for the past few hours came over and sat beside me. His name was Sediq, and even in comparison with the other mujahedin he was obviously very poor. Instead of the second-hand army boots which most of them had, he wore a pair of battered baseball shoes, and the one shirt he possessed was threadbare and rotting at the seams. Possibly because he was a stranger to the rest of the group, the others tended to ignore him and thus he had attached himself to me. I had taken off my boots and socks and was cooling my feet in the water. He pulled off the baseball shoes and, as he rolled up his trousers, I saw his right leg was wrapped in a filthy makeshift bandage, wound round with black thread to keep it in place. He gingerly removed it, revealing a patch of suppurating flesh the area of the palm of my hand. After carefully folding the bandage and putting it to one side, he balanced his foot on a small boulder and began flicking drops of water on the raw surface of the wound, breathing in sharply through clenched teeth as he did so. I had a tube of antiseptic cream in my satchel and I squeezed some into his hand, adding that he was on no account to tell any of the others. I knew that if they learned I had medicine of any description I would have a barrage of requests for it and my supplies would soon be gone. He was embarrassingly grateful but I was glad to give it, especially since he had not asked for it, unlike some of the men in Teremangal who demanded ointments for scars that were already white and long since healed.

For a while we sat in silence with our feet resting in the cold flow, listening to a flock of sparrows in the branches of the trees above us; then Sediq began to sing. It was a simple, rather tuneless song and clearly he was improvising. It was about a young man who had travelled far from his own home, without friends, living in the shadow of sadness. One night, he had a dream, a beautiful dream, and a great light appeared to him. In the morning when he awoke a stranger came to him, a man from a distant country, who became the young man's friend. The name of the stranger was Abdul.

In other circumstances it might have been a mawkish display of sentiment but, as he sang it, the song was without affectation and seemed a natural token of friendship. When he had finished he took a naswar box from his pocket. Then he unclipped a safety pin from the collar of his shirt and began to clean his teeth with it, using the lid of the box as a mirror.

Meanwhile, someone had found a chaikhane and the Professor called out to us to join them. We stepped into a small, low-ceilinged room lit by a single window. The men had stretched themselves out over the floor and some of them were already asleep. Others were talking quietly among themselves or leaning against the walls, their eyes wide and unseeing with fatigue while a few villagers stood together by the door looking at us with gently bemused expressions. The master of the chaikhane apologised for having no food but provided us with generous supplies of tea and sugar. When it was time for us to go he refused all payment.

By now the sun was directly overhead and our pace slowed. Walking became an automaton-like plod between occasional patches of shadow while the sweat poured into our eyes and the river glittered tantalisingly below us. We overtook men from other groups resting in the shade of trees and then we too slumped down in the dry grass, battling to stay awake, with the hypnotic murmur of the river in our ears.

Eventually we came to a barren plateau with grey, treeless mountains rising up on either side of it – the sort of place that nineteenth-century travel writers might have described as having a 'wild grandeur'. But I was too tired to appreciate it and all I could think of was sleep. I had dropped back behind the main body of the group when a man with a thick mane of hair and a large nose strode alongside me in a pair of battered wellington boots. He informed me he was on his way to Kabul. I expressed a polite lack of interest, but he was unperturbed and obviously a fanatic conversationalist. So, for the next two or three miles, I had to endure a series of questions and unrequested monologues. At regular intervals I told him I was tired, bored and ill, none of which seemed to have any effect on the ceaseless flow. Finally, in desperation, I told him that I was dying.

At this he paused, swivelling a bloodshot eye in my direction, and looked at me in the same way I imagine the Ancient Mariner fixed on the hapless wedding guest.

'Take my photograph.'

At this I had a sudden, glorious spark of inspiration.

'I will take your photograph if you stop talking to me.'

He stopped in the middle of the path with his eyebrows furrowed in concentration: it was clearly a difficult bargain.

'Two photographs.'

Taken aback by such alarming quick-wittedness, I just managed to recover the situation by telling him I would take one photograph there and then: provided he said nothing more to me, I promised to take another later. This seemed to satisfy him, so I photographed him scowling at the camera and we continued on our way in silence. Half a mile further on we arrived at a chaikhane where he demanded his second photograph. I reluctantly agreed, feeling he had somehow had the better side of the bargain.

Afterwards I sat down beside one of the mujahedin who pointed to his feet and grimaced with pain. He was in low spirits.

'This is a desert,' he said, gesturing at the sunbleached grass, thorn bushes and the rocky peaks in front of us. 'No houses, no trees, no cigarettes. Nothing. Not like Nahrin.'

I had to agree it was a depressing place.

'But some places are worse,' he continued. 'Tomorrow, or the day after. There it is more dangerous . . .' he nodded to himself, adding as an afterthought, 'And there is no water.'

The conversation lapsed and I could feel myself about to fall asleep when someone presented me with a bowl of grey rice. I wasn't hungry, but I crammed the food into my mouth and chewed at it mechanically, washing it down with mouthfuls of sweet chai.

The pack animals with Nazim Khan were still a long way behind, and since no one seemed to know where we were going I found a space to lie down between two mujahedin under an awning of tattered cloth and brushwood. One of them was already asleep, the other sorrowfully examining a huge, plum-sized blister on his big toe. I tried to make a few notes in my diary but the buzzing of the flies and the hot windless air were like a drug. In a few minutes I too was asleep.

The sound of a truck revving woke me. Somehow or other it had managed to reach the chaikhane, and the plan was for some of us to ride in it for the last few miles to where we could stay the night. The rest of the group would follow us on foot. I barely had time to scramble on to the back of the truck before it set off, rattling and lurching between boulders until it reached the beginning of a track following the winding course of a wide valley. The sun was setting and the hills in the west were already in shadow. The younger mujahedin called out in joyous mockery to the people we rushed past, casting a cloud of dust behind us.

Every two or three miles the truck halted to allow some passengers to get off while others clambered aboard. The driver kept the engine running and refused to bargain with anyone. Those who hesitated were left behind. The signal for departure was a thunderous roaring of the engine. Then, with a chorus of '*Borou bekheir!*' we were on our way once again. At first I worried that we might lose touch with the rest of the group: where were we going? how long before we reached our destination? And how would the rest of the group find us? The mujahed with the plum-sized blister shrugged and smiled. '*Sabr ku* – be patient, Abdul. All will be well.'

As it turned out we travelled no more than ten or fifteen miles, and at twilight the driver set us down at a collection of half a dozen dilapidated houses. In front of one of them a fire had been lit between some stones and a man was sitting on a chair beside it. A little distance away a lopsided tent was billowing in the evening breeze. A youth sauntered up with a sly look on his face, flourishing a pistol.

I sat on a rock and opened my diary to write a few lines before the light faded completely. The youth was undeterred and continued waving the pistol in a tiresome manner. I was about to lose my temper when the tension was eased by the appearance of a mujahed who told us he was from the Panjshir. He asked to see the youth's pistol. After weighing it in his hand and taking a sight along its barrel he returned it with a deprecatory air. Somewhat deflated, the youth put the gun back in its holster and slunk away.

The Panjshiri led us into one of the houses and we sat around a lamp and talked about the future of the war. He said that he expected the Resistance to conquer their enemies within six months, helped by twenty million dollars from the United States and one million pounds from Great Britain. He spoke with certainty of the bravery of the men of the Panjshir, but his tone changed to scorn when I asked him about the role of the mullahs in the war against the Soviets.

'The mullahs that are left are not interested in our struggle, all they are interested in is sleeping and eating . . .'

A voice called out of the shadows: 'What are you saying, brother? I am a mullah.'

The man from the Panjshir was unabashed. 'I have no quarrel with you. There are good mullahs too, and for all I know you are one of those. But most mullahs do nothing for us; only when their village is threatened or attacked by the Shuravi do they ask us for help.'

Another voice called out from the corner of the room.

'Maulawi Sahib is no ordinary mullah. He has made the journey to Peshawar with us to buy arms for the *jehad*. He shares our life. He is a brave mujahed. Be careful what you say, for he is our leader and we love him dearly.'

'Peace be with you, brother. As I said, I have no quarrel with you or any man who fights the Shuravi,' said the Panjshiri. 'Let us drink tea together and you can tell me how the war is going in your part of the country.'

A lamp was lit and the light shone on several unfamiliar faces. The mullah whom the others called Maulawi was a plump Uzbeki with a round, almost hairless face and a wall eye which gave him a slightly quizzical expression. His clothes, including his turban, were of good cotton material, over which he wore a full bandolier and a Kalashnikov. His five companions, by contrast, were dressed in a collection of dull green parkas and military style trousers. One of them was wearing a Russian-issue fur hat whose ear flaps hung down over his thick black beard, giving him a strong resemblance to the Wolfman of horror movies, a similarity made even more striking when he smiled, which revealed a row of sharp white teeth.

I was too tired to follow the conversation beyond the customary questions and answers exchanged when different groups met. Instead I let my thoughts wander, silently greeting the faces of friends until one in particular seemed to return my gaze. I wondered whether perhaps, in that moment, a subtle thread connected us. But even as I asked myself the question I lost the image of her face and found myself once more in the dimly-lit room where the men were spreading out their petous for the evening prayer.

Maulawi led the prayers in a fine resonant voice, pronouncing the words fluently which revealed, as I thought, his religious training in the madraseh school. When performed well, the chanting of the nemaz expresses the twin tendencies of praise and longing that are central to all the great religions, and it was clear that the members of the group were inspired by Maulawi's fervour.

As he finished the rest of the group arrived, hollow-eyed and footsore. Once again the owner of the chaikhane had no food to offer us and so, after sharing a few dry nan, we settled down for the night. I had been unable to find my petou which was somewhere among the baggage; the Panjshiri who was beside me covered us both with his own.

I tried to thank him but he interrupted:

'There is no need to thank me. If I had no petou I would expect you to do the same for me. Good night, Abdul. Sleep well. Tomorrow is a long journey.'

We set off by starlight. The hills were dark masses whose features slowly emerged as the path climbed to a windswept plateau. It was a desolate landscape. The thin sunlight struggling through the clouds on the horizon emphasised the bleak, unfriendly nature of the place. The colours of the rocks shifted through a spectrum of dull lilac to pink and were beginning to settle into a dusty yellow by the time we came to a stonebuilt hut with a roof of sun-dried mud.

The pack animals and their drivers were already a good way behind. The rest of us were roughly divided between those who wished to push on while the air was still relatively cool and those who wanted breakfast. The Professor and a few others of us decided to see whether we could get some chai from whoever lived in the stone hut. An old man came out to greet us and after welcoming us courteously invited us inside. He was a shepherd, and during the summer months he pastured his flocks in the mountains. I asked him whether it was a lonely life. He laughed and replied that he often made chai for travellers like ourselves.

While our host poured some water into a blackened teapot and fanned the embers of a fire, the Professor asked him about other groups of mujahedin who had passed along the trail. Unlike some of the other mujahedin, the Professor was unfailingly polite to all those who gave us hospitality, but on this occasion I noticed him treating the old man with particular respect. When the shepherd went out to get some more sticks for the fire, I asked the Professor why he spoke with such deference.

'He is *ruhani*, a spiritual man. Men who live by themselves in the mountains are often strong believers. They have few distractions and are closer to God than people like ourselves. He is very poor, but he gives what he can. He is a very good man.'

I glanced around at the interior of the hut. The rough adobe walls were bare except for a tattered poster of State propaganda which showed a gigantic ugly-looking cowboy, representing the United States, wielding a club at a mosque. The club was riddled with holes, from which emerged the heads of vicious-looking men armed with machine guns, presumably mujahedin. Someone had been unimpressed with the picture for they had added a swarm of childishly formed jets and helicopters attacking the cowboy. In the sky, a different hand had painstakingly written the words '*Allah akbar* – God is Great' in thick black letters. Apart from the low doorway the only lighting was a small window, partially blocked with branches of dry thorns. The floor was covered by a couple of thick, goats' hair blankets. In one corner there were a few plates, half a dozen tea glasses and a small bundle of clothes and blankets. It had the uncluttered simplicity of a monk's cell.

After finishing our tea we said goodbye and I saw the Professor press some money into the hand of the old man. Then we carried on, past herds of camels grazing on the skyline, and descended towards the plains of Lowgar. The path was steep and my knees began to ache. Sediq stepped effortlessly from rock to rock, choosing the most comfortable way down while I stumbled clumsily after him, jarring my spine and longing for the path to level out.

The sound of gunshots echoed from the peaks above us, but Sediq was unalarmed: it was probably lookouts of other mujahedin announcing our approach, he explained. We stopped for a short rest and were soon joined by Maulawi who was limping heavily. We sat down and looked out over the landscape, already vanishing into a haze of dusty light. As Maulawi pointed out the route we needed to take, it was difficult to believe that the dun-coloured country below us was at war and that we were about to enter one of the most dangerous areas, the province of Lowgar.

A couple of miles farther on, we came to a long scree stretching all the way down from the path to the road below. By now I was heartily sick of the jolting descent, so I squatted down on my heels and launched myself off down the slope using my pack as a counterweight. As I gathered speed, I heard whoops and cries of encouragement from the others. Then I realised I had no effective way of slowing down or steering; luckily there were several large boulders jutting out from the scree and I came to a bruising halt against one. Looking up, I saw Maulawi had already set off after me. Trailing a cloud of dust behind him, he hurtled past me, roaring at the top of his voice until he was abruptly silenced by another uncomfortable-looking boulder. The next moment he was up and laughing.

'You and I are both lazy, aren't we, Abdul Baz?'

He rubbed his broad backside and pushed off down the slope again. Gingerly, I followed him, this time taking care to aim for a boulder that was closer.

We reached the bottom trailing a small avalanche of shale and gravel and sat down to wait for the others. They caught up a few minutes later, still laughing at our ungainly descent, and we arrived at the next village in good spirits.

There were horses tethered under some trees and men drinking chai in the shade of a chaikhane. They were from Hesb Islami, another faction of mujahedin, and the air was charged with tension and mutual distrust until we discovered they were travelling in the opposite direction to ourselves, towards Pakistan. Once this was established, the atmosphere between the two groups changed and the men started talking easily with one another, except for one of the Hesb Islami, a man with small brown eyes, stoatish features and a thin black beard, who sidled up to me and asked a series of probing questions. Why had I come to Afghanistan? Was I American? How could I, a foreigner, begin to understand the war? Did I even know the meaning of the word '*jehad*'?

His gloomy face and unrelenting seriousness reminded me of party bores who bludgeon one with talk about the moral issues of the day.

'Do you believe in God?'

'Yes.'

'None of your people understands the meaning of God.'

I mumbled something about there being holy men in all religions.

'You worship wood and stone. You are *but-perast*, idol-worshippers.'

The word *but-perast* is usually a term of abuse and I began to feel annoyed.

'The cross is our *mehrab*,' I replied. This silenced him for a moment.

'You Christians have three Gods, but in truth there is only one. *La ilaha illah lahu* – there is no god but God.'

The man drinking chai next to me paused with the glass half-way to his lips: 'Listen.'

Most of the mujahedin had picked up their guns before I was able to identify the distant noise of a helicopter. It was the first time I had heard one inside Afghanistan so the sound carried no menace for me, but the others were wide-eyed and shouting in nervous excitement.

The Professor was already in the doorway. Pulling on my boots I hurried after him, tripping and stumbling over my laces. We took cover under some bushes by the edge of the river and waited. I felt oddly detached from the sudden activity around me, as if I were in the middle of a game of grown men playing cowboys and indians.

'If they see the horses they will shoot at them; we are safer here.'

The Professor was out of breath and I noticed him flicking the sweat from his moustache. The sound of the river vanished into the mechanical thudding of blades beating the air as the helicopter, a Mi 8 troop carrier, came into sight. A sporadic crackle of gunfire started up from the hilltops around us. There was an answering burst of machine-gun fire from the helicopter which continued on its way without altering its course. As I watched it disappear over the jagged skyline, I thought of the men inside it, gazing down over the wrinkled brown landscape, clenching their sphincter muscles in case a stray bullet or rocket tore its way through the floor of the aircraft. In a few minutes they would have covered a distance that would have taken us a day's march.

The Professor's arm was pressing down on my shoulders.

'Wait. Another is coming. Don't show your face.'

As the second helicopter appeared, its shape seemed more sinister, like a swollen metallic insect, heavy with malevolent intent. It was flying higher than the first, well out of range of any bullets, and the gunfire echoing among the rocky crags only accentuated the powerlessness of the mujahedin. I realised then how the war was more than mere lines and arrows on a map representing opposing forces and the movement of troops. There was another dimension – the air– in which the Soviets had total supremacy. The sky was no longer innocent.

The Professor and I remained in the shelter of the riverbank, but no more helicopters went over and after ten minutes or so he judged it safe enough to return to the chaikhane. Sediq, who had taken cover among some rocks farther down stream, followed us and we found the others reminiscing about their recent exploits. For the younger ones, armed with their Lee-Enfields, it had been a clear victory. The older men were silent.

Plates of rice were produced and I sat down next to an amiable-looking man but almost at once I became aware of an appalling smell emanating from his shoes – a pair of disintegrating plimsolls around which a small cloud of flies was circulating busily. After several days' marching everyone's feet smelt, and I had become immune to the usual level of gamey smells. I waited for my nostrils to adjust but, if anything, the stench seemed to intensify. Even opening my mouth for another handful of rice was a daunting prospect. I edged away as tactfully as I could and found a patch of shade beside the river.

Next to me a teenaged boy was stripping down a Lee-Enfield and oiling the parts with an expression of solemn concentration. He proudly showed me the gun's workings; it was over fifty years old.

The rest of the group arrived. After eating, they lay down in the long grass beside the river and busied themselves sewing patches on to their shirts or grooming their moustaches in the mirrored tops of their naswar boxes.

The dappled light flickering on the pages of my diary, the soft swish of the horses' tails whisking at the flies and the sound of the river acted like a charm of peace, and the spell was almost undisturbed by the brief appearance of two more helicopters in the distance; so far away they seemed like flying ants skimming across the mountains.

Several times I asked members of the group where we were, but none of them seemed to have any idea and when I showed them a map of the region they frowned with puzzlement. Even those who could read were uncertain. All I could elicit from them was what I already knew; that we were approaching the plains of Lowgar. However, knowing where we were or where we were going was more or less irrelevant: I had no choice but to follow along with the rest of the group, and our route might change at a moment's notice depending on the presence of Soviet patrols. Besides, my companions had only the slightest understanding of their whereabouts, and cared even less. When asked how far it might be to the next staging post their replies were all different: 'two hours', 'three hours', 'six hours', 'a day, *Insha'allah*'. In the end I realised that my attempts to think in terms of hours or distance were an unnecessary distraction. I consoled myself with the wisdom of the Persian poet who advised the traveller first to overcome the constraints of time and place before his footsteps bordered on the threshold of eternity and remembered the words of the Qur'an: 'He is with you wherever you are.'

In the early afternoon we set off once more. The trail was a narrow path along the course of the river with cliffs on either side. As I watched the cavalcade of men and horses winding through the rocky gorges, it was as if a line of *The Thousand and One Nights* had come to life, and the forty thieves were setting out on another foray from their secret cave. But instead of a robber chief with a hooked nose and a scimitar reeking of blood we were led by Nazim Khan. He looked suitably picturesque on a white horse, but his narrow shoulders, beardless face and woollen hat several sizes too big for him were unlikely to strike terror into the hearts of anyone; nor would the others have made very convincing brigands.

We passed through an area where, according to a mujahed, three thousand families had lived before the war. There was almost no one left. As if an earthquake had devastated the land, hardly a house remained intact. Splintered roof beams jutted from piles of rubble, crumbling earth walls protected empty gardens, tangles of weeds and clover flourished at the edges of broken irrigation channels and, in the orchards, the air was pungent with the smell of fallen fruit rotting on the ground.

Rounding a bend in the river we came upon the rusting hulk of a Russian tank, partly submerged in the water. Immediately Sediq unshouldered his anti-tank rocket, struck an heroic pose aiming at the wreckage and clamoured to have his photograph taken. Further on there were fields of cannabis. I asked one of the mujahedin what would happen to the harvest. He didn't know: in that part of Afghanistan only the old men smoked it.

'They smoke and they dream. They forget the war and they are happy. Mujahedin are not allowed to smoke it; our commanders say it makes our spirit weak,' he smiled. 'But sometimes, a few of us smoke in secret.'

In the late afternoon we arrived in a thickly wooded valley. Here and there little streams criss-crossed the valley floor and we made our way more slowly, savouring the cool air and the shadows cast by the mountain walls on either side of us. We stopped at a makeshift tea-stall under a mulberry tree where a majestic old man with a flowing beard was drinking chai with two younger men whom he introduced as his sons. He was the leader of another group of mujahedin and claimed to have several hundred men under his command. It was easy to believe him; he was an impressive character, well over six feet tall with broad shoulders and a strong, enveloping handshake. Thick eyebrows overhung a pair of watchful brown eyes and, with his aquiline nose and thick grey beard, he had an aura of unshakeable authority. I asked if I could take his photograph and he seated himself on a fallen tree, his sons on either side, guns resting in their arms, gazing impassively at the camera. I was just about to press the shutter when Nazim Khan materialised from nowhere and inserted himself at the back of the group with an expression of oily self-satisfaction.

While the horses were watered, some of the men performed their nemaz, led by one of the chieftain's sons who called out the prayers in a fine resonant voice. I was still bathing my feet and dusting them with talcum powder as the group set off again. I had to hurry to catch up with them.

The track rose gently upwards and in a short while emerged from the forest into scattered groves of apricot trees. Some of the group climbed into the boughs and shook the branches, raining down tiny golden fruits, which we gathered in handfuls. The path grew steeper and soon we were scrambling up a dry gully towards a cleft in the skyline. It was hard going and I allowed myself to fall back behind the pack animals. It was a big mistake; the dust stirred up by their hooves hung in the air and stuck to the back of my throat. When the slower animals were lashed by the drivers the shock triggered long sighing farts and occasionally a soft patter of dung. The sight of a horse's haunches in front of me began to pall. Humming furiously to myself I overtook the baggage train and stomped my way up to the top of the pass.

It was sunset and the last rays shone over a barren, undulating landscape. Our track stretched between the shadowed hills towards the west, disappearing into the distance. There was no sound; not a bird, not an insect. The evening breeze plucked at our clothes, chilling the sweat on our faces. The men stood in a line, facing the glowing horizon, while Maulawi led them in prayer. I sat to one side, contemplating the next stage of the journey that lay before us. The country was how I had always pictured Central Asia; desolate, treeless and utterly alien. For the first time I felt alone.

For a while the going was easy. The path sloped down into the plain and the younger mujahedin ran whooping down the steeper parts in competitive displays of energy. But as we pushed deeper into the arid waste the group grew silent and the pace became slower. Except for the halt at midday we had been travelling almost continuously since the early hours of the morning. Now it was dusk and we still had another eight or nine hours' march in front of us. Several of the men were already limping but no one complained. The stars emerged in a moonless sky and a warm wind buffeted us in the darkness.

Intermittent glimmerings played along the horizon. We had entered the plains of Lowgar. Several times there were the sounds of gunfire but they were far away. We came to a ruined caravanserai where the faint glow of a lamp was just visible at the window of a darkened building. Three of us went to the door which was opened by a sorrowful old man who offered us food in return for a small amount of money. We sat silently in a lamplit room and a few minutes later he appeared with three steaming bowls and some rounds of stale bread. The bowls contained nameless parts of an animal half-submerged in a yellow broth. I could only muster the mildest enthusiasm for eating as I dipped my bread in the hot, salty liquid, but my companions masticated everything with disconcerting relish. We paid hurriedly and left to find the others had gone on without us, leaving a solitary mujahed to show us the way. He was anxious in case we lost touch with the group and muttered resentfully at the delay. The wind had picked up again and the men and animals had vanished without trace into the shifting night air.

However, in half an hour we had caught up with the stragglers. Another effort and we were with the main body, where the sense of urgency which had been spurring us on dissolved, our pace slowed, and we slipped back into the rhythm of semi-conscious footsteps.

Fatigue can anaesthetise the body so that one no longer feels or cares about what one is doing and I let my mind wander. I remembered stories of Japanese soldiers during the war who slept even as they marched. The thought was deeply seductive; I closed my eyes. It was quite comfortable: my legs continued moving, there were no sounds to disturb me except the occasional pebble knocking against my boots, no need for a pillow . . . A thud and a stab of pain in my knee woke me. I had stumbled into a boulder beside the track. It was a useful lesson: next time I fell asleep I would do so with my eyes open.

I fumbled in my knapsack for the headphones to my Walkman and put on a tape of the Brandenburgs. There was an instant transformation. The stars shone and my feet lifted effortlessly. I sped past the others, and had almost reached the leaders when a sharp dig in the ribs made me unclip my earphones. The figure beside me was very agitated: he was afraid that the tiny red light glowing on the tape recorder might reveal our presence to Soviet patrols. Although it was invisible more than a few feet away I guiltily covered it with my hand.

Suddenly a penetrating light blossomed in the sky. For a moment I thought it was a particularly bright shooting star, but it remained almost motionless, bathing the landscape in an eerie glow. The hairs at the back of my neck froze and my throat went dry as I realised what it was: the flare of a Soviet patrol. Instinctively, none of us moved; the brilliance was hypnotic and I wondered how anyone could fail to spot us, standing in a disorderly tableau of men and horses on the skyline.

At last the light went out and in the dark my heart beat like a fist on a door. I could hardly breathe. With infra-red binoculars they could pick us off at will without being seen. I took a swig from my water bottle to loosen my throat and handed it to my walking companion of the past few miles. 'The big light is very dangerous,' he whispered. 'The Shuravi are close.'

It seemed a rather unnecessary piece of information.

'Yes,' I whispered back. 'But what are we going to do?'

There was a pause and I heard deep gulps of water being swallowed. Another pause, then a subdued belch. I hissed my question again. Silence.

'I don't know. Only God knows. We are in the hands of Allah.'

The flask was passed back to me, noticeably lighter than before. Some way behind us there was the clink of a bridle. Everyone was waiting for some kind of signal, but nothing happened.

Sitting with my back propped against a rock, I considered the situation. There had been no more flares – why? Perhaps they had seen us and were now waiting for us to move before firing another. Alternatively, it had been a signal, or a nervous guard frightened by a noise in the darkness, or even a drunken act of high spirits. I grew calmer, found a more comfortable position and stretched my legs. How many more hours would we be marching? And when would we be able to sleep? I remembered a long forgotten line from a school hymn: '. . . teach me to live that I may dread, the grave as little as my bed.' I was very tired.

I dozed off and was woken by Nazim Khan, still astride his horse, calling my name. The group was on the move. I stumbled to my feet and fell in with the nearest mujahed, who greeted me with the sympathy of another laggard.

'Ho, Abdul! This is a long road. Are you tired? My feet are very painful, especially the right one – big blisters all over it. It's all right if like Nazim Khan you have a horse but for people like us, Abdul, it's a long hard journey, isn't it?'

I agreed, faintly amazed he had such energy for conversation.

'My friend has a donkey. He said I could ride it but he's loaded the animal with bales of material for his mother and sisters. On top of that Nazim Khan asked him to carry some ammunition because he's too mean to buy enough mules. He let me ride it for a short way but the creature fell over and wouldn't get up.' He sighed. 'I'm a big man and it's a small donkey.'

I made a clumsy attempt to translate the saying, 'If wishes were horses, beggars would ride.' He groaned companionably.

'Truly spoken, Abdul. The world is not an easy place. Every man has his burden.'

He had all the characteristics of a true grumbler but I couldn't help liking him. I sensed a warm-hearted and lazy rogue. He moaned again.

'I've eaten nothing for hours – only those little apricots.'

I had an idea: what if he listened to the Brandenburgs?

His head was so large that the earphones only just fitted. The effect was instantaneous – he gave a deep sigh of pleasure and his pace quickened. It was hard to keep up with him, and we progressed rapidly along the line of trudging silhouettes.

Half an hour later we came to a body of men waiting by a pool of water. I could just make out the shapes of a few trees. The men were members of our group waiting for the vehicle which would take us on to our halt for the night. I was lightheaded with relief and celebrated with a gulp of water from the pool. It tasted bitter, but I was too thirsty to care.

One by one the others limped in until we were all present except for the baggage animals and their drivers, who were making their way separately to the rendezvous. Many of the men were in the last stages of exhaustion and slumped down on the ground as soon as they saw us. At last the rumble of a heavy engine was audible in the darkness. A vehicle flashed its lights briefly before coming to a halt a couple of hundred yards away.

The transport was a large, rickety bus. As many as possible squeezed themselves into the seats, while the rest of us climbed on the roof and hung on to the luggage rack. For several miles we rocked and jolted across open country until we reached some kind of road and gathered speed.

The Plough swung to and fro above us and the night air rushed past. A mujahed, noticing I was cold, insisted I share his blanket. 'We don't want you to go back to England and say that the mujahedin didn't keep you warm.'

We compared the names of constellations and he told me the times of sowing and harvest.

The bus lurched to a halt. The driver, it seemed, was refusing to go any further: it was too dangerous. We offered him more money but it was no use. It was time to start walking again. Like zombies we shouldered our packs and weapons to trail after Maulawi, who miraculously seemed to know the way. An hour later we arrived at our destination, a small mosque with a straw-covered floor and a lamp burning in a niche in the wall.

The first stage of the journey was behind us: we had crossed the plains of Lowgar and for the time being we were safe. I tried to calculate how long it was since we crossed the border from Pakistan: incredibly, less than sixty hours had passed since I said goodbye to Sa'id, Ali and Mahmoud.

A mujahed had rolled his petou into a pillow and beckoned to me to lay my head on it. Without a word we lay down, shoulder to shoulder, and slept.

3

Wardak

I woke jaded and unrefreshed. Groping my way out of the mosque, I found Maulawi washing in a stream in preparation for the early morning prayer. Mists hung over little rivulets that ran between fields of corn; here and there solitary figures squatted on the ground relieving themselves. The sun gleamed a dull yellow as Maulawi chanted his prayer, joined by the five other men in his group.

Nazim Khan and the others were still asleep. Instinctively I was unwilling to stay long at the mosque, so I decided to go ahead with Maulawi. We passed patient oxen treading circles of newly harvested corn, while old men or small children followed them, tapping their flanks with goads. Men and women stood in the straw threshing rhythmically, or casting grain into the air in clouds of chaff. We skirted round a huge bomb crater in the middle of the path; there were others clearly visible in the fields on either side. A helicopter went over in the distance. The day grew brighter. As the colours intensified I felt I was emerging from the confused and sinister limbo of the previous night into the light of another, real world.

We entered a town and ate some grapes in the shadow of a fruit seller's awning. Our guns attracted no attention. Men on bicycles rode slowly past and little girls, their heads covered in gaily-coloured *chador*, staggered by carrying vessels of water. At midday the others joined us and a guide took us to a set of deserted rooms facing on to the road, where there were stalls selling shish kebabs and nan, fruit and chai. It was the first appetising food we had seen for several days. After gorging ourselves we lay back to relax for a few hours until another truck arrived to take us on. Even my grumbling companion of the small hours, Rahim, was relatively content.

'These kebabs aren't bad, Abdul – better than those little apricots. There could be more meat in them, but we must thank God for what he have.'

He told me of his family; he had three sons and his wife was very beautiful. It was hard to believe him. He had a squat nose and a heavy jaw; he breathed heavily through his nose and mouth at the same time and his narrow eyes had a squint which gave him a shifty look. Rammed on top of his head was a grimy woollen hat. The other mujahedin wore theirs neatly rolled but Rahim didn't bother: his head was too big and he hadn't been able to find a hat large enough. Instead he wore it in such a way that it looked a cross between a cossack hat and a tea-cosy.

While the others oiled their guns, they talked about the presents they had bought for their families. They had bolts of brightly embroidered fabric which was impossible to buy in Afghanistan, combs, bangles and tiny pairs of shoes. All these they unpacked and laid out for one another's inspection, exclaiming with scorn or admiration as they heard the prices paid for each item.

I wandered off to look around the town. It was mid-afternoon and the heat was oppressive. I took refuge in the shade of a chaikhane. A knife-grinder was busy sharpening a bundle of blades, some men were shoeing a horse and, nearby, a man was operating a primitive water pump, drawing water up from a well and sluicing it into an irrigation ditch. Superficially at least life seemed normal, except for the armed men, walking the streets hand in hand. They were from a large company of Hesb Islami, sixty or more, who were going to share the transport with us later that afternoon.

On my return to our temporary billets, the presents had been packed away and the guns stacked neatly in a corner of the room. Ten minutes later a vast cattle truck lumbered round the corner and shuddered to a halt. An interval of barely-controlled pandemonium ensued as the two groups boarded the vehicle. Rasputin-like figures carrying mortars jostled with wiry Uzbekis with bandoliers of bullets hanging from their shoulders, all pushing and shouting their way to the best places. Sacks of flour, boxes of ammunition, bundles, knapsacks, guns and fruit were manoeuvred perilously aboard: more men, more belongings, the flow seemed endless. The driver, with a wet strip of cotton knotted around his head, sat in the cab smoking a cigarette and staring fixedly into space. There were no serious injuries and the whole operation had the atmosphere of a crowd of well-behaved football supporters. Eventually close to a hundred men squeezed themselves on to the truck. The driver tossed his cigarette out of the window, the engine kicked and roared into life: we were off. *Borou bekheir!*

I had managed to secure a cramped position on the baggage rack directly over the driver's cab. One of my neighbours, a half-wit with a face like an adenoidal sheep, laughed uproariously when I told him that my name was Abdul Baz. It was not a comfortable ride. A

melon and a rocket launcher were pressed into the small of my back
and at every pothole the barrel of the half-wit's Kalashnikov jabbed
into my kidneys. Branches smacked the sides of the lorry and swept
across our hunched shoulders. We clutched at the leaves of mulberry trees flashing past and if we were lucky we were rewarded
with handfuls of crushed berries.

The road rolled on through earth-coloured villages. Women
huddled round wells covered their faces as we approached, dogs and
chickens scattered in all directions. Ragged children rushed at the
dust of the lorry, squawking and screaming and trying to tap the
passing wheels with sticks. Soon we had left them all behind and
were climbing through valleys of green shadow surrounded by cliffs
of bare rock. At sunset, the lorry stopped and we were deposited
beside a slow-moving stream.

We waited in the gathering gloom for the pack animals to arrive.
The air was alive with mosquitoes. The others wrapped their petous
around their shoulders for protection, but my petou was with my
pack. I cursed and stamped as the insects began to strike through my
cotton shirt.

The Hesb men started off ahead into the dusk leaving us to take
refuge from the bloodthirsty insects in the village mosque. It was a
fine wooden building. Inside an array of lamps were flickering from
simply carved wooden pillars and a few villagers were kneeling in
prayer, seemingly oblivious to our presence. We stacked the guns in
a corner and talked quietly among ourselves. The men seemed
nervous. There was a state outpost on one side of the valley through
which we had to pass and Nazim Khan went over the procedure if
we were surprised by a Soviet patrol. The close, airless heat of the
mosque was oppressive and I grew thirsty. A few subdued villagers
were standing outside the door. I asked one of them where I could
get some water. He took my bottle and bent down to fill it from the
open drain running at our feet. I stopped him just in time. When I
asked him whether there was any clean water several of the men
beside him shifted uneasily; at last, one of them volunteered to fill
my flask from a nearby well. The man's behaviour puzzled me until I
reasoned that he resented the danger our presence brought to his
village.

The lead-driver of the baggage train finally appeared. Although
the men and animals were tired from the three-hour journey, they
only halted for a brief rest. Then we set off in silence, leaving the
lights of the village behind us, to climb a narrow path into the
mountains at the head of the valley.

The fine sand of the path muffled our footsteps. Above us, a mosaic of stars sparkled like the haphazard lights of a vast and distant city. The only sounds were the occasional dull knock of horses' hooves, bound with rags, and the creak of ropes securing the ammunition boxes. At one point for no apparent reason we stopped. Five, ten, fifteen minutes passed. Once again I thought of infra-red sights and wondered what the delay was. Then Nazim Khan rode up from behind and without any explanation we continued on our way. A shadow came alongside me and pressed an apple into my hands.

The landscape grew less hilly and the constellations on the horizon appeared so close it seemed one might reach out one's hand to touch them. By now the outpost was safely behind us. The men began talking to one another in low voices and when we stopped in the shelter of some rocks the Professor lit a cigarette. His face was smiling in the light of the match.

'We are safe now; thanks be to Allah. Are you tired, Abdul? Were you frightened?'

The others laughed in the sudden blackness as the flame went out.

I ignored his question and asked how much further we had still to go.

'Another two hours, maybe three, and we can rest.'

A breeze blew softly about us and the delicate crescent of the new moon became visible. It seemed a good omen.

By the time we reached our halt for the night the men were hungry, but there was no food. Not for the first time, I felt irritated by the lack of organisation. Nazim Khan disappeared with someone carrying a lamp, leaving us to settle down for the night. My petou was still among the baggage and I was lent a thin cotton one by an old man lying beside a mound of corn for threshing. The air grew cooler and I burrowed into the straw, doing my best to ignore the penetrating hum of mosquitoes.

We struck camp while it was still dark and walked on towards the dawn, under a sky threaded with lilac clouds. My companion was the Wolfman look-alike from Maulawi's group, who loped easily up and down the steep paths. We crested a hill and came to a collection of gravestones, finely carved with ornate script. Below us lay a misted green valley enclosed by rocky hills. We sat and watched the first rays of the sun touch the tops of the poplar trees and spread across the adobe roofs towards the fields of ripening corn. The houses were surrounded by tall, mud-brick walls, set with strong wooden gates, most of which were closed, but through one I glimpsed a hand beckoning from a doorway and a small child running across a courtyard. Beside the gate lay an old dog with

chewed ears, sunning himself on a mound of refuse like Odysseus'
faithful hound, Argos.

The sun grew higher and in the next village we came to a little boy
offered a cup of water to one of the mujahedin. The path led along a
winding stream and the young mujahed in front of me stopped to
pluck an apple from a tree growing on the bank. His hand rustled
among the leaves but the fruit fell through his fingers into the water
with a bright splash and floated away. Somehow the sight moved
me deeply, and as I walked away the moment echoed uneasily in my
mind.

It was full summer: the trees were laden with apricots and apples,
the fields colourful with hollyhocks, convolvulus and lavender. But
at the edge of almost every village there were ragged flags fluttering
over the graves of the *shahid*.

At the next village, I caught up with the Professor who was
looking for somewhere to buy cigarettes. A man led us to a tiny
room piled with matches, tinned milk, cigarettes and biscuits. The
owner of the shop invited us to have a pot of milky tea and we talked
about the war. He was an intelligent man and answered my
questions clearly.

In the immediate area there were three hundred houses. So far
fifty people had died as a result of the fighting. Prices of the most
elementary goods had doubled or trebled and many items were
unobtainable. It was difficult to continue running the shop. Nevertheless, he was prepared for the war to continue for another thirty,
forty, fifty years — however long it took before the Russians left
Afghanistan. I asked him how he received news of what was
happening in other parts of the country. He called through a
doorway and a young man like an Orthodox monk appeared
cradling a transistor radio. They listened to Voice of America and
the BBC, which sometimes got things wrong. Kabul Radio was
useless. Had any people left for Pakistan? At this he was silent.
Looking at the young man holding the radio, he shook his head
slowly.

'Only the bad people have left. A few. Not good Muslims.'

While we were talking an uncomfortable spasm gripped my
stomach and I was courteously shown to a secluded privy at the end
of the garden. The walls were of woven willow branches and it hung
over a briskly flowing river. It was a delightful place and I dawdled,
swinging my legs in the sunlight until I heard the anxious cries of the
Professor calling my name among the sunflowers. When we made
our farewells to the owner of the shop, he pressed a packet of
cigarettes into my hand, refusing every attempt at payment.

By now we were a long way behind. We struck off in the direction we hoped the others had taken, asking people working in the fields whether they had seen a group of men and horses, and at last we came on their tracks in the damp mud running between the fields of rice.

By midday we reached a chaikhane where we found the main group already eating. Maulawi's men invited me to join them. A large bowl of soup was produced into which they tore pieces of nan until the liquid was absorbed, leaving a soggy mess of bread. I ate a few hand-fuls but the presentation dulled my appetite and in the end I settled for a nan and a glass of green tea. Through the doorway I watched a flock of sheep go by with curious swaying rumps, and I remembered Herodotus' description of the sheep whose tails were so huge that their owners harnessed them with little carts to carry them.

Some distance from the chaikhane was a river. During the after-noon the men wandered down to it in ones and twos to wash their clothes. Some stripped to the waist and soaped themselves. I was mildly surprised for, by nature and religion, the Afghans are a modest people. I was caked with sweat and dust, the light was beckoning on the water and I decided to take a swim. Still wearing my trousers, I waded in. The water was warm but the current was stronger than I expected. I clambered into mid-stream to let the full force of the water sweep me past the Professor and the others until it flung me into a natural wall of boulders further downstream. Bruised but glowing, I knelt in the shallows and noticed bright, golden particles twinkling in the fine silt. I trickled some mud on to a rock. Sure enough, as the sun dried it, the sediment revealed miniature flakes of shiny metal. Gold!

Back at the chaikhane I showed some of the sparkling dust to a mujahed. He cupped it in the palm of his hand, blowing gently on the dust until only a few yellow specks remained. Carefully brush-ing one to the side of his hand he pressed it with his fingernail, splitting the glittering flake in two, then shook his head with a smile and rubbed the palm of his hand on his trousers. Fool's gold.

Once the hottest hour of the day had passed, we continued. The trail stretched across a still-baking plain of sun-bleached rocks. Gradually the group disintegrated into a broken line of figures shimmering in a haze of heat. A mujahed on a horse trotted up and began talking to me. Was the weather the same in England? Did we have sheep? And what about pigs – surely we didn't eat such dirty animals? All the while he let his horse amble in the middle of the path while I stumbled along at one side. I began to resent the man's comfortable complacency, and my answers grew more curt until I ignored his questions altogether. He made several more efforts at conversation which were met with silence until with a laugh, he kicked his horse forwards, leaving me in a cloud of dust to contemplate my unfriendliness.

At the other side of the plain the trail entered another range of hills and my spirits were beginning to wilt when I heard someone singing lustily at the top of his voice. The singing stopped and a voice called my name.

'Ho! Abdul Baz. When you are tired you must sing! That's how to climb these mountains.'

A handsome young man in a grey turban caught up with me. He had an open face, bright eyes and strong white teeth. His name was Amin'allah, he had just finished his madraseh training and was now a mullah. I liked him immediately. After talking for a while he stepped out, calling over his shoulder:

'Now we will sing together; first you, then me. You see, the journey will be easier.'

I ransacked my memory for a suitable tune. At last I found one:

Some talk of Alexander, and some of Hercules,
Of Hector and Lysander, and such great names as these,
But of all the world's great heroes, there's none that can compare,
With a tow row row row row row row for the British Grenadiers.

I bellowed the words while Amin'allah clapped his hands in time.

'Again, Abdul, again.'

The song had taken almost all my breath away but he ignored my protests.

'Again, Abdul. Sing about Iskandar again!'

I sang another round with the blood pulsing in my temples, and quavered to a halt halfway through the chorus. 'Ra ra ra, Abdul Baz!' echoed in front of me.

We passed a small mound of rocks beside the path at which Amin'allah broke off singing and stroked his beard, murmuring a prayer. Further on he discovered a tiny spring trickling in a shadow between some boulders. He brushed the surface to clear it of stray particles and drank a mouthful from his cupped hand to reassure me that it was clean.

'Drink, Abdul. This water is from the heart of the mountain. It is very pure.'

I knelt down and put my lips to the surface: it was piercingly cold.

I had already forgotten the delight of chilled water and gulped greedily to wash the thirst from the back of my throat, almost draining the little pool.

At last a gap in the mountains opened before us and we saw the small, fortified town where we were to spend the night. From a distance it was extremely picturesque: massive adobe guard towers rising above a jumble of flat roofs surrounded by trees and green fields. Close to, it was a less appealing sight. The only sign of life was a solitary cur which shrank away at a well-aimed stone from Amin'allah. The crumbling mud walls were zig-zagged by great cracks. A sense of apathy pervaded the filthy streets.

We placed our packs and guns on the flat roof of our sleeping quarters. Below us the horses mouthed at their bits and, once their loads had been removed, rolled in the dust of the courtyard. Beside me the leader of the drivers, a gaunt and kindly Uzbeki called Sufi Imam-Uddin, massaged his legs. Then he glanced at the sky and ran his fingers through his beard; there, shining faintly in the west, was the silver ringlet of the new moon.

Supper was a wretched affair. We gathered in a mosque and ate in almost total darkness. Half a dozen plates of wet, gritty rice were distributed among us with a single onion among five men and water from a large, cracked jug. There was no bread. The men ate with a silent intensity. They were clearly disappointed with their welcome. Maulawi tried to rally their spirits with sparks of humour but they fizzled out in an atmosphere of weary gloom.

After the meal Amin'allah spread a horse blanket in a corner of the roof and arranged my pack as a pillow, resting his gun and bundle beside it. I was taking off my boots when a shadow opposite hissed my name in mock urgency:

'Abdul Baz! Look out, the enemy's coming!'

I was in a bad mood and the joke seemed in poor taste, so I replied:

'I don't care; wherever they are it's all the same to me.'

The tone of the voice changed abruptly:

'It's all right for you. Look at the war, take some pictures and leave. What do you understand about it?'

There was a pause, then the same voice muttered the word 'kafir' scornfully in the dark.

There was a shocked silence. 'Kafir' means unbeliever and is a deep insult to any Muslim. I had to act quickly. If I let the insult pass unchecked I could see a serious gulf widen between me and the rest of the group. I leapt to my feet, grabbed at the shadow and my fingers closed on the man's shirt. I tugged it roughly.

'What did you say?' I shouted as fiercely as I could, though my knees were unsteady with nerves.

The man said nothing. I sensed his antagonism weaken, so I pressed home the attack:

'I am one of the Ahl e Ketab, the people of the Book. Who are you to say I am an unbeliever?'

Amin'allah separated us. Someone switched on a torch and I saw the man's face. His eyes were unsure, and blinking in the glare of the light he looked so delicate and thin that I felt sorry for him. The beam of the torch swung into my eyes for several seconds then shifted back to the man.

'The foreigner's mad. I said nothing. Suddenly he attacked me.'

Once again the brightness flashed into my eyes. I turned to address the anonymous light.

'You heard what he said. Although my religion is different we have the same God.'

The brilliance rested on my face for a few moments, flickered briefly over the man opposite, then vanished with a click. From the darkness where the light had been a tired voice uttered the words, '*Tamam shod* – it is finished'. Amin'allah took my hand, placing it in that of the man opposite. As we shook hands, I noticed that his, like my own, was greasy with sweat.

Later, I sat leaning against the low wall that ran around the roof. The evening wind was cool on my forehead but the heat of the day still radiated from the crumbling adobe at my back. The moon balanced on the silhouette of the nearby fort.

A tap on my shoulder stirred me from my reverie.

'Abdul Baz, *o baradar* – brother. Take some of this.'

My invisible neighbour tipped some naswar into my hand. I inserted the powder under my tongue and savoured the hot, bitter taste. It was also the taste of success. I had been called *baradar*. Now, in a sense, I was their brother.

A cock crowed: it was dawn. The jumble of empty blankets around me showed the men were performing their nemaz in the mosque. After about a quarter of an hour they returned talking excitedly and smiling. Nazim Khan had decided to make a late start, a sheep was to be slaughtered and the rest of the morning was free. Some chai was produced. I sat in the sun drinking, then allowed myself the luxury of a cigarette.

A little later Amin'allah asked me to accompany him to the mosque. Inside there was a crowd of villagers and mujahedin sitting on the floor listening to a middle-aged man in a white turban and brown robes. At his side two younger men stood in respectful silence. They were itinerant preachers lecturing the assembly on the need for every man to set his life in the way of *jehad*.

'Townsmen, it is your duty to help your brothers in this holy war. It is your duty to God, the compassionate, the merciful. He will reward you. Already – who knows? – He has decided that you will become a *shahid*, a martyr and your reward is certain: *behesht*, the kingdom of Paradise.'

Here and there a head nodded in solemn acquiescence. He continued, his voice rising in volume:

'The present war against the Shuravi is part of a greater war: the Islamic revolution. All over the world our brothers in the faith are awakening to a new spirit of religion.'

Suddenly he pointed towards me.

'This man comes from a distant land, but he has heard of the bravery of the mujahedin. The word is spreading. Soon every country will know of the strength and glory of Islam.'

At the end of the sermon, I talked with one of the younger men. He told me that his organisation had offices in London and Paris, but was reluctant to tell me more. He asked whether I was a Muslim but when I replied that I was a Christian he lost interest and politely disengaged himself.

Meanwhile, a sheep had been selected from a flock inside the courtyard of the ruined fort, slaughtered, and was already roasting over a blazing fire. The smell drew us into a hungry circle, our attention fixed on the smoking meat and the steaming cauldron. At last the food was ready, and we filed past to receive a chunk of meat on a nan bread and a cup of salty broth from the cauldron. In the distance a Soviet jet crossed the sky over the plains of Lowgar.

At one o'clock we shouldered our packs and set off into the blazing heat, to cross another treeless expanse of sand and rocks. On the way I barely avoided an argument with one of the mule drivers who seemed to take a perverse delight in whipping his animal across my path.

We crossed another range of hills and entered a series of valleys. Under a willow, I found the Professor who had rolled up his trousers to bathe his feet in a stream. With his white skull cap, carefully trimmed moustache and pot belly, he looked exactly like a McGill seaside postcard. I pulled off my boots and socks and sat down beside him. For several minutes we gazed in silence at our feet, pale and unfamiliar beneath the rippling surface. The Professor offered me a cigarette and we puffed away, blowing the smoke at the insects hovering around us.

'Abdul, my friend, war is a terrible thing.'

The words sounded curiously out of place in the translucent shade of the willow tree.

'It changes the hearts of men.'

In the undergrowth a bird trilled and there was a flutter of wings and leaves.

'The men are not getting enough to eat. Some of them say that Nazim Khan is keeping money back from them. Imagine, a brother Muslim.'

'Is it true?'

'I don't know. Nothing is certain.'

An air of gentle melancholy descended. A minute later a gruff voice shouted our names.

'Wakil. Abdul Baz. Ho there! What are you doing, playing in the water?'

Rahim lumbered into view.

'God, my feet are painful, covered in blisters. Look, I had to loosen the laces.'

The Professor suggested he bathed them in the stream.

'Can't do that. If I take my boots off I won't be able to put them on again.'

Rahim stood about, grumbling good-naturedly about nothing in particular while we dried our feet. The shadows were lengthening when we set off again with the Professor in front, myself in the middle and Rahim bringing up the rear.

The valley broadened out into a wide plain and we saw another adobe fortress, equally picturesque, rising above fields of corn and framed by a range of amethyst-coloured mountains.

We followed the curve of a river and arrived at the evening's halt just as the sun was setting. The men were oddly subdued; the reason why became clear when I discovered that we were in the heart of Hesb Islami territory. Nazim Khan was even then engaged in delicate negotiations as to whether we could remain in the vicinity.

A couple of young men sauntered up dressed in the dark grey clothes which were the characteristic uniform of Hesb Islami. They seemed friendly enough and one of them spoke excellent French. He had come from Algeria to join the *jehad* and had already been in Afghanistan for six months. He claimed there were several other volunteers like himself from different parts of the Islamic world including Turkey, Egypt and Iran. It was good to speak French and I tried to prolong the conversation, but he had to go. Nevertheless, he promised to return later in the evening when, *Insha'allah*, he would introduce me to his commander Sa'id Ahmed Shah.

Nazim Khan returned having gained permission to stay over-
night, provided we kept to the area surrounding the inn. We ate a
meagre supper of bread, soup and rice, watched over by a few Hesb
guards armed with Kalashnikovs and, when we had finished, we
laid out our blankets under the eaves of the inn. It was a warm,
windless night and the men lay awake, talking in soft, unhurried
cadences.

'*Vite! Vite! Lève-toi.*'

The Algerian had returned. The Professor asked me sleepily
where I was going. I told him I didn't know, which was partially
true: it seemed undiplomatic to say I was visiting a Hesb Islami
commander.

'Don't go, Abdul. It's very dangerous. Stay here.'

With an uneasy feeling of disloyalty, I ignored the Professor's
warnings and followed my guide into the darkness. Our path took
us along a dry river bed. I could see nothing at all and stumbled
blindly after the cries of my unfortunate dragoman as he stubbed his
toes in the pitch blackness.

A blood-curdling scream followed by the sound of a magazine
clip being rammed home stopped us in our tracks. A flashlight
searched our faces and a disembodied voice asked for the password
which my guide returned in a slightly shaken whisper. There was a
second's pause and then the order to continue was given in gentler,
almost apologetic tones. I prayed there were no more over-zealous
guards hidden in the night but ten minutes later it happened again
and, by the time we saw the dim glow of a window, I was distinctly
on edge.

I was shown into a room where several figures were seated round
a lamp. The man I judged to be Sa'id Ahmed Shah rose to greet me.
Although his native language was Dari he preferred to speak Arabic,
the holy language of the Qur'an. The Algerian acted as interpreter.
The rest of the men in the room were silent.

He told me that he was thirty but his face looked older. He was
married and had four sons. When he learnt that I was the same age
as him, and still unmarried, he asked mockingly how I managed for
women. Did I buy them in the bazaar? I replied that in my country a
man might live with a woman before marriage.

'Then does he marry her?'

'*Insha'allah.*' He gave a knowing smile.

'And if that man does not marry her, can she marry another?'

I told him that in my country both men and women might
have several lovers before marriage. As the Algerian translated,
Ahmed Shah's eyes narrowed in disbelief and his lip curled with

disapproval. I sensed the conversation was about to turn sour and asked him about the fighting in the surrounding countryside.

Ahmed Shah was personally in command of 3,500 men. In the past five months there had been sixty-three bombings in the region of Saidabad and, out of a population of 12,000, 1,800 had been killed. Medical aid was unnecessary; instead they used traditional, Afghan methods of healing which included preparations of hashish for wounds. Prayer was the most effective treatment of all. No, they didn't need any weapons either, although walkie-talkies would be welcome.

We talked of Islam. He lectured me for a while and I countered with a series of doctrinal questions which prompted him to ask why I hadn't converted to the faith. My reply, that the great religions were different paths up the same mountain, amused him.

'At least you are one of the Ahl e Ketab – the People of the Book. But your knowledge of God is a pale shadow of the Glorious Qur'an. That is the reason Europe and America are so degenerate and why we want no help from you.'

When he spoke of his religion he adopted a cloying gentleness of manner. But the lamplight could not soften the marks of war on his face, and when he described the numbers of Soviets he had killed he smiled without humour. There was a dangerous and unpredictable quality about him. I thought that for all his outward piety he seemed the sort of man who might use religion as a pretext for brutality. I was about to ask him what he would do, once the war was over, when he murmured something to the Algerian. Ahmed Shah was tired, he had been travelling for several days without sleep, and the interview was over.

Once more we ran the gauntlet of invisible sentries. I got back to find the Professor chain-smoking and fretting over my absence and he extracted a promise from me that I would not go off with another group again.

The stars were still bright in the sky when we set off. By sunrise the small party of men I was with had lost touch with the main body. We plunged into a deep valley rustling with trees, but there were no familiar tracks in the dust; we were lost. Steep mountains rose up on either side. The Professor asked the way from a bent old man who pointed waveringly towards the mountains to our left and uttered the word '*Jang!*' – war. The Professor stepped out briskly in the opposite direction.

So began a difficult climb out of the valley. We slogged up a goat-track with the sun blazing overhead and the rocks underfoot throwing the heat up into our faces. I counted fifteen false crests before I gave up, past caring. One of the men lay down by the side of the path, covering himself with his petou. He was shivering and his eyes stared blankly at me when I pulled the blanket from his face. Malaria? Dehydration? There was nothing I could do, so I trudged on. No one else stopped to help him.

An hour later we reached a plateau and a miraculous vision appeared before us: a solitary tree and an old man in its shade. A few sheep grazed a patch of grass by a trickle of water.

After a while, the companion we had so callously abandoned limped into view and we resumed our journey. I was walking some way ahead of the others when I caught sight of a group of nomads approaching with their camels. Suddenly, a wild-looking ruffian emerged from their midst, and ran towards me shouting and cursing in a strange dialect. I nodded politely but this only enraged him further and he pushed the barrel of his Kalashnikov at my throat. Just in time, the Professor defused what might have been an unpleasant situation. I had been mistaken for a Russian.

We made our way down into another valley where we found a dreary collection of makeshift dwellings. The Professor decided to call a halt. We ordered some chai and collapsed in the sweltering shade of a tent. I was beginning to run a fever and had some difficulty in following the Professor's conversation. Outside the tent a dog tied to a tree was struggling to free itself.

'It is not good to be here,' said the Professor. 'Behind those mountains . . . ,' he gestured towards a line of dun-coloured hills a few miles away, '. . . are Hesb Nasr.'

He waited for the name to take effect and seemed disappointed when I showed no reaction.

'They are bandits. They take people's money and guns, then kill them.'

He drew his fingers across his throat with a lugubrious expression.

'Or sometimes they skin them alive,' he added, tracing a line across his foot, up his leg and slowly along the length of his body. He smiled as if he had told a faintly risqué story.

'Oh.'

'We must wait for the others till sunset. If they haven't arrived by then we must go back to Peshawar.'

The thought of enduring the rigours of the past week all over again made the prospect of being skinned alive seem a risk which was almost worth taking.

Some hard, tasteless apricots were produced, and two children with pockmarked faces watched us as we ate the fruit listlessly. A squadron of flies swarmed around our heads. Through the awning I saw the dog free itself and lope away . . .

The Professor shook me awake from a confused, sweating dream; there was still no sign of Nazim Khan and he was nervous about staying where we were.

'It is too dangerous. Two men were here earlier, they were bad men, probably from Hesb Nasr. We must go into the mountains and sleep near the nomads. We will be safe there.'

The sun was low in the sky as we limped back up the mountains. The nomad chief welcomed us and invited us to share supper with him. We seated ourselves on a black felt carpet and his sons poured water for us to wash our hands. As the sun set the nomads and the members of our party prayed together, facing slightly away from the splendour of the west, towards the invisible radiance of Mecca. I sat to one side, contemplating the men and their faith and the mountains, seemingly on fire, in the distance.

After supper, a mound of cushions and cotton quilts were brought for us: I smoked a cigarette and watched the shadows of the mountains. The mujahed beside me was already snoring as the moon swam into a sea of stars. Hours later, Nazim Khan and the others arrived. Half-awake, I glimpsed their torches floating in the darkness, then slipped back into a dreamless sleep.

4

Bamiyan

We started at dawn, taking a route that avoided the territory of the
Hesb Nasr. It meant a long detour across a monotonous, stony plain
broken at intervals by gullies, some several hundred feet deep. One
moment there was a cavalcade of men and horses in front, the next
moment they had disappeared. It was easy to understand the origin
of travellers' tales of powerful wizards and enchanted caravans
vanishing without trace.

At noon we rested briefly by a stagnant pool under a grove of
poplars where there was a roguish old Uzbeki with a chai stall
doing brisk business, selling warm bread and chai at exorbitant
prices. From there the landscape changed, becoming less harsh. We
entered a range of gently undulating hills and valleys. Whenever
possible I walked alone; the blisters from the previous day had made
me irritable and the strain of being continuously in the company of
the mujahedin was beginning to tell. But solitude was hard to come
by. One mujahed in particular, a man with a long, stupid face and a
hat with drooping canvas ears, made my life a misery. Whenever I
thought I had finally escaped him, he would pad noiselessly up
behind and abruptly hiss my name. If I slowed down he dawdled, if I
accelerated so did he. I stopped and let him overtake me only to find
him lurking in wait round the next bend. It began to be surreal,
reaching a grotesque climax as he intoned garbled fragments of
English:

'I am a clock. You are my book. This is Friday.'

My head began to spin. He started reciting an obscure version of
the alphabet: 'A-B-D-F-N-G-R-P-S . . .' and my patience snapped. I
spun round and shouted a string of choice Anglo-Saxon expletives.
He gave a fishy smile and was silent for a few minutes; then the
litany of rubbish began again. Barely able to control myself, I told
him he had the brains of a sheep and that I preferred my own
company. As an afterthought, I added that I was practising *zikhr*
meditation, and found his presence intrusive.

In a wretched village of tumbledown mud hovels I rested by a
pool and watched him shamble past, still mumbling to himself. Two

little girls were washing chatties with sand and a tiny old man, bent like a dwarf with rheumatism, was bathing his misshapen ankles in a dribble of water. None of them took any notice of my presence. I sat on the water's edge, a momentary visitor to their world. The old man hobbled off and the little girls rinsed the last of their pots and trotted away. I remained for a while longer listening to the trickle of water falling into itself, watching the light and shadow of a cloud's reflection, passing across the sky beneath the troubled surface of the pool.

For several hours I journeyed by myself, following the bootmarks in the dust, now and then glimpsing the horses and mules which were taking a different route on the other side of the valley. In the late afternoon I reached the brow of a hill overlooking a dusty plain. Sediq and a few others, including the idiot hanger-on, were sprawled on either side of the path examining each other's weapons. I perched myself on a rock, and was enjoying the view when I heard a burst of sniggering. Turning round I found the tube of an anti-tank rocket smilingly aimed in my direction by the idiot. At his shoulder, Sediq was explaining the firing mechanism. As tactfully as possible I told them that, in England, pointing an anti-tank rocket at a person's head was a serious breach of etiquette.

They talked about the merits of their weapons, but I had seen and heard enough about their guns; the topic bored me and I took no part in the conversation. Disgruntledly, I began to write my diary and later, when they set off, I ungraciously refused their invitation to keep pace with them.

I was the last to arrive at our halt for the night and the group was already gathered around Nazim Khan listening to his description of the following day's itinerary. He beckoned me to sit beside him. The next moment there was an almighty bang and a slap of hot air hit me in the face. Six feet away, an anti-tank rocket had exploded. The launcher was propped on the ground, still pointing in my direction – the rocket had missed me by inches. By the time anyone realised what had happened, the rocket had detonated itself harmlessly on the hillside a quarter of a mile away.

There was a stunned silence. Then everyone began shouting at a man with a smoke-blackened face: Sediq. The thought that I had almost had my head blown off was oddly finite. I felt nothing and went off to get some corn plasters from my pack. As I was loosening the cords of my pack a mujahed with a disarmingly simian face wandered up to me.

'*Allah faz'l*,' he murmured. 'God is excellent.'

Our accommodation for the night was a long, low building. Before the war it had been a roadhouse, now it was a staging post for groups of mujahedin passing through. Inside, a poster of Ayatollah Khomeini, flanked by the charred flags of the United States and the Soviet Union, gazed unsmilingly down at us from the walls. Supper was dull but plentiful, provided by some taciturn men who seemed inoffensive enough, although the Professor described them in a whisper as friends of the Hesb Nasr.

I stretched out for the night beside two brothers who had been working in Iran for a year. They were full of praise for Ayatollah Khomeini and the government of Iran. Both brothers had saved a lot of money and were on their way back to their wives and families in the north. They were simple, likeable fellows. Their main topic of conversation was the colour of tea. One liked black tea, Iranian style, *chai siah*; the other preferred green tea, *chai sabz*. Throughout the journey, at almost every chaikhane, they would wink at me, raising their different glasses of tea, and shout the respective colours with enthusiasm.

I woke to find the brothers gone and the room half-empty. I scratched myself and realised why. Fleas. Groping my way outside to the concrete patio, I inserted myself in a narrow space between two sleeping forms. A penetrating hum passed over my head, then another. Mosquitoes. An hour or so later the cold concrete and the mosquitoes drove me back into the flea-ridden warmth.

At daybreak we marched out under a silver-blue sky. The road wound up into another range of mountains following the meandering course of a river. Throughout the morning a bearded youth kept pace with me. He was a tailor's son from Nahrin and had just spent a year in Peshawar, an experience which had greatly inflated his sense of self-importance. Whenever there was a minor difficulty, such as a river crossing or reloading the mules, he stood in people's way, shouting useless advice and confusing everyone. However, he had a huge pouch of naswar and supplied me with generous pinches of the stuff as we walked along.

'This is better than cigarettes. Too much smoke in your chest and you can't climb the mountains. But with this' – he shovelled another batch of naswar under his tongue – 'your heart beats strongly and the mountains are easy.'

It was true. The miles seemed to roll by effortlessly, and at midday we came to a squat, windowless inn at the foot of a pass. In the distance, between wisps of cloud, were mountain peaks capped with snow.

Through a low doorway, I could just make out Nazim Khan and

several mujahedin plunging their hands into a large metal bowl. They called out to me to join them. I was about to step into the meaty-smelling gloom when a battered vehicle rattled to a halt behind me. Rahim's vast head poked over the side of the truck.

'Come on, Abdul, climb aboard. It'll save you a few miles' walking.'

In an instant I had joined him on the roof and we were jolting along between hilly meadows. Red-veiled women crouched in small groups, sickles in their hands, harvesting the corn; little boys splashed in the shallows of a river; in a green field, a dog leaped and bounded after a butterfly. The truck drove into a stream running across the road. The engine shuddered spasmodically and then stopped.

Water was sluiced over the bonnet and there was a sinister hiss. Then the engine was switched on again; nothing happened, only a metallic cough and a brief poltergeist-like knocking. In front of us the road climbed towards the clouds at the top of the pass. The sky darkened and a few spots of rain fell. Anxiously, we hung over the sides of the truck and watched the driver extract unlikely-looking bits of rubber and metal from the engine's interior. It looked as if we would be there for some time. Rahim produced some naswar and together we lapsed into a companionable reverie of boredom, under a tarpaulin.

An hour later we were moving again, gears grinding at every turn of the road and after a lurching, swaying climb we reached the top of the pass. Another range of mountains stretched out before us in the distance, paling into the horizon like veins of shadow in alabaster. From the summit, the road rattled down into another sunlit valley, through carefully-terraced fields of corn and barley and, at last, we arrived at another hostelry which had been built into the overhang of a large cliff. The afternoon sun fell across the sloping ground in front of a crumbling adobe building and there were the rusting remains of a jeep and a truck in the corner of the inn yard. It was the end of the road; further on there was only a narrow track along the banks of a rushing torrent.

Inside the inn, we found several men sprawled out asleep beside the remains of a meal. On the walls were more posters of Khomeini, Rabbani and a large news sheet displaying the photographs of the fifty or so local commanders of Jamiat Islami, together with their names and brief details of their lives. Many of them were in their early thirties. There was a range of physical types: Pathans, Uzbeks, Tajiks and others I could not identify. Some looked as if they had stepped from the pages of Thomas Hardy's Wessex, while others looked Mongolian. In one corner of the room there was a lurid picture of a mujahed bayonetting a Russian invader off the top of a mountain.

Just as dusk was falling, the others arrived, footsore and weary. On the way they had heard the sounds of gunfire in the surrounding hills, presumably a skirmish between Hesb and Harakat factions who were in dispute over the valley's administration. Rahim and I had been asleep for several hours and heard nothing. Looking at the exhaustion on the group's faces I was glad I had taken the lift on the truck.

The evening meal included some pieces of meat and vegetables, and the men's spirits revived. After eating, several people sang and I was called upon by Amin'allah to give another rendering of 'The British Grenadiers'. Next to me Maulawi was in fine form, smiling and clapping his hands in time with the tune. There were a few glucose tablets left in my kit bag and I offered him some. His response was cautious but at last I persuaded him to take one, while the others watched his expression carefully. To my amazement he puckered up his mouth and called for a glass of tea to wash the taste away. The others laughed and teased him for his greed in accepting an unknown medicine, then they lost interest and the conversation turned to other matters. But I was still puzzled by Maulawi's re-action. As I looked at him, I noticed his jaws move slightly and, his tongue rolling around the inside of his cheek, and he turned towards me with a grin on his face. Then it dawned on me: realising that the others would have clamoured like children for my remaining supplies of glucose tablets if they had suspected they were sweet, he had pretended they were bitter. It was pure Zen: quick-witted pantomime and astute psychology. I looked at Maulawi with a new respect.

Later he introduced me to a friend of his called Yusuf.

'And what do you think of Ayatollah Khomeini?'

I described the superficial view of him held by most people in the West and dissociated myself from it.

'I admire and respect his desire to establish an Islamic society, but as an outsider I find it difficult to understand . . .'

My voice trailed away; I was on uncertain ground.

'His methods?'

'Perhaps.'

'How could you? How could any Westerner, any non-Muslim understand . . .', this time Yusuf was lost for words, 'the true meaning of Ayatollah Khomeini's message to the world. In Europe and America you think of the hostages, the war with Iraq, the political prisoners and executions. You forget your own history. How many people died as a result of the revolution in the Christian religion four hundred years ago?'

I thought hard for several seconds before I realised he was talking about the Reformation. I hadn't expected this sort of conversation; it was unnerving.

'Ayatollah Khomeini is a new force in the Third World. He is neither capitalist nor communist. He uses the language of religion to speak to the hearts of men. That is why he is so important; he is raising the consciousness of the Third World, not by political ideology or machines or money, but by the word of God.'

We talked about the *jehad* and his hopes for the future. The war was a test of Islam; many people would die but, in the end, victory was certain. The struggle in Afghanistan was a battle between a dying political system and a living religion. The Russians were mad to think they could conquer a people who were under the protection of God; it was like a fly attacking an elephant.

As we talked I felt as if I had passed through an invisible barrier into another dimension governed by fundamentally different laws where the world that I had previously known had only marginal significance. Here, a man's body was a shadow, death was a process of life and the only truth was the mystery of God's purpose.

An hour later I said farewell to Yusuf and went out into the inn yard. The stars stretched across the shadows of the mountains and a horse whinnied softly in the darkness. A bright crescent of light shone in the night sky, the moon of Islam, a recurring symbol of the faith, utterly beyond the power of man to dislodge from its place in heaven.

We left the inn before dawn, following the course of the river down through narrow gorges, hidden from the sun, with the chill of the night still clinging to the rocks. In places the torrent plunged into deep caverns, smoking with spray, to re-emerge in an explosion of white water. The thunderous drumming of the river reached an intensity that made conversation impossible as the noise snatched our words away, dashing them into the seething water rushing past below us.

At one point the path crossed a swiftly flowing stream. A bridge of saplings with flat stones placed on top of them spanned the current and I watched a mule, laden with ammunition boxes, being led across it. The animal was nervous and just as its front legs reached the other side its hind legs missed their footing. It toppled into the swirling waters, almost pulling the driver in as well. Two men leapt to his assistance and grabbed the halter to take the strain, while another, cursing, jumped into the foam and started beating the mule like a madman. For a minute or so it looked as if the ropes tying the mule's load would have to be cut, and the ammunition lost, but somehow the creature was whipped and hauled on to the further bank with its burden intact. I crossed over and the driver showed me his hand: across the back of it and between his thumb and forefinger a runnel of flesh had been torn away.

Further on we came to the steaming surface of a hot spring where several of us stripped to our underclothes and immersed ourselves in warm, rust-coloured water to wash away the grime of the past few days. By now the sun was almost overhead and its rays began to penetrate the cliff walls on either side of us. Thereafter the path left the river and with the sound of the waterfall still thrumming in our heads we descended into a valley of yellow corn enclosed by fantastically coloured rock formations of deep purple and green. After the cool of the past few hours it was like entering a furnace: one of the drivers wove a garland of leaves around his head to protect it from the sun. At midday we arrived at a glade of poplars from where a truck would take us on to the next stage of the journey.

'How do you like Afghanistan?'

The words, spoken in English, took me by surprise. The man's name was Hassan, the leader of another group of thirty or forty mujahedin who were independent of any of the other major factions. He was an university graduate, as were all the men under his command. The strain of two years' guerrilla fighting showed in his face; his eyelids were raw with lack of sleep and a nervous tic flickered at the edge of his right eye.

'Because we refuse to join the other parties, they mistrust us. Only ten days ago we had a skirmish with some of the Hesb Islami. We killed eight of them without casualties on our side. It was their own fault – they attacked us and we defended ourselves. My men have been carefully trained and each one of them has studied books on guerrilla warfare, but the Hesb Islami men knew nothing of such things.' He shook his head wearily. 'They didn't even know how to take cover.'

The truck arrived and we said goodbye to one another, and as he walked away I thought of his precarious life, leading a handful of men in a running war against the Russians while under continual threat of attack from rival groups. I wondered how much longer he would survive.

We clambered on to the truck and set off. The road followed a river which, as we descended, changed from a powdery blue torrent to a lazy brown meander. We stopped at several villages along the way. On each occasion Maulawi was welcomed with obvious affection by people who embraced him and kissed his hand. In the late afternoon we arrived at the ruins of a small town called Bafaq. It was a tableau of desolation. A month before it had been attacked by helicopter gunships and nearly all the drab, nineteenth-century stucco buildings had been damaged or destroyed. A strong wind was sweeping through the street, raising a grey cloud of dust that covered people's faces and turned them into expressionless masks with darting eyes. One of the townspeople invited me to have tea with him and I listened to his description of the day when the helicopters came, while he shelled pistachio nuts and his brother stroked the head of a tiny bird cupped in his fingers.

It was Maulawi's last evening with us, for the next day he was returning to his own village. During the time we had travelled together I had come to enjoy his cheerful good humour and the prospect of bidding him farewell saddened me. After an unappetising bowl of rice garnished with an already-gnawed sheep's vertebra, we talked about Persian poetry. Hafiz was a charming sensualist, Sa'adi was a man of wisdom, but as for Jalal Uddin Balkhi Rumi – there was a true poet! One could read his verses for a thousand years and still not reach the hidden depths of meaning:

> Count me not one of these men; recognise a phantom circling
> If I am not a phantom, O soul, why do I circle about the secrets?

He laughed and asked me why I was not a Muslim.

By way of reply, I described the passage from E.M. Forster's short story called 'Mr Andrews', in which a Christian and a Muslim arrive, after death, at the Gate of Heaven. Standing hand in hand before the gate, each man pitied the other for the imperfections of his faith and instead of saying 'Can I enter?' as they had intended, they cried out 'Cannot *he* enter?' And from the gateway a voice replied, 'Both can enter'.

We discussed the different beliefs of men and the names of God. Maulawi told me some of the hundred names of God and added that some men believed there were as many as a thousand names, although he did not know what they might be.

Just as we were going to bed a party of Hesb Islami entered the town. For some reason, their arrival worried Nazim Khan who gave me strict instructions not to leave the room where I was staying, and ordered two mujahedin to sleep one on either side of me, both armed with pistols.

The following morning we loaded a truck with the guns and ammunition and climbed aboard. It was a sad contraption, falling apart with rust, and when the engine started it threatened to push its way through the disintegrating bonnet. However, the men were in good spirits for the worst of the journey was over, and as we rumbled across the plain and into a series of winding gorges a mujahed beside me told me about his family in Nahrin.

Suddenly, a figure stepped into the middle of the road. The driver sounded the horn but, instead of moving aside, the man merely waved his hand, motioning us to halt. Beside me, Rahim fumbled with his rifle but it was too late: as he did so a volley of shots exploded from the cliffs around us. We had driven into an ambush. I looked round. No one had been hit. Either our attackers were useless marksmen, or they were aiming away from us. After several seconds the firing subsided and the driver switched off the engine. For a moment there was utter silence.

The figure in the middle of the road unhitched a megaphone from his shoulder.

'Nazim Khan! You are surrounded. If anyone raises a gun my men will fire, only next time they will kill. Do you understand?'

To emphasise the point another scatter of shots rang out.

'Enough! I wish to speak with Nazim Khan.'

No one on the truck moved. Nazim Khan was sitting in the driver's cab with Maulawi and the Professor. Cautiously we scanned our surroundings. In front and behind guns pointed down at us from rocks and crevices in the cliffs. Thirty yards to our right, among a collection of boulders, slight movements were visible. On our left there was a wide sweep of open ground sloping down to a river. A high-pitched whine came from the megaphone.

'Nazim Khan! I know you are there. Come out!'

The door of the cab remained firmly closed.

'You refuse to come out so we will come and get you.'

The figure with the megaphone beckoned two men from behind some rocks, who walked slowly towards the truck. Behind me someone hissed:

'Don't shoot them. Wait and see what happens.'

One of the men banged on the door of the truck.

'Nazim Khan. Which one is Nazim Khan?'

The door opened slowly and as Nazim Khan emerged the man pulled at his hair, flinging him to the ground.

'*Bizhra!* – Coward!'

The word hung in the air and we all avoided each other's eyes. Nazim Khan scrambled to his feet and I glimpsed his face; it was as white as paper. The other man kicked him in the small of the back and he stumbled forwards, half-turning over his shoulder as he shouted back to us:

'Don't shoot, for the love of Allah, don't shoot. Don't . . .' A rifle butt slammed into the back of his head.

One of the men unfastened Nazim Khan's pistol. Then, gripping his arms, they dragged him away and disappeared behind an outcrop of rocks at the bend in the road.

'Get out of the lorry,' said the megaphone.

We clambered down, some of the men with their guns still strapped to their shoulders.

'Go to the side of the road and don't move.'

A few of us edged away from the truck, discreetly choosing the meagre protection of a low bank that would give us cover against any shooting from our right. The sun grew hotter. The brothers who had been in Iran were enviably phlegmatic:

'Abdul Baz, you see the men up there. They have guns. If we don't give them our weapons, all our weapons, they will kill us. Perhaps they will kill us anyway.'

I lit a cigarette. Another shot rang out above us. Our ambushers were nervous. I wondered whether I was witnessing the last moments before a massacre.

'Put your guns in the truck.'

Reluctantly the men unshouldered their weapons and placed them in the back of the truck. There was a buzz of flies. Minutes passed and the sweat began to pour down our faces. Some men moved slowly to one side and squatted down to urinate. I did the same, taking the opportunity to check the lie of the land in case the shooting started. Perhaps I could run underneath the cliff, over the road and then across fifty yards of open ground to some rushes by the river's edge; dive in and hold my breath. It was pretty hopeless. Having my head or shoulder blown off on a road in Afghanistan seemed a prosaic way to die.

There was no sign of Nazim Khan reappearing so the Professor and Maulawi set off towards the bend in the road, each holding a white length of turban above their heads. There were no warning shots and the men encircling us eased their positions, letting their heads show above the rocks.

Half an hour later Maulawi and the Professor reappeared with Nazim Khan and we smiled with relief. Something had been agreed. At least we should get to know what was happening.

A large bruise covered one side of Nazim Khan's face, almost obscuring the eye; his lips were bloody. He spoke with difficulty.

We had no choice, he said, but to surrender our arms. The leader of the ambush was called Khial Muhammad – he was mad and wouldn't listen to reason. The men were to stay behind while he, the Professor and Maulawi were taken with the guns and ammunition to Khial Muhammad's village. He turned in my direction:

'You will come with us, Abdul!'

Several of our ambushers emerged and took charge of the lorry. Nazim Khan and Maulawi got into the driver's cab while the Professor and I hoisted ourselves into the back. Then a strange thing happened: the five men who had been travelling with Maulawi nodded to our ambushers and they all climbed aboard together and began turning over the Kalashnikovs, rocket-launchers and DSHKR guns like children with a collection of new toys. The truck lurched off leaving the rest of the group in a cloud of dust surrounded by men with guns. As we rattled along, I asked the Wolfman who our ambushers were and what he thought they might do with us, but he said nothing, and merely drew his hand across his throat and smiled.

It was only then that I realised that Maulawi and his men might actually be traitors. Why else were they so at ease with our ambushers? But in what way were they in league with them? They seemed to know each other, although they had not greeted one another with the embraces customary between men of the same group or village. Had we been captured by Soviet sympathisers or a rival group of mujahedin? Remembering Maulawi's impassioned discourses on Islam it seemed unlikely he would have anything to do with the Soviets. But who else would wish to take our weapons?

Half an hour later the truck drew up, the arms were swiftly unloaded and our captors spirited them away into some trees at the side of the road. Nazim Khan disappeared in the company of Maulawi and his men, and then our captors drove off, leaving the Professor and me by the side of the road. My sense of unreality intensified when some old men appeared, greeted us courteously and invited us to accompany them for a glass of tea. We followed them through a field of ripening corn to a courtyard in the shade of a huge mulberry tree. A pot of steaming green tea and two warm nan loaves were placed before us while the elders of the village appeared in twos and threes.

A little later Nazim Khan and Maulawi emerged from a nearby building followed by the village chief who, I later learned, had organised the ambush. He seated himself at one end of a large carpet in the shade. Nazim Khan took his place at the other, sunlit end of the carpet while the rest of us arranged ourselves on either side, facing one another. Khial Muhammad, who seemed to be the leader of the men who had ambushed us, spoke first, saying how fortunate the village was; now they had guns they were safe and could defend themselves against the Shuravi. The arms were necessary and God had been generous in providing them. Sweat was pouring from his forehead and several times he seemed to lose the thread of what he was saying. I looked around at the faces of the old men. Only a few nodded their heads in agreement; most were grave and solemn. There were murmurings of the bad reputation that would come to the village.

Then Nazim Khan made his reply. The guns were for the *jehad*, for the people of Nahrin to defend themselves. He appealed to the elders: surely it was wrong for a Muslim to steal from his brother Muslim? The arms had been bought in Peshawar, then carried for ten days with great difficulty over rivers and mountains. Now all the efforts of the men were wasted. For the love of Allah, where was the justice?

At this the old men looked even graver, and several took Nazim Khan's part to remonstrate with Khial Muhammad. He smiled sardonically. The old men could think and say what they liked; the arms were staying with him. He rambled on with a malarial glitter in his eye: a spy had told him that some of the arms were destined for Abel Khan, the lord of the neighbouring territory. He had already killed several of his, Khial Muhammad's men, and if he received any more arms he would pose an even greater danger. Taking the arms was an act of self-defence. Further discussion was pointless; the arms remained with him. Brushing aside any other comments from the assembly, Khial Muhammad walked away.

The rest of the afternoon was spent in a series of discussions under the shifting light of some fruit trees on a slope overlooking the village. By now the others who had been left to follow us on foot had arrived, and together we listened with a growing sense of hopelessness as Nazim Khan and the Professor tried in vain to persuade the elders to censure Khial Muhammad. It was useless. He was beyond their authority, and besides, the younger men in the village supported him.

Our attention turned to the ambush. How had Khial Muhammad known about the truck and the load of arms? Was it really just coincidence that Maulawi lived in the neighbouring village? And why had Maulawi's men been allowed to keep their weapons? They protested their innocence, but the perfunctory way in which they expressed their regrets implied that they were not unduly troubled by the morning's events. Had the smiling Maulawi secretly contacted Khial Muhammad the previous evening? Had he, indeed, planned it all along, all the way from Peshawar? Nobody knew.

That evening Maulawi invited us to have supper at a nearby mosque and afterwards to stay the night there. Before the meal he led the prayers for our group and later was brave or brazen enough to sleep among us. The backbreaking efforts of the past ten days wasted, the men in the group accepted the rice impassively. Their attitude was Homeric and reminded me of a passage in the *Odyssey* in which, after a swathe of men had been devoured by Cyclops, the survivors sat down and ate by the seashore: then, when they had finished eating, they lay down and fell asleep. But the stoicism of my companions' actions could not disguise the lines of exhaustion and disappointment in their faces. One by one they stretched out to sleep. The lamps were extinguished and I was glad to find oblivion in the cramped darkness.

In the morning Nazim Khan and the Professor made a final attempt to retrieve the weapons. All they managed to extract was a single, derisory Kalashnikov and a warning from Khial Muhammad that if Nazim Khan remained in his territory another day he would personally kill him.

We set off through a waterless landscape of grey, weather-worn rocks. Whichever way the road turned the wind was against us, whipping sand into our faces and making every step a double effort. The cliffs on the far side of a dried-up river valley vanished in clouds of dust and the leaves of the few trees we passed were no longer green, but bleached a pale yellow. Khial Muhammad's threats were at the back of everyone's mind and we didn't rest until late afternoon when we reached friendly territory. The ruler of those parts was Abel Khan, a friend of Abdul Haq of Nahrin, and his son happened to be in the village where we had stopped for chai and nan.

Abel Khan's son was about twenty-five, plump, with soft features and long black hair, like the dark-eyed princes in the murals of Tchehel Setoun in Isfahan. He had spent four years in America and England, and his English was almost fluent. Shortly after the Russians invaded he had returned to Afghanistan to fight. He told me he had no regrets, although he asked me to send him some tapes from England: The Who, the Beatles and Roxy Music.

'When I was in the States I used to smoke a lot of dope and got into heavy rock music. I still listen to it sometimes. I put on a tape and sit beside one of the rivers here; it is beautiful. Occasionally, when I think of the life I used to have in London and Washington, I feel sad, but I must be here. This is my country and these are my people.'

He invited Nazim Khan, the Professor, Amin'allah, Rahim and me to stay for a couple of nights with his father. It was decided that the rest of the group would continue on towards Nahrin since the long, difficult journey back to Pakistan was clearly impractical. A meeting place three days' march away was agreed. We drank another pot of chai together and then it was time for the young man to leave. Forty or fifty villagers gathered round as a prancing black horse with crimson saddle trappings was led forward. Two men with Kalashnikovs emerged from the crowd; one held a stirrup while the other gripped the horse's bridle. Then they cleared a passage through the people and in a cloud of dust he was gone.

The moon rose. One by one the group gathered their belongings and filed past Nazim Khan to say goodbye. Several embraced him tenderly – a couple of the younger mujahedin were close to tears. It was a poignant moment: the guns they had carried so proudly were gone, their labours had come to nothing and ahead of them lay a journey unarmed through dangerous territory, to arrive at last in Nahrin empty-handed. In silence we watched them vanish into the moonlight.

5

Pul e Khumri

When I woke the sky was a featureless expanse of grey cloud. For breakfast we ate some gritty bread, wrinkling our eyes against the stinging particles of sand that blew through the chaikhane. The full extent of the group's loss was just beginning to sink home and for an hour or so we sat in a leaden gloom while the Professor worked out the cost of the captured weapons. Nazim Khan sat hunched in a corner watching an ant dragging a raisin across the dusty floor. Even Rahim was silent.

At midday a messenger arrived from Abel Khan to tell us that a truck would take us to his house in the late afternoon. The news stirred us from our torpor and we washed our clothes in a nearby stream. Another group of mujahedin arrived who listened to our descriptions of the ambush with unsmiling expressions and disapproving clicks of their tongues. By the time the truck arrived the sun was already low on the horizon.

In the back of the truck a woman was lying on a trestle bed. She was very ill. Each time the truck lurched or jolted another woman who was sitting at her side reached out and held her head while a gaunt man, presumably her husband, gazed down at the heavily wrapped body with a look of impotent anguish on his face like a Giotto fresco. The rest of us did our best to avert our eyes from the nakedness of his grief, but the sense of suffering in our midst weighed heavily in our hearts; and even after the three of them were set down in the twilight of a little village their presence seemed to remain with us.

The stars emerged and we entered a sinister landscape of looming cliffs, lit here and there by splashes of moonlight. The engine kept overheating and several times we had to stop while the driver poured water into it from a drum lashed to the back of the truck. Only one headlight was working, and after a particularly vicious series of potholes it, too, dwindled to a thin gleam, then died away completely. We pulled to a halt once more. The driver rummaged through a battered biscuit tin of nuts and bolts but there was nothing remotely like a screwdriver. My Swiss Army knife was commandeered and together we attacked the headlight. As the driver's head craned over my shoulder, I caught the unmistakeable sweetness of alcohol on his breath.

After twenty minutes it was obvious that the headlights were beyond repair. The driver slumped back into his cab and switched on a cassette recorder leaving the rest of us to ponder our predicament. Even in broad daylight the road was treacherous, but at night, with no headlights . . . It seemed tactless to mention the driver's cavalier disregard of the Qur'anic prohibition against alcohol.

The prospect of a night spent in the back of a truck was unappealing. I suggested someone should sit on the front bumper holding a flashlight, and for the rest of the journey I found myself clinging like a limpet to the bonnet with one hand while shining a meagre beam of light on to the track with the other. Several times I lost the bank of gravel that marked the edge of the road and we ground into boulders with a sickening thud, but somehow we arrived at our destination. I had no idea which way the road went. We ploughed up an earth bank, swung erratically to the right, narrowly missing someone asleep on a charpoy outside his house and pitched down again at an angle of forty-five degrees, finishing up balanced precariously on the edge of a steep gully. The truck emptied in a flash leaving the driver alone in his cab, like the captain of a sinking ship, laughing uncontrollably to himself.

The five of us were shown to our rooms, which by lamplight reminded me of those one might find in an Edwardian seaside hotel. Some bedding was laid out for us and for a few moments I delighted in the luxury of clean sheets before sinking into a heavy sleep.

No one disturbed us and the room was bright with sunlight when I awoke. A vast breakfast of tea, bread, yoghurt and melons was brought to us. During the meal members of Abel Khan's family visited us and questioned us about the ambush. In the course of the conversation it emerged that for the past year there had been a running feud between Khial Muhammad and Abel Khan. Now that Khial Muhammad was better armed they were afraid. Perhaps Abdul Haq would help his friend, Abel Khan, fight Khial Muhammad? Cynically, I wondered whether Abel Khan's hospitality might have an ulterior motive. No sooner had we finished eating than another meal arrived, equally vast: this time a pile of saffron rice scattered with raisins and bathed in a cream sauce.

In the middle of the afternoon I managed to stir myself, heavy with food, and staggered outside to view the surroundings. A marble mosaic courtyard below our window became a flight of steps between a series of terraces planted with flowers and fruit trees. It was easy to imagine the steps descending to a brilliant blue swimming pool or a private beach somewhere in the south of France. But looking out across the trees to the sun-bleached grass and rocks on the other side of the valley I realised how fragile the illusion was. Behind me, the house where we were staying stood solidly between two worlds; a flat roof over Georgian-style windows opened wide to reveal a shadowy interior of rugs and gold-embroidered, Day-glo curtains. At the entrance a doorkeeper with a bushy grey beard dozed contentedly on a three-legged stool. The fierce heat impelled me back into the shade of my room where I found Rahim snoring loudly, sleeping off the combined effects of our two meals.

The last of the setting sun had barely slipped behind the mountains when a third, and even more gargantuan, meal arrived: mounds of rice, bread, onions, meatballs and chunks of beef with yellow melons to follow. One by one we fell back from the meal on to our cushions, stunned by the sheer quantity of food, until only Rahim was left, eating with a look of grim determination on his face as if the honour of our party depended on him.

We went to bed early. Pulling the sheets over me, I experienced an uneasy sensation in the hinterland of my body, but it was so slight that I turned over on my pillow and was soon fast asleep. It was a physical premonition of difficulties to come. Some hours later I woke. The moon was touching the tops of the trees when I made the first of several treks to an expanse of evil-smelling waste ground where I was painfully reminded of the less romantic side of travel.

An audience with Abel Khan had been arranged for breakfast but, at the appointed hour, it was a physical impossibility. Summoning dwindling reserves of politeness, I made my excuses and remained in bed. I could feel events were gathering for a climax of epic proportions. I dosed myself with iodine and within minutes felt an invisible fuse burning down into my stomach. Should I station myself by the spittoon? It looked a bit meagre for my purposes. Staggering across the richly carpeted floor of my bedroom, I reached the window. The doorkeeper greeted my sudden appearance with an ingratiating smile. I just had time to glimpse the smile on his face freeze as the meals of the previous day made a series of dramatic encores over the marble courtyard outside my window. I felt better immediately, like a soul newly released from Purgatory. With a sense of humble virtue, I washed and crawled back into bed.

Amin'allah woke me in a state of high excitement: Abel Khan was on his way; I should prepare myself immediately. I had barely finished dressing when he arrived, flanked by a dozen servants and retainers. He was around fifty years old, plump and leaning heavily on a walking stick. The short distance from the Palace to the annexe where we were staying had visibly tired him and his face was beaded with perspiration. We introduced ourselves, exchanging glances of mutual sympathy, and he teetered into an adjoining room, followed by at least half his entourage. We seated ourselves on cushions and looked at each other; I knew instinctively we had nothing to say and I thought I glimpsed the same realisation mirrored in his eyes.

But the air of keen anticipation among his retinue could not be disappointed; it was our duty to converse. Abel Khan's English was not good and the audience began with the curious remark:

'I pissed many happy days in Birmingham.'

I replied that I had never been to Birmingham and enquired after his health.

'Thank you, it is not the best but by the grace of God I am still alive.'

He sighed disconsolately and taking a small tin from his waistcoat pocket inserted a pink lozenge into his mouth. There was a long pause while I groped for a happier topic of conversation but my mind was an utter blank. Abel Khan, with far more experience of such occasions, filled the growing lacuna with a request for chai. Another silence of cosmic proportions threatened to engulf us and I could sense the Professor at my side fidgeting uneasily.

'Abdul Baz can speak some of our language, sire. He says that Khial Muhammad should return the weapons.'

A flicker of interest passed across Abel Khan's face and he changed to Farsi:

'Khial Muhammad is a dog.'

He placed another sweet in his mouth and looked round at the assembled faces, all vigorously nodding in agreement.

'A dog. Abdul Haq should send five hundred men and kill him unless he returns the arms.'

From there on the conversation became more general, and for the next hour it revolved around the same predictable topics. Mad, foolish, unbrotherly Khial Muhammad, treacherous Maulawi and brave Nazim Khan whose skill had, without doubt, saved the lives of the rest of the group. I was enduring agonies of boredom and caught the eye of one of the younger advisers whose woebegone expression betrayed a fellow sufferer.

'You are ill, Abdul Baz?' Abel Khan interrupted at last. 'My doctor will care for you.'

A heavily bearded youth was called, who questioned me in detail about my symptoms while everyone listened with rapt attention. To make sure, he lifted my shirt and jabbed my stomach repeatedly with his fingers. After nodding sagely for a while, he prescribed four different sets of pills and recommended plenty of fresh fruit. It was, I thought, extremely unsound advice.

Another immense banquet was set before us in honour of our departure: rice, a variety of stuffed meats and sauces, followed by grapes and melons. Since it seemed probable that such a meal would merely compound my miseries, I settled for bread and yoghurt. Then gifts were presented. Nazim Khan received a Kalashnikov and the Professor, as his adviser, a suitably distinguished *chapan* of dark blue silk. Secretly I hoped for a similar garment and could barely conceal my disappointment when I was given some material that looked like a set of embroidered tea-towels.

After a protracted leave-taking, we piled into a small truck. For a while we followed a dirt track, but this soon degenerated into a back-breaking ride through a series of dry watercourses that would have tried the agility of a mule. We surged up improbable-looking gullies, grabbing wildly at each other for balance, while I performed extraordinary feats of sphincter control. Heat, discomfort and illness combined to make me feel faint. Seeing my condition, an old man with kindly eyes gave me a *stamboul*, a tiny dried melon-like fruit, which he told me to hold to my nostrils. A delicate scent emanated from it and almost immediately I felt refreshed. Farther on, someone spotted a kowk, a small partridge-like bird, and the jeep slammed to a halt. Nazim Khan unshouldered his Kalashnikov to take a shot, but took so long to draw a bead on it that the bird was safely hidden among some boulders by the time he was ready. The others teased him mercilessly although, had he managed to hit it, there would have been nothing left of the bird except a mass of bloody feathers plastered against a rock. Eventually we emerged from the tortuous canyons into a less jagged region of scrub-covered hills. For a while there were no villages and the only people we saw were a man and his wife on a mule, like the figures in Samuel Palmer's 'Flight into Egypt'. Then the hills subsided into a rolling plain of wheatfields, with a harvest moon, heavy with golden dust, resting on the horizon.

It was dusk by the time the jeep jolted to a halt on the edge of a small valley. There we found the rest of the group waiting for us: they had almost given up hope of our arriving and when they greeted us the relief on their faces was visible in the moonlight. We ate a hurried meal and then set off together into the warm radiance of the night.

We journeyed on for several hours through the silent hills with the dust from our footsteps drifting around us in slowly moving clouds, glowing in the light of the summer moon. At last we heard the sound of dogs barking in front of us and we arrived in a village of empty streets and small, darkened houses. A tiresome wait followed, briefly enlivened by the appearance of a village cur which darted out of the shadows growling viciously until a rain of well-aimed rocks and stones sent it yelping out of range.

Some men were preparing to lie down where they were on the bare ground by the time a villager appeared to take us to a place where we could stay the night. By the light of a lamp we spread ourselves out on the floor of a mosque and lay down to sleep.

The men spent most of the next morning dozing in the baking shadows of the mosque. I wrote my diary and was the only person left awake apart from Sediq, whose eyes kept flickering nervously in my direction. I couldn't forget the incident with the anti-tank rocket; the sight of him still made me angry and he knew it. The perpetual expression of unease on his face made it all the more difficult to like him. Eventually he slumped back on the dirty grey bundle of rags that was all he possessed, and fell asleep. I studied the faces of the sleeping mujahedin. They had a curious innocence; without the lines of bitterness or frustrated greed that disfigure so many Western faces. These men were farmers and shepherds, made ascetic by the effects of hunger and fatigue. Their faces had a gaunt strength. No double chins or marks of surplus flesh clouded their physiognomy. Instead, want and necessity had sculpted their features in well-defined contours and each man's individual character was clearly visible.

Outside the white light of the midday sun beat down on the dust and stones. A donkey brayed in the distance. Flies wandered over the eyelids and nostrils of the man beside me. I looked at the watch on his wrist; it had stopped. I had the sense of being lost in a forgotten corner of the universe where life was mere existence distorted by a bad dream. But I was still awake and I realised that I was alone in another people's nightmare. Someone grunted softly from the depths of sleep; the sound was oddly comforting; I pillowed my head on my knapsack.

. . . She was laughing and I kissed her . . .

The snores of an Uzbeki by my shoulder woke me. In the twinkling of an eye she was far away and I was left in the airless shade of the mosque with her absence in my heart.

It was time for the midday meal but the heat had dulled our appetites and we pushed handfuls of rice and bread into our mouths mechanically. We needed as much strength as possible: a long march and a dangerous crossing lay ahead of us. After we had finished eating the men talked of the remaining part of the journey and their homecoming. We had to pass close to the Soviet base at Pul e Khumri and find a way across a stretch of territory criss-crossed by tank patrols. Originally the plan had been to send several men ahead of the main group, armed with anti-tank rockets, to lie in wait and knock out any tanks that might appear. Now we had no weapons except for Nazim Khan's Kalashnikov; worse still, it was a full moon. The prospect of being under Nazim Khan's command in such circumstances filled me with concern. Nevertheless, the men's deep faith was reassuring: they were under the protection of God, their lives depended on his will, and if it was their destiny to die it had already been decided. *Insha'allah.*

More troubling was their return to Nahrin; what could they say to the commander of Nahrin, Abdul Haq? What would they find on their arrival? The previous evening someone in the village had spoken of heavy bombing, with scores of people dead and wounded. The men's conversation faltered and their eyes were unseeing as they contemplated the possibilities of their homecoming.

While the drivers were saddling the horses and mules the others filled water bottles from a nearby well. My stomach trouble hadn't cleared and I persuaded Nazim Khan to let me ride one of the horses.

The fiercest heat of the day was over by the time we started and the colours of earth and sky, which had been bleached by the midday sun, were returning in the yellow light of the afternoon. After a couple of hours we saw a village on a hilltop in the distance and decided to stop there for chai. Drawing closer, we found it was almost completely deserted. Doors and shutters were locked and nettles were growing in the streets. The roofs of several houses had collapsed and the mud walls, exposed to wind and rain, had begun to dissolve back into the earth. At the summit of the hill we came to a chaikhane where a small group of men was sitting. Their clothes were ragged and they were so poor that the Professor was reluctant to accept the handfuls of dried mulberries and glasses of thin, brackish tea which they offered us.

We decided to wait another hour until sunset before continuing our journey but many of the mujahedin shrank from talking to the villagers. Possibly they saw the stricken village and its few pitiable inhabitants as ghosts of their own, uncertain future.

Behind us, the last of the sun cast a horizontal light across the land and we journeyed on under a darkening sky towards the east. We passed three men kneeling in prayer on the chaff of the threshing floor and, in the twilight, a young man filled my water bottle from a well. The water was cool and slightly bitter. The line of men and horses moved on silently through the dusk with the fine sand of the pathway drifting at their feet like smoke. The terrain grew mountainous and the path skirted the edges of ravines that fell steeply away into warm darkness. Cliffs and crags passed in an aqueous light, which, as I gazed on it, seemed increasingly familiar. Then I remembered: the background of the 'Mona Lisa' and the hills of ancient dust receding into shadow.

Nazim Khan called a halt at the foot of a ravine. Once again he reminded us of the danger. No cigarettes, no talking. Several men took the opportunity to relieve themselves, others whispered together in the dark. Rahim tapped me on the shoulder and poured a mound of naswar into my hand. Those of us who had horses remounted and we set off once more. The pitch-black walls of rock on either side of us fell away and we entered a wide open plain of boulders and sand, glowing softly in the moonlight. High above us the moon shone with such brilliance that it seemed as if its light transferred a gentle heat, while the horizon seemed to move within itself like the uneasy surface of the sea at midnight. I was riding a white horse; there was moonlight, there was danger. The sense of adventure was distinctly ambiguous. I tried to convince myself that fear was an illusion and that the armies of the night were shadows of my own imagination. I was acutely aware of my body as a fragile receptacle of flesh and bone on the gleaming target of the horse and I felt a fierce wonder and thankfulness to be alive on a summer's night among the mujahedin. I loved life and was afraid to die.

Four or five miles away the lights of the Soviet base twinkled in the darkness. We came to some deserted buildings and dismounted, taking shelter behind a wall. Nobody knew the way. Suddenly several figures detached themselves from the shadows on our left and challenged us in low voices. They were men from a group of Hesb Islami. For half an hour the Professor and Nazim Khan negotiated with them while Amin'allah and another man were sent off to reconnoitre. In the distance a couple of flares went up and there was a short burst of machine-gun fire. The Professor returned to assure us that all was well. Five or six of us sat down in a patch of moonlight.

'How are you, Abdul Baz? Are you afraid?' asked the Professor.

I sensed that in some way I had acquired a talismanic quality for the group and decided it was better to preserve the fiction for the time being. I replied that I was hungry and would like a shish kebab.

The Professor laughed.

'You are always hungry, Abdul Baz. And a hungry man is some-times a passionate man. Perhaps, like me, you are thinking of your beloved?'

The thought stopped me in my tracks; what on earth would she make of the conversation we were having? And what would she be doing now? I tried to picture her in my mind's eye, but as I did so it seemed as if I was entering a dream, another, impossible world away.

'I don't think about her.'

'You aren't worried she is with another man?'

It seemed unnecessary to say we had parted and for all I knew she indeed might already be with someone else.

'No, I don't worry.'

'She must be a good woman who loves you very much.'

One of the younger mujahedin entered the conversation.

'How do you say this in your language?' he said, shaping his hands and fingers in an unmistakeable gesture which made the Professor give him a good-natured cuff on the side of the head. I told him and asked, in turn, how it was pronounced in Dari. He whispered the word in my ear. I pretended not to understand so he tried again, louder. The others heard and there was a ripple of laughter.

Amin'allah and his companion joined us; they had been unable to find the path we were looking for and had heard the sound of tanks. A hurried discussion followed, with the group roughly divided into those who wished to send out another scout party and those in favour of pressing on. Nazim Khan vacillated between the two until someone pointed out that it would be dawn in a matter of hours and he reluctantly gave the order to go on.

It was a beautiful, windless night, full of the fragrance of mint and lavender and the sound of insects. Stepping along the raised banks between the rice fields with a glint of light reflecting here and there on water, I thought of other moonlit walks in Japan. A haiku formed itself in my mind. 'Under a bright summer moon, hiding in the sound of the cicadas.' I was behind the leader of the drivers, Sufi Imam-Uddin, who had rolled up his trousers and whose thin legs strode rhythmically in front of me like those of an elderly scout-master. A few hundred yards away, some tracer wheeled away into the night and we crouched down for a couple of minutes, then set off again.

We discovered a man standing like a stork in the middle of a field who was quickly press-ganged into service as a guide. When he tried to run away two mujahedin grabbed him.

'Brother,' said the Professor, 'we mean you no harm, but if you try to deceive us we will surely kill you.'

Half a mile further on Nazim Khan called another halt, ostensibly to wait for the horses and mules to catch up; in fact our unwilling guide had somehow given us the slip and we were lost. Somewhere ahead of us was a river but no one knew where it was, or how we were going to get across it. For the next twenty minutes we stumbled blindly to and fro between little streams that criss-crossed the area. At last we heard the sound of rushing water and came to the river. A grey expanse of water, thirty or so yards wide, was flowing by in front of us. Here and there irregular flashes of moonlight glinted on its surface. Was this the best place for crossing? No one knew. Had we evaded the Soviet patrols, or were they still in front of us? As other members of the group arrived the men began to raise their voices, some arguing that we should cross immediately, others that we should try to find another safer place further downstream. Nazim Khan tried to pitch his voice above the confusion but the men ignored him.

The uncertainties of the past few hours had unnerved Nazim Khan; without waiting to test the depth of the water he kicked his horse forwards and called out to us to follow him. I wrapped my camera, diary and tape recorders in plastic and put them in my satchel. Meanwhile, the Professor had commandeered a horse and I hoisted myself up behind him, clinging to his waist.

The water was cool and, as it rose to my knees, the thought of a swim seemed appealing. We got further out, the river began swirling at our waists and the horse started to swim, but it was clear that our double burden was too much for it.

'Get off, Abdul, otherwise the horse will drown.'

I heard a note of fear in the Professor's voice. With a sudden shock I realised that I had reached the point of no return and was on my own. The water glittered enticingly.

I let the current lift me from the saddle and struck out confidently for the shadow of the other side, twenty or thirty feet away. I took a couple of strokes and then, to my horror, I realised my hiking boots had filled with water and were like lead weights around my feet. I just had time to take a deep breath before I went under.

If I could hold on long enough, I told myself, the current itself would carry me on to the further bank. But in the meantime I had to have air. I struggled towards the surface.

It was so close that I could see the opaque grey ceiling of air a few inches above my face. I put all my energy into a wild, flailing effort and my mouth and nostrils broke the surface sufficiently to take another breath before the waters closed over my head a second time. The second time. One more breath and it would be the third time. A flame exploded within me and my body kicked and struggled in the dark water. For a moment my face was in the air and I saw the shadow of the bank a few feet away. As I sank one of my boots knocked against something. I pushed up and surfaced by a wall of slippery mud; beside me a horse was kicking and floundering. *Avoid the hooves. Avoid the hooves.* In a panic I dug my fingers into the mud and clawed myself half out of the water. There were noises, hoarse shouts and despairing cries. I didn't care. I was alive.

For several minutes there was chaos. Men and animals struggled on to the bank and gathered in shivering groups. After a while it became apparent that, by some miracle, no one had drowned. It had been a near-disaster. The drivers had cut the loads from the horses and most of the baggage, including my rucksack with all my medicine, my maps and clothes, had been washed away. I had nothing but the clothes I was wearing and the contents of my sodden satchel. I checked the Walkman. It was still working and the sound of the Brandenburgs resounded improbably in my hands. It was a wonderful moment.

It seemed impossible that the noise and confusion could go unnoticed by the patrols and for the next half hour I steeled myself for a sudden flash of lights or a burst of machine-gun fire. Everyone was in a state of panic, half-running to keep up with the man in front, leaving the man behind to follow as best he could. The members of the group were beginning to lose touch with one another, and those in front appeared completely lost.

There was a dull grinding of tanks and heavy gunfire over to our right. We hurried across a stretch of wasteland covered with charred bushes. Someone whispered the word 'mines' and the mujahed behind me yelped in fright, but there was no stopping now. We were within a few yards of the road and, suddenly, there it was, a dull asphalt surface stretching across our path. We hurried over in twos and threes, then bolted like rabbits into a tangle of grass and thorn bushes on the other side. I had forgotten my illness until then. A wave of exhaustion hit me and for several minutes I struggled with the temptation to lie down. A familiar voice called my name:

'Lose all your things, Abdul? So did I. Everything.'

It was Rahim, stolidly grumbling at his misfortune. 'My friend decided his donkey was drowning and cut away some of its baggage – the part which belonged to me. Shawls for my wife and turban silk I was going to sell in the market, the money I kept in my hat – all of it lost in the river. In his wisdom Allah saved our lives but took everything else. The life of a mujahed is hard.'

The sky was lightening from dark to grey when at last we stopped for a rest. Some of the men threw themselves down in the dust of the road, and slept.

The chill of the early morning air struck at our damp clothes, and we sat in small groups shivering and smoking cigarettes. Someone produced some hashish. After emptying a cigarette he filled the tube of paper with lumps of the sticky resin. It was unpleasantly strong and I could only manage a lungful before passing it on.

We were still smoking when Nazim Khan remounted. By now it was almost home territory and at the entrance to the next valley Nazim Khan loosed a volley of shots that echoed from peak to peak. For four or five hours we walked without break. The sun climbed overhead and the rocks began to quiver with heat. I passed men sprawled on the ground with their horses nearby, heads bowed, too tired to go on.

I found Rahim lying beside a small cavity in the cliffs; a curtain of hornets was hovering in front of it. When I poked my head inside I glimpsed a rusty can and a puddle of muddy water.

'Are you thirsty, Abdul?'

I nodded.

He stretched his arm into the hole and drew out the can – it was half-full of cloudy water. I took a couple of gulps and handed it back to Rahim who drained the remainder. The next moment he spat it out and held out the can; writhing at the bottom of it was a colony of minute, silvery-green worms.

Towards midday we stopped at a farmhouse where an old man gave us chai and some boiled eggs. My strength had given out completely and I persuaded Nazim Khan to provide another horse for me.

The horse's owner was a squat Uzbeki with a low forehead, whose eyes narrowed resentfully when Nazim Khan ordered him to lend me his animal. There were no stirrups; a couple of mujahedin had to help me up and I only managed to stay on by twisting my fingers under the ropes securing the saddle. Our progress was painfully slow; the horse was exhausted and my half-hearted commands and kicks had no effect. The Uzbeki tore a branch from a tree and gave it to me.

'Use this. Hit him hard – he's a lazy beast.'

I tapped at the horse's flank a few times.

'Harder, harder!'

I gave another couple of thwacks and the horse momentarily

quickened its pace, then settled back into a slow walk. The Uzbeki murmured something under his breath then shouted at me again.

'Hit him, you fool, don't let him sleep. Hurt him!'

It seemed pointless and I said so. The next moment the Uzbeki had snatched the stick from my hand and brought it crashing down on the horse's rump. With a snort it started forward over a dry river bed, littered with uneven boulders. Again the stick came down, the horse whinnied with pain and with a series of farts broke into a trot. A stinging blow landed on my back and I heard the Uzbeki shouting and cursing at the top of his voice. Another crack and the horse broke into a wooden canter, and still the Uzbeki was close behind, lashing and beating at its flanks. Out of the corner of my eye I glimpsed his face, ugly with rage, sweat and spittle glistening at the corners of his mouth. He was in a blind fury and I realised that he would whip the horse until it stumbled or I fell off. Somehow I had to stay on. Once more the stick cut across my shoulders and then again on the horse's side, splintering as it did so. The Uzbeki cursed and began to fall behind. A stone whistled past and another struck the horse's legs; but the sudden exertion was too much for the animal, its breath became harsh and laboured and in another fifty yards its ungainly canter gave way to a jolting plod. The Uzbeki caught up and I offered to get off and walk, but he refused.

'You are ill and I am strong. Besides, Nazim Khan will beat me.'

There was no malice in his voice. Whatever had enraged him was now forgotten and we continued on in silence. Had I unwittingly transgressed some unwritten code, thereby insulting him? Or had he been angered by Nazim Khan's peremptory command to lend me his horse? I didn't know, nor could I be bothered to find out. I was simply grateful not to be walking.

The next few hours passed in a series of disconnected images.

A man with a hideously scarred face and a stump where his right arm should have been greeted us and embraced the Professor tenderly. I noticed what I thought were slices of water melon placed on the shoulders of a horse, presumably to cool the skin where the ropes had chafed it, but when I looked closer I saw that it was an expanse of raw flesh. What had seemed like the black water melon seeds were flies, feasting on yellow serum which frothed at the edges of the wound like a sherbet dip.

We came to a field of melons. The Uzbeki told me to get off, and then ran to a brushwood shelter and emerged with a plump, middle-aged woman at his side, who was his mother. He shouted to the members of the group to wait while he gathered armfuls of the round, heavy fruit which he then tumbled at our feet. His mother stood at one side smiling with happiness that her son had returned safely, in such a state of excitement that her *chador* slipped repeatedly from her face.

In the late afternoon we entered one of the outlying villages of Nahrin and, after wending our way through leafy, walled streets, we arrived in the courtyard of a little mosque. One by one I said farewell to the members of the group. The two brothers who had worked in Iran smilingly shouted '*chai siah*!' '*chai sabz*!' for the last time. Sediq gave me a fumbling handshake and looked away; Latif, who had taught me to pronounce the words '*la ilaha illa lahu*' embraced me and commended me to God. The Professor promised to contact me soon and Rahim vowed that he would buy me as many shish kebabs as I could eat when we met each other again. Amin'allah was staying with friends nearby and said that we would find each other easily.

The time I had spent in the men's company and the distance we had travelled together had led to several deep but unspoken friendships. Now that we were saying goodbye to one another it seemed extraordinary that our lives should part so easily and suddenly. I remembered the end of term at school and how the leavers said goodbye to one another: relief, regret, stoicism in face of the unknown. It was the same now. When they had gone I sat down by the side of a still, green pool and watched some children filling vessels of water. I was a stranger, an observer, an unnecessary mouth to feed. The others were returning to the welcome of their family and friends. I was alone.

Just as I was beginning to feel sorry for myself, an old man emerged from the doorway of the mosque with a glass of chai and some dusty sweets which he placed on the ground beside me. He looked into my eyes, then gazed up at the sky and looked once again into my eyes. Then, after a moment he nodded and smiled. The gentleness of his presence was healing, and I became more at peace.

6

Nahrin

Towards evening a man led me to the home of Abdul Haq, commander-in-chief of Nahrin and the surrounding area. Abdul Haq was away in the mountains and would not be back till the following day, but his second-in-command and a dozen fellow mujahedin were staying at the house. Lamps were lit and we seated ourselves under the portico, where plates of rice and lamb were brought for us. When the meal was over, pillows and cotton quilts were laid out and I lay back to sleep with the sound of cicadas sussurating in the moonlit garden.

The next morning I was woken by Amin'allah. News had reached the mujahedin that the bombing raids were to be increased and it had been decided that I should spend the daylight hours away from Abdul Haq's home.

'Unfortunately there are informers in Nahrin,' said Amin'allah. 'They tell the Shuravi where the most important houses are. Then the jets come and bomb the place. The Shuravi have tried to hit this house several times but so far, by the grace of God, they have not succeeded.'

We were walking through an orchard of peach trees when we heard the sound of a helicopter in the distance. Amin'allah ran to a low mud wall and threw himself down on the ground.

'Hurry, Abdul, hurry. Soon the jets will come.'

I took cover beside him and we waited, peering up through the branches of the trees to catch a glimpse of the helicopter which was circling over a village a couple of miles away. After several minutes it swung away over the plain towards the town of Nahrin and the drumming of the rotor blades grew fainter. I wanted to wash my clothes in a nearby stream, but Amin'allah was adamant:

'Don't move. First the Shuravi send in helicopters to see where the people are. If they see a group of men gathered together they talk to the jets by radio and tell them where the group is. Sometimes the helicopters themselves shoot rockets. They fire at anything – houses, men and women working in the fields, even animals. It is more difficult for them to see us if we are still. Have patience.'

I picked at the dirt under my fingernails with a bit of straw and listened. I could just hear the helicopter through the sound of the wind in the trees. Then, almost inaudibly, another sound emerged, grew louder and a metallic speck swept over the horizon trailing a roll of thunder across the sky. There were a couple of dull explosions, a minute's pause, another rumble of thunder and the jets circled over the town and pitched low over the hills for another bombing sweep. As the bombs dropped Amin'allah murmured the words: '*Ay Khoda, Khoda* – Oh God, Oh God' – as if he were uttering the responses of the confessional. Then the jets disappeared into the distance, leaving a widening cloud of dust and smoke over the town, and as the last reverberations of their engines died away Amin'allah turned to me and said:

'More people killed, more *shahid*. Three or four, maybe more. Who knows? This is our life now; any day the jets can come, and more of us are killed. Today we have been lucky, it was a short attack. Sometimes it lasts longer; an hour, even more. If you stay here for a while you will understand our life a little better.'

I spent the rest of the day in the peach orchard writing my diary and sleeping. At sunset a mujahed brought us news that Abdul Haq had returned to the village and was expecting us. We set off through the gathering dusk towards the Commander's house.

The lamps were already lit and plates of rice arranged before us when Abdul Haq took his place at the evening meal. He welcomed me and apologised for the difficulties of the journey. He was shorter than I had expected but had a remarkable presence: an aura of intense energy surrounded him, and his men's demeanour showed they accepted his authority completely.

Nazim Khan was present at the meal and Abdul Haq questioned him closely about the journey. At the descriptions of the ambush and the river crossing Abdul Haq's eyes narrowed slightly and his gaze became more searching. I found it difficult to believe we were the same age. His features were ascetic; but instead of the harsh lines I had seen in the face of the Hesb Islami commander it seemed as if the war had stripped away every trace of false emotion to reveal this man's essential nature, a man of intelligence and humanity.

Once the meal was over a succession of people came before him with requests for letters of introduction, permission to travel to Peshawar, payment for supplying the mujahedin and other, more trivial matters. He was clearly exhausted, but he treated each person in turn with kindness and patience, and when at one point his second-in-command tried to discourage further demands he brushed the suggestion aside, and did not retire to bed until the last bit of business was satisfactorily completed.

The moon was shining through the trees when I opened my eyes. Cocks were crowing in the lanes of the village and a donkey coughed and brayed in the cool air. One by one the shadows beside me shifted, grunted and staggered to their feet to go to the mosque for the early morning prayer. I lay under the covers for a while longer, savouring the moment on my own and wondering what the next few days would bring.

After hearing my plans to write an article about the life of the people of Nahrin, Abdul Haq had appointed a mujahed to act as a guide, to show me round the town and help with any difficulties I might encounter. My guide was called Muhandis, or Injineeah, a title given to anyone who had attended a course at university. He was twenty-eight years old with amused brown eyes and a well-combed moustache and beard. The previous evening he had displayed a dry sense of humour in conversation and I was looking forward to his company.

The sky was a deep green and the planet Venus was still bright above the horizon when we set off. My illness had weakened me and my legs were like water so that I was soon trailing behind the others; as a result, the journey to Nahrin took twice as long as it should have done.

On the outskirts of the town a clear rushing stream flowed in the shade of some poplars. This, Muhandis explained, was the main water supply for the town. I was about to drink from it when the donkey which was carrying our things came to an abrupt halt a few yards upstream from where I was. There was a hissing sound and a yellow cloud trailed away in the water between the donkey's legs. I made a mental note to restrict myself to drinking chai while in Nahrin.

Almost immediately we had entered the town I saw signs of bombing: a derelict house with broken walls, its orchards splintered and uprooted by the blast. Further on we passed a site where several people had been killed when the school building in which they had sheltered took a direct hit. The place looked like a small quarry with two craters, ten to fifteen feet deep, in a waste of broken timbers and fragments of stone. Muhandis pointed to the shattered remains of a tree which had been tossed to one side by the explosion.

'It was a great tree. Three men with their arms outstretched could only just touch their hands around its trunk. It had been there for two, perhaps three hundred years, and now' – he made a brief gesture – 'it is gone.'

Muhandis was anxious that I should take photographs of the wreckage and destruction but I refused. Most of my film had been lost in the river and I had only three rolls left for the remainder of the journey.

We ate a meal of kebabs and chai in a chaikhane on the edge of the bazaar. Muhandis tried to persuade me to remain in the darkest corner of the room while he bought some items for me in the bazaar.

'Most of the people in the town are good men, but it is better not to let too many people know you are here. There are Khad agents in the town. Your safety is my responsibility and if anything happens to you Abdul Haq will be very angry with me.'

He imitated the stroke of a whip and smiled. 'Perhaps I would be beaten.'

How could I write about the town if I was hidden away and talked to nobody? I asked. Reluctantly Muhandis agreed and together we made our way to the bazaar where I bought soap, batteries, toothpaste and a toothbrush, a skull-cap and turban – all to replace those which had been washed away with my pack. By now my beard was a fairly respectable length and I found that I could pass as an Afghan. As long as I remained silent, my presence drew almost no comment, although occasionally men asked whether I was from the Panjshir and once someone asked if I was a Russian prisoner. Muhandis tried to parry such questions with the reply that I was a friend who was travelling through the town, but the pretence grew threadbare when it came to bargaining over material for the turban. By the time we left the bazaar news about me had spread and several shopkeepers nodded and smiled in our direction as we passed by.

We returned to the chaikhane where we ate kebabs and grapes. Two kowk rattled and squeaked in wicker cages beside us. Muhandis told me that they were fighting birds. They were caught young and raised to maturity when they were pitted against other birds; a particularly fierce one could fetch tens of thousands of afghanis and the rearing of such birds was a useful means of making money for those who had little hope of earning it any other way.

A little boy sidled up to me and showed me his hand: a diminutive finger had grown from the side of his thumb. Muhandis laughed and told him he was lucky.

'When you pick your nose you can clean both holes at the same time.'

This observation seemed to please the boy who grinned shyly and sat down beside us. Not to be outdone, a man flourished his hand revealing misshapen stumps where his third and fourth fingers should have been; a Tajik with a bristly shaved head and a neck like a bull roared with laughter. By now there was a party atmosphere and Muhandis begged me to sing a song so I gave a performance of 'Yonder come baby all dressed in blue' with a tuneless backing from the bull-necked Tajik, humming raucously in my ear.

I was tired, and in the middle of the afternoon Muhandis led me to the place where I was to stay. I followed him up a flight of uneven mud stairs, along a narrow corridor and into a room not much larger than a cupboard, where two mattresses had been laid out, covering the floor. Half a dozen rifles were stacked in one corner; in another a pile of overripe melons exuded a sickly sweetness and the air was hectic with flies. Muhandis looked at me and a sly grin spread across his face.

'This is a safe place, Abdul. Not many people come here.'

'I can see why.'

His grin broadened.

'There is a bed for you and a bed for me and blankets. Look, there is even a curtain.'

He twitched a sweat-stained combat jacket hanging over a small aperture in the wall.

'You can rest here in peace and safety. I will come back in an hour.'

With a lingering smirk of encouragement he left me to settle in to my new surroundings. The décor had a distinctly surreal quality. A tethering stake had been driven into the crumbling plaster of the wall and from it hung a tiny ball of string. The ceiling was painted black and in the middle of it a single dusty bootmark had been printed on its surface. I lay down on one of the mattresses and closed my eyes. The sharp scent of charcoal caught my senses and for a while I listened to the inconsequential noises of the street below.

I was deep in conversation with someone whose face I recognised, but whose name I could not remember when I was woken by the sound of knocking, and Muhandis pushed his head round the door.

'Come, Abdul. If you want a bath we can go to the *hammam*'.

For days the members of the group had told me of the wonderful *hammam* in Nahrin. By now I was drenched with sweat so I agreed with enthusiasm. Visions of white marble and clouds of steam lit by shafts of sunlight evaporated when we arrived at the bath house, pushed open a rickety door and stepped into a vault of dank shadows. It was six o'clock in the evening and the *hammam* was

empty. Muhandis volunteered to guard my clothes while I went into
the washroom wrapped in one of the *hammam*'s towels: a strip of
khaki-coloured cotton. Feeling like a latter-day participant in some
Eleusinian mystery, I fumbled my way through a door made from
strips of packing case branded with the gnomic letters CCCP into
the bowels of the hammam. There was a smell of stale sweat,
standing water and a hint of something even less agreeable. A couple
of frogs hopped away from my feet. I plunged my washing bowl into
a dark hollow in the wall and was rewarded with a cupful of tepid
water. After washing as best I could I was heading back for the
changing room when I caught sight of something on the floor. In the
dim light it looked like a vast frog asleep in a circle of dusty sunlight.
Breathless with excitement at the sight of such a gigantic specimen I
tiptoed closer only to discover a neatly coiled turd left by a previous
denizen of the bath house. The Nahrin baths were a far cry from the
RAC club.

Later, when I told Muhandis of my close encounter he showed
neither surprise nor sympathy, but merely remarked with an
enigmatic smile, 'It is not our custom.'

In the evening I had dinner with Abdul Haq and a group of mullahs.
When the usual round of handshakes was being made I was
momentarily disconcerted to discover that the oldest and holiest of
the mullahs had no right arm. Nevertheless, warm greetings were
exchanged and we settled down to a modest banquet of meat and
rice. Naturally enough, the topic of religion was soon raised and, in
authoritative tones, the one-armed mullah informed the hushed
assembly that the Bible prohibited the use of tobacco. I pointed out
that the Bible had been written two thousand years ago, whereas
tobacco had only been discovered in the last five hundred years. For
a split second the mullah was silent and I wondered whether I had
committed an unpardonable solecism. Then he launched into a
vigorous questioning of my beliefs. How could anyone, even a man
as holy as Hazerat Issah, the Prophet Jesus, be physically resur-
rected? And how could God, who is beyond all mortal comprehen-
sion, father a son by a woman of Galilee? And why did Christians
drink wine, clearly forbidden by God through his mouthpiece the
Prophet Muhammad? And what was the point of worshipping
images of wood and stone?

I replied that Christianity, like Islam, has both an outer meaning
(*zaher*) and an inner meaning (*baten*). Therefore, it was as difficult
for a non-Christian to understand the meaning of such things as it
was, say, for an uneducated Muslim to interpret the flight of the

Prophet on the wonderful creature Burach.

'Who can tell?' replied the mullah. 'Only the one in whom all secrets are known.' And, with these words, the catechism came to an end.

The air in the room was very close, and we took it in turns to fan each other. Once the meal was over I made an excuse to go outside where I planned to smoke a guilty cigarette; I found another member of the party beside a gurgling stream with a glowing cigarette already in his hand.

'Don't worry, Abdul. Some religious people have narrow thoughts. Look at me. I believe I am a good Muslim, but I am smoking tobacco. For me it is not *haram*. God knows better than the mullahs.'

Just then the door behind us opened. At once my companion dropped his cigarette with a faint hiss into the stream and stood up to greet the mullahs who were making their departure. I quickly followed his example and together we bade them a respectful farewell. The other members of the party set off in twos and threes into the night.

Muhandis and I went back to the room cluttered with guns and melons. The atmosphere was hot and stifling and sleep was impossible, so we moved our mattresses on to the flat roof outside where a couple of mujahedin were sitting, talking quietly in the moonlight. One was a watchmaker, the other a lawyer who asked me about the English legal system. He was surprised to hear that the laws of England, unlike Qur'anic law, had little relation to any holy book, and he had difficulty understanding how people could be persuaded to obey them. The conversation shifted and I asked him about the war.

'Almost all the conscripts in the State army, seventy-five per cent or more, support the mujahedin. When they are sent against us they fire high in the air over our heads. Once they have received a rifle and a new pair of boots many of them join the mujahedin. That is why the Shuravi put minefields round the military camps; not only to stop us getting in, but to prevent the soldiers getting out.'

He laughed contemptuously.

'They are afraid of their own army. The Shuravi have good weapons, but the Afghan conscripts are only issued with carbines when there is a battle. Once they are back in barracks the arms are taken away again. The Shuravi themselves aren't bad fighters, provided they have air support. But without it they become afraid. The Cubans are different: when one of them is shot the others keep going. They are very brave.'

'And the mujahedin?'

'Many of us are brave, although there are also cowards. But even the cowards fight, because this is a *jehad*. In the West you think we are fighting because the Shuravi invaded our country and we want to be free. That is only half the truth. The Shuravi bomb our mosques and religious schools, they try to teach our children communism and tell us that Islam is a backward way of thinking. It is true that Afghanistan is a poor country, but the most precious thing we have is our faith; without it we have nothing. We are fighting to protect our religion.'

'And your families, your wives and children?'

For several moments he said nothing.

'It is hardest for them. The journey to Pakistan is expensive and dangerous, so most of them remain in the towns. We go to our camps in the mountains, but they have to stay behind – that is why most of the people killed in the bombing are old people, women and children. My wife worries for my safety while I am away fighting the Shuravi, and all the time I am afraid in case she is killed in the bombing.'

We continued talking till the wick of the kerosene lamp burned low and the moon had moved a handspan across the sky. Eventually the others lay down to sleep, but my mind was restless and I sat up for a while longer, writing my diary by the light of the moon.

The next day I went for breakfast to a flyblown chaikhane near the caravanserai. To begin with I was stared at so that I felt like a solitary chimpanzee having a tea party in an invisible cage. But telling my onlookers to go away was a mistake: once they discovered I could speak some of their language their reserve vanished. Were there shish kebabs in England? Did the people of my country take naswar? And did they know about the war in Afghanistan? Why wasn't I married – was I too poor to afford a wife? Had I seen the bombing? Where was I going? Question followed question till my head was spinning and I knew I had to have a haven where I could collect my thoughts. Eventually Muhandis found a more secluded place for me: the walled garden of a deserted house belonging to a man called Moheb.

A month earlier the neighbouring house had been bombed and three people killed. Moheb's brother had sent his family away into the country, leaving the house empty and forlorn. The windows were broken and the plastered front was pitted with holes and fragments of jagged metal; but the vines had survived. A little brook flowed through the garden and close by was a leafy trellis from which the grapes hung down in golden-yellow bunches. The explosion had covered them with a bloom of fine powder. The first time I ate the sun-warmed fruit particles of grit crunched in my teeth and I thought of the people hit by the blast. From then on I washed the grapes in the water of the stream.

One afternoon two of Moheb's brothers came to the garden and together we harvested the grapes. The elder brother was a small, wiry man with a huge moustache. His name was Hussein. He told me how before the war he had worked as a mechanic in the Persian Gulf. He came back to join the mujahedin: the year before he had been shot in the leg while fighting the Russians. Luckily the wound had healed, but the scar was still an ugly pink and he could only walk for short distances. The other brother, Jemal, was round and stocky with sorrowful brown eyes. Before the invasion he had been in the Afghan army, and had formed a bad impression of the Russian advisers who had been sent to Afghanistan.

'They were animals. They never washed before meals and they used to piss next to us while we were eating. When the invasion happened there were thousands of them, but none of them knew why they had come. They were told they would be fighting Chinese and Americans – they were surprised when all they found were Afghans.'

We filled several large wicker baskets full of grapes. As we cut the sticky bunches from the vines and dropped them into each other's hands, I thought of bombs falling and remembered the parable of the labourers working in the vineyard who each received a penny for their toil.

Later we were joined by the Professor and Muhandis who had accompanied Moheb, the owner of the vineyard. He was tall and thin, a man of forty or so, whose high forehead and steady brown eyes revealed a fine character.

While Hussein and I washed in the stream the others wandered round the garden. Half an hour before sunset a friend of Muhandis' knocked at the door into the garden and, sitting down beside us, unwrapped a small lump of hashish from a crumpled scrap of newspaper. He prepared a couple of cigarettes and we passed them between us, sitting back under the vines, shafts of sunlight flickering through the leaves.

Neither the Professor nor Moheb was used to smoking hashish, and they drew on the cigarettes out of politeness rather than any real desire. The Professor confessed he had smoked more when he was younger.

'Ten, fifteen years ago I used to – then it was very good with my wife,' he smiled and made a sucking noise with his clasped hands.

'But now I only smoke occasionally. Abdul Haq forbids the mujahedin to use it; anyone caught with it is beaten. He is right; if you
smoke and bombs are falling it is easy to go mad.'

He lowered his voice.

'The friend of Muhandis, the man who brought this *charas*,
smokes too much. He is afraid of the bombs so he takes *charas* and
then he is even more frightened. Look at his face; you can see he is a
sick man.'

It was true: he was a young man but his brow was furrowed by
lines of anxiety and his eyes were weak and evasive.

The Professor cleared his throat.

'But sometimes, Abdul, when there is no danger, it is good to
smoke. These moments of peace are very precious to us; but *ah jan*!
if you had come to this town before the war . . .' He turned to a girl
of five or six who had silently appeared and was playing with
Muhandis by the banks of the stream.

'This is Moheb's daughter. She has never known peace.'

Muhandis had a Kalashnikov strapped to his shoulder and the
little girl was holding on to its barrel as she steadied herself to dip her
feet in the water. The war was suddenly incomprehensible. I asked
the Professor whether he thought the people of Europe and America
could possibly understand what it was like for the men and women
of Afghanistan. His reply was straightforward.

'Of course. Why not? You have mothers, wives, brothers and
children. In the same way we worry for their safety, so would you.'

The logic was irrefutable, but I knew the reality was different, and
said nothing.

It was time for the nemaz. The little group of men stood under the
vines in the last rays of the sun: Moheb with his brothers on either
side, Muhandis, the Professor swaying slightly as he rose to his feet
and Muhandis' friend, his face unresolved and sad, drifting off into
a perplexed reverie in the middle of his nemaz which he performed
several paces away from the others.

After praying Moheb invited Muhandis and me to come to his
house for the evening meal. Then he and the others set off, leaving
me to follow with Muhandis who first wanted to show me more
evidence of the bombing. It was as if he needed to show me the
destruction to convince himself it was real. We looked at the
remains of a house but there was almost nothing to show there had
been a building there: only piles of rubble and splintered timbers
jutting from mounds of earth and stones. A hole had been dug into
the side of one of the craters.

'Four people died in that house. They had taken shelter in the cellar. Three bodies were never found, only a few pieces of bone and flesh.'

Thirty yards away a large earthenware vase, still intact, was balanced in the upper branches of a sapling where it had been tossed by the blast. A small boy with protruding ears and an expression like an alarmed rabbit sidled up to us and whispered to Muhandis.

'He wants you to take his photograph.'

I noticed a couple of others hovering uncertainly behind a broken wall and an image flashed into my mind of a group of children giggling for the camera at the bottom of a bomb crater.

'Tell him I don't have my camera with me – maybe tomorrow, *Insha'allah.*'

Muhandis picked up an irregular slab of metal the size of a dinner plate with cruelly jagged edges.

'This is part of a bomb.' He pressed it against his stomach, gave a mock cry of agony, then tossed it aside with a laugh.

We gazed at the devastation in the gathering twilight.

'This happens everywhere in Afghanistan,' he said.

I glanced at him and the look in his eyes was a little like the amazement I once saw in an Oxford villager's face as he stared at the wreckage after a thunderstorm in which the familiar landmarks of tall trees had been torn away.

At dinner Moheb told me of his family: before the war it had been one of the most prosperous in Nahrin. But the business had declined, prices in the bazaar had doubled or tripled and now he was having difficulty looking after all the various relations who were dependent on his household. There had been another brother with the mujahedin, but six months before he had been killed, leaving a young widow and a child. The shadow of his death was still visible in the brothers' faces. Several times Moheb asked me about the Christian doctrine of the resurrection. I told him the parable of the seed planted in the earth.

'In truth,' he murmured, 'Hazerat Issah was a wise man.'

I had dinner with Moheb several times. We used to sit on a raised platform of earth outside the walls of his house in the cool of the evening while his elderly father, frail as a withered leaf, shuffled his rosary and whispered to himself. The younger girls of the household brought us food and water, since their elder sisters and the women of the house were not permitted outside the home: the presence of a male foreigner might have had unpredictable repercussions. Nevertheless, on a couple of occasions I caught a glimpse of heavily veiled figures looking down at me from the parapet over the main gate, and heard women's voices and the sound of laughter.

One evening two strangers arrived from the north of Ishkamesh. They were tough-looking characters, strong-boned, burly men with beards like Quaker sea-captains, but as they listened to Moheb's description of the bombings of Nahrin the muscles of their faces tightened with alarm. One tugged at his beard nervously while his companion rocked backwards and forwards groaning softly. Moheb was unable to give them any words of reassurance.

The meal was over, the pots of tea had been cleared away, and we were preparing to go to sleep when we heard the sound of footsteps in the alley leading to the house. Muhandis rolled over towards his gun as a shadow approached the circle of lamplight, all elbows and knees and timidity.

It was a boy of seventeen from a nearby town who had heard that Moheb was a good man who might let him stay for a night or so. His mother and father had been killed in a bombardment and their house destroyed. There was a heavy silence. One of Moheb's brothers grimaced with disbelief. Even if the story were true, the family's own resources were sorely stretched by the presence of Muhandis and myself. But Moheb nodded his assent and a few minutes later the boy was eating hungrily from a bowl of rice.

I had already settled down to sleep when Moheb tapped my shoulder and produced a radio which was able to pick up the World Service. This was an unexpected bonus since my own had been emitting a disagreeable growling since its immersion in the river. I lay back with the Milky Way above me, listening through the static and the Soviet interference to the news of coal miners on strike and the latest score in the Test match: England seemed to be losing.

Almost a week had gone by and still there was no bombing. An air of foreboding spread over the town like a cloud, and I found myself drawn into a downward spiral of unease which I could only halt by a great effort of will. Instead of wolfishly smiling enquiries about English girls, Muhandis lapsed into longer and longer silences.

There were several false alarms, when helicopters crossed the sky like bloated dragonflies, or aerial reconnaissance planes circled over the town for minutes at a time. But still no attack came.

One afternoon, I was sitting in the walled vineyard. From the next door garden came the sound of a man chopping wood with long, steady strokes. The throb of a helicopter became audible and the workman's rhythm faltered for a few seconds; then, when it was almost directly overhead, his axe was silent, but as the clatter of the helicopter's blades receded into the distance the chopping began again. The event struck me as a simple metaphor for the Afghan resistance.

The next attack happened without warning, when a single jet dropped its bombs in a couple of sweeps on the edge of a town several miles away. By the time I'd fully realised what was happening it was all over, except for a column of dust-coloured smoke rising above the houses in the distance.

The wearisome tension had been broken, for the time being at least. That evening I shared a meal with Muhandis and the watch-maker whom I had met on the roof in the moonlight. We greeted each other like old friends and I understood how the bombing drew everyone in the town even closer together, instilling among them that rare affection, bordering on love, which survivors have for one another. During the day we were constantly at risk; only when the sun had set was the invisible siege lifted. Then the life of the people reasserted itself; little lights sprang up along the sides of the road where the fruitsellers and stallholders offered their wares by the light of hurricane lamps, men walked arm in arm from one chaikhane to the next, and there was an almost festive spirit to the passers-by.

I tried hard to find out the numbers of people killed in the raids and the percentage of people who had left for Pakistan, but replies varied so widely that I realised any specific figures I attempted would be meaningless. I had to contend with an innocent lack of knowledge or else an understandable tendency to exaggerate – sometimes to extreme lengths. Whether it was Soviets or civilians killed the replies often varied by a factor of ten. This annoyed me intensely until it occurred to me that exaggeration helped the people come to terms with the enormity of what was happening to them. Some of them, I am sure, also hoped that by their multiplying the number of casualties aid would appear more readily.

It was time for me to be moving on. I had already stayed several nights with one family, the danger to whom increased on each occasion. Khad agents were active in the town; I could not stay too long in one place. Besides, I wanted to travel further north to meet Qazi Islamuddin, the Jamiat commander of Ishkamesh.

7

Ishkamesh

The truck going to Ishkamesh had been captured from the Soviets several months before and, although its engine sounded like a hen-coop full of broody chickens, it was in good enough condition. Moheb had decided to come some of the way with me, and had climbed into the cab between the driver, myself and a young man with grey-green eyes whose mouth and chin were ragged with impetigo. He had been fighting in the Panjshir for the past year and was on his way home to his wife and his recently-born child whom he had not yet seen.

The truck climbed painfully into the mountains above the town with the phantom chickens in the engine shrieking as if they were being slaughtered, until the road levelled out and it was possible to hear what the young man beside me was saying.

'The past few months have been difficult, but now the offensive is over I can take a rest with my family for a few weeks. I will see my child and eat some good food and drink clean water. That is one of the greatest difficulties in the Panjshir: we need tablets to purify the water. Sometimes we have to stay in places where the water is dirty, the men drink it and become sick. Also vitamins: it is very hard to get enough vegetables. That is why my mouth hurts and my gums and teeth are rotten.'

I prepared myself for the inevitable request for pills or medicine, but instead he produced a pear from his pocket and pressed it into my hand.

'Take it, it's delicious.'

I tried to explain that he should eat it instead but he misinterpreted me.

'Don't worry, it's not poisonous – look, I'll take a bite to prove it.'

A crisp white bitemark appeared on the fruit which he thrust once more into my fingers. To refuse further would have been impolite and I took a modest nibble.

'Finish it,' he urged. 'I've several more.'

Was impetigo infectious? I couldn't remember. I told myself that good manners were more important than hygiene and took another bite.

At a village of mud brick houses the lorry rattled to a halt and deposited some of the passengers, including my neighbour, who pushed another pear into my satchel. Moheb also said farewell, and before I could thank him properly he too had slipped away. The rest of us stood aimlessly around the truck waiting for more passengers to arrive. A toothless friend of Moheb's passed round a smouldering cigarette full of hashish. At last everyone was ready and an old man with a long white beard and a soup-stained shirt climbed in beside me. He looked like Father Christmas in a turban.

The chickens cackled into life once more and we inched up another mountain at the speed of a cardiac patient carrying a heavy suitcase. Father Christmas held on to the dashboard with both hands, a Kalashnikov wobbling between his legs as we lurched in and out of impossible gullies into the gathering dusk. Another hour and we stopped for nemaz; Father Christmas vanished into the dark, and his place in the cab was taken by Qazi Islamuddin's father. He was a huge Tajik with a shaven head, who carried on an animated conversation about his son with a man hanging on to the lorry outside the window. Clouds of dust blew into the cab and the view of the road through the windscreen was almost completely blocked by the shoulders of two men who were clinging on either side of the bonnet. The driver could only have steered the truck by memory or instinct, for by now it was almost dark and because of the risk of Soviet patrols he was driving without headlights. Several times he stroked his beard and murmured a prayer to himself: I assumed he was praying for much-needed divine assistance but he later told me that such prayers were customary when passing a grave or cemetery.

On the outskirts of another village we pulled to a halt and I got down from the cab to stretch my legs. A silhouette beside me pointed to the sky and asked:

'Do you have stars in your country?'

Another showed me the Plough, telling me it was called 'the Seven Brothers'. In return I told him one of the few words I could remember from my lackadaisical studies of Ancient Persian – 'haptoiringa' – the name for the same constellation. I also tried to find another group of stars for him – the Seven Sisters – but sadly they were invisible.

I had had enough of the inside of the cab and for the last part of the journey to Ishkamesh climbed into the back of the truck. Half an hour later we saw beams of light wavering above a ridge and

rounding a corner we found ourselves caught in the full glare of a
jeep's headlights. I counted fourteen or fifteen mujahedin squeezed
into, and on top of, the vehicle. One of them towered head and
shoulders above the others: this was Qazi Islamuddin who introduced himself with the greeting, 'How is your health mine is very
good thank you,' accompanied by a meaty handshake. These were
the only words of English he knew.

Somehow space was made for me in the jeep, and we jolted off
towards our refuge for the night, a small arsenal of guns and rocket
launchers bumping against our ribs and shoulder blades. Qazi
Islamuddin had a seat to himself next to the driver. I felt as if I were
in the company of a group of prep school boys on an adventure
outing in the charge of a genial and bearded headmaster.

We ate in the shelter of a village mosque, where Qazi Islamuddin
expounded on the character of the Afghan people.

'We are warriors and very brave. We eat a lot and we fight a lot.'

To my ears, the words were heavy with unintended irony. My
first impressions of Qazi Islamuddin and his men were that they
suffered from boredom and frustration. In contrast to the heavy
fighting of previous years they had only fought the Soviets once in
the last nine months, in the early spring, and the lack of combat was
weighing heavily. Qazi Islamuddin had a cassette player to console
him and he put on a tape from Iran of boys' voices chanting the
words *Allah u Akbar, Khomeini, mard e Khoda* – Allah is great,
Khomeini is a man of God', over and over again like a mantra, until
the cadences acquired a mesmeric quality. But I was being sum-
moned by other, unavoidable commands. My stomach trouble,
which for several days had been slumbering like a snake in hiber-
nation, had stirred once more. I was directed to a derelict building
and a crumbling staircase leading to a darkened room. I struck a
match and in one corner I glimpsed a jagged hole in the floorboards.
Holding a lighted match in one hand while I loosened the cord of my
trousers with my other hand was not easy. I was just positioning
myself when there was a crunch of dry wood and my right leg shot
through the floorboards, almost hurling me into the blackness
below.

Later, as I made my way back to the mosque, I wondered whether
I had been at the receiving end of an Afghan practical joke, or
perhaps there had been some other more sinister motive.

Still shaken by my near escape, I lay down beside the men whose
faces I had hardly seen. But, as a golden moon rose over the grassy
eaves of the mosque and shone into the branches of the mulberry
tree above our heads, any misgivings I may have had about my

neighbours vanished in the glory of a summer night in Khunduz.

The next day was market day. Qazi Islamuddin had offered to help me buy a horse so we drove in the jeep towards the main town of Ishkamesh with the early morning glow slanting across the rolling plain.

The previous year the Soviets had attacked the town and destroyed the bazaar, but the shops and stalls had been rebuilt and the avenues between the wooden stalls were thronged with men and animals. The horse market was ten minutes' walk away from the main bazaar in a large square of open ground filled with hundreds of horses and men moving here and there in a haze of dusty sunlight. Finding a suitable mount, let alone bargaining with an Afghan horse-trader to a reasonable price, would have been impossible without Qazi Islamuddin. We looked at various animals. All the time I was painfully aware of my ignorance: I sensed the sharp eyes of the horses' owners noting my inexperience and imagined them making quick mental adjustments to their asking prices. Some of the horses were sorry creatures, sway-backed and long in the tooth; but others were fine steeds with muscled flanks and bright eyes. I was looking for a horse which pushed smoothly forwards at a good pace and had the stamina to take the high passes of Nuristan. I tried riding several: the first was limping uncomfortably; another pranced and swung its head dramatically and kicked its hind legs in the air, to the great amusement of a crowd of onlookers; while a third was hopelessly docile. I finally chose a six-year-old roan horse with an intelligent eye and in good physical shape. A mujahed went off to buy a saddle and other fittings and the rest of us breakfasted on warm nan, apricot jam and tea.

A large group of Hesb Islami men were passing through the area on their way up to Badakhshan and there were armed men everywhere. An oldish woman with a plump, pock-marked face tried to sell a hen to one of them but he waved her away:

'Listen, Mama – the only thing I have in the world is this gun,' he grinned. 'And that's no use to you, is it?'

She shook her head ruefully and waddled over to the master of the chaikhane, but the price he offered was too low for her and she wandered away clucking disapprovingly.

After breakfast, Qazi Islamuddin went on a tour of the bazaar, a dozen mujahedin trailing listlessly behind him. The bazaar traders greeted him politely enough but without the reverence that had been shown to Abdul Haq.

At midday we ate a meal at a kebab stall and I studied his face carefully: it was intelligent, but noticeably different from the photograph of him which I had seen, taken two or three years earlier. The features were gradually being absorbed in characterless flesh and his eyes had an anxious shadow to them.

As he was about to tear a nan in half he paused, tossed it several times in his hand, and threw it to one of his men, telling him to weigh it. Sure enough, it was underweight and the luckless baker was brought in, a thin man with an enormous nose, twisting his fingers till the knuckles were white and scratching nervously at his ankles. A messenger hurried to fetch the Hesb Islami commander of Ishkamesh, and the two commanders discussed the case. The shortfall was small; nevertheless, the man had been dishonest. Perhaps he should be beaten?

The group left for prayers and the baker followed them, grinning sheepishly at the remaining customers who looked the other way and continued sipping their tea. Ten minutes later there were shouts of laughter in the street and the baker reappeared, his face blackened with mutton fat and soot, surrounded by a small crowd of people mobbing and jeering at him.

For a while I talked with people in the chaikhane but as the day wore on I grew tired and found a corner in the shade from where I could watch the passers-by. On the other side of the street Qazi Islamuddin was entertaining several visiting commanders of Hesb Islami. Dogs sunning themselves in the middle of the road snapped at their fleas. Two old men met in a joyful embrace, one grasping the other's beard and kissing him passionately on the cheek. Fruit sellers splashed glittering arcs of water in front of their stalls to keep down the dust.

We returned to Qazi Islamuddin's house for dinner. My fellow guest was a Hesb commander called Mustapha Jan, in charge of several thousand men bringing arms from Pakistan, who were breaking their journey for a few days before continuing north. He was well-educated and we had a conversation over a wide range of topics. First of all he established his political views.

'You ask me whether I wish a democratic form of government. I will ask you a question in reply. What is democratic? If you mean capitalism as it is in the West, the materialistic pursuit of riches, the immorality and the loss of religion, my answer is no. If you mean a political system which has evolved among the Western peoples for the past two thousand years, then my answer is still no. But if you mean an Islamic government, by Muslims for a Muslim country and its people, my answer is yes! For that is Islam.

'As for my attitude towards communism, I will tell you this:

better than communism is socialism, and better than socialism is colonialism for at least it permits a certain measure of religious freedom. But these are all bad. Better than all of them is Islam.'

He laughed mischievously and exchanged a smile with Qazi Islamuddin. 'Now tell us about your religion.'

I was doing my best to explain my beliefs when he interrupted me.

'But how can God become a man or a man become a God?'

Always the same question, the personality of God in Christ and, as always, I was unable to give an adequate reply. I said that I admired the purity of the Muslim concept of God.

'And your forefathers seven hundred years ago in Palestine: what did they believe, and why did they try to destroy our religion?'

I told him the story of St Francis of Assisi who visited the court of Saladin in order to convert him to Christianity. The saint wished to prove the power of God's love and offered to walk across a bed of red hot coals in the certainty that God would protect his feet from harm. Saladin's reply was simple.

'I can see you are a holy man, but you need not walk across a bed of red hot coals to prove it. I do not wish your feet to be harmed.'

Mustapha Jan was silent for a few seconds, then he asked:

'And which do you think is the best, your religion or Islam?'

I replied with another story of two men, a Crusader and a Saracen. They were comparing swords and the Crusader brandished his sword and claimed it was the better. Placing a thick steel helmet on a post and raising his long, heavy broadsword with both hands, he brought it crashing down, cleaving the metal in two. The Saracen was silent. Then he drew his scimitar, forged in the city of Damascus, and held it out, blade uppermost while, with the other hand, he unwound a silk ribbon from his turban and tossed it into the air. As it floated down on to the scimitar's blade the silk fell in two. The Crusader was silent.

At this, both commanders smiled. The discussion turned to the course of the war and Qazi Islamuddin described how it had changed.

'In the beginning we had nothing and only a few people were prepared to fight the Shuravi. Gradually we acquired weapons, we learned how to use them and began to win battles. Our support grew and the Shuravi had to bring more men against us. Still we fought and so the Shuravi changed their tactics. They took the war into the air where we could not follow them and threw down bombs on our towns and villages to frighten the people away. By this, the Shuravi hope to deprive the mujahedin of their support. So far they have not succeeded. But there is another war also, and in this the

Shuravi are very strong. They are trying to defeat us by destroying our economy. Prices have doubled and trebled for essential items, they destroy irrigation channels and burn our crops. If we have any produce to sell, transporting it to the larger towns is almost impossible.

'In some areas, in the north, there are already food shortages. The Shuravi have no pity; if they cannot force us to leave our country, they will try to starve us into surrendering. But God is great and even if we have to eat grass we will never surrender.'

'One thing the Shuravi do not understand, cannot understand,' added Mustapha Jan, 'is our religion. A man who believes in God is stronger than a man who has no religion. Ten, twenty, thirty years from now the Shuravi will grow tired of the war, like the American people tired of the war in Vietnam. Communism began a hundred years ago and already it is old and confused. But God is eternal. Perhaps now you understand, Abdul Baz, why this *jehad* can only end in victory.'

When the Hesb Islami commander rose to leave, Qazi Islamuddin enfolded him in a long embrace. It occurred to me that perhaps this display of affection was also intended for my benefit: two commanders of different groups showing their underlying unity for the foreign correspondent. However, my scepticism probably derived from the ingrained mistrust which the English have for seemingly extravagant gestures.

Qazi Islamuddin retired to bed but I talked for a while longer with the mujahedin who guarded the gates to the house: young men who, although they had no education, had a natural courtesy and sensitivity.

Later, after the lamp had been extinguished, I lay awake listening to the sound of horses shifting their hooves in the straw of the courtyard. The men who lay beside me knew almost nothing about me or the country that I came from. They had welcomed me with kindness. It was good to be with them. My previous life seemed curiously meaningless or irrelevant. I tried to remember friends, one friend in particular, and the last night we were together; drinking a bottle of wine and listening to the Police. But although I could recreate her image in my mind's eye I felt unmoved: I was more at peace where I was, and the last thought as I fell asleep was that I had finally arrived in Afghanistan.

In the morning I was taken to see a village which had been attacked the previous year – broken mud walls and huge craters in a stretch of open ground. But there was far less destruction than I had seen in

Nahrin. Grass was growing over the piles of rubble; at times it was difficult to distinguish the effects of helicopter gunships from the remains of buildings that had been allowed to fall into disrepair. Stones dislodged by the passing of the years or the blast of a high explosive bomb can look very similar. I needed to be by myself.

Returning to Qazi Islamuddin's house I came to a glade of poplars by a stream. I sat down in their shade and watched the street in front of a walled farmhouse. A man came out of the house to rinse a spittoon in the brook; twenty paces downstream someone scooped a cup into the water and drank from it. There was the sound of children's voices and in the distance a cock crowed. A dog wandered into the shade and slumped down to lick its paws. A doorkeeper dipped a flail into the stream and splashed water over the road in front of the gate and then, with a sidelong glance in their direction, splashed another dollop over some urchins who were watching him. It must have been like this before the war; time passing so slowly that change of any kind was infinitesimal. I remembered the legend I'd heard of the mountain of sand, higher than the sky, and the mythical bird that levels it, one grain at a time, until its labours are finally completed on the day of the Resurrection.

To travel from place to place is to travel through time, and in every place the quality of time is different. Here, now, it seemed to stretch in all directions. And I felt I understood why the Prophet Muhammad had ordained the observance of prayer five times a day; to act as markers for the faithful to lead them through the desert of eternity.

At sunset Qazi Islamuddin took me to a *kargah* in the mountains. We drove across a plain dotted with ancient tumuli and other, more recent burial grounds, over which the ragged flags, marking the graves of *shahid*, hung limply from branches in the windless air. We stopped at one of them and Qazi Islammudin pointed to a small mound with a boulder at one end.

'My brother is buried here. He was killed by the Shuravi.'

The earth was already overgrown with dry grass and weeds. One death is much like another after the event. The young man of last autumn and the inhabitants of the plain two thousand years ago were united in the same silence. I couldn't remember any words of condolence and so I asked how old his brother was when he was killed: he was younger than me.

The last part of the journey was in pitch darkness and I had no clear idea of my surroundings until dawn the next day. A series of stone cabins had been built at the base of a rocky cliff that reared up into a semi-circle of jagged peaks above us. It was a well-chosen spot. The mountains behind us were impassable and, in front of us, a rocky scree sloped gradually down towards the plain hundreds of feet below.

Qazi Islamuddin gave me a tour of the site. A spring had been tapped and the water channelled towards a plot of vegetables. Further on there were the remains of a mosque and other buildings which had been destroyed in the fighting at the beginning of the year.

'The Shuravi reached as far as there,' he said, pointing towards a ridge half a mile away.

'There was snow on the ground and the cold was terrible. They even brought tanks with them, but we destroyed most of them.'

There was no sign of any rusting metal hulks and I asked him what had happened to the remains of the tanks.

'The Shuravi didn't want it to be known that we can destroy their tanks so they removed what was left of them.'

Qazi Islamuddin kept his eyes firmly on the path and I said nothing, although I was mildly surprised that the Soviets should have been so litter-conscious.

'This is our fortress,' he continued. 'The Shuravi will never take it, and if they try we will defeat them again. Since the winter we have placed guns in the hills around the camp to protect us against air attacks.'

It crossed my mind that the weapons might have been better employed in the defence of the town below. We retraced our foot-steps along a path littered with spent cartridges and mule droppings, stopping at the field of vegetables for Qazi Islamuddin to inspect and sample the onions and tomatoes. The war was far away and for the first time in several weeks I felt safe, but Qazi Islamuddin was deep in thought and his silence touched me with a curious melan-choly. At last he spoke.

'When the war began, as I told you, we had nothing. I made this camp. We fought the Shuravi again and again; we survived. But the war has changed and for months the Shuravi haven't come near us; only their planes and helicopters which bomb us from the air. And there is little I can do to stop that.'

I sensed his longing for the early days of the conflict when resistance had been improvised from nothing and the fighting had still been on the ground: a time of heroes and feats of battle. Now the struggle was different – a wearisome siege from the air, with long periods of inactivity.

Two brothers came to the camp to obtain letters from Qazi Islamuddin in preparation for a journey to Pakistan. For an hour or so we sat and talked together on either side of a small, glistening stream. They were in their fifties, with iron-grey beards and eyes without guile or weakness. The talk was of religion: the younger of the two told me of a prophesy that Hazerat Issah would appear in Damascus in our lifetime. His brother added that the Third World War would occur in eight to ten years' time, after which the whole world would be Muslim. They also asked detailed questions about Christianity and listened attentively to my answers. When the time came for them to continue on their journey I felt I was bidding farewell to friends.

I also talked with Qazi Islamuddin's driver who was older than the other mujahedin. Before the war he had owned an hotel and garage in Kabul but soon after the Russians entered the capital he sold everything, moved to Ishkamesh and then joined the mujahedin.

'I used to get a lot of Westerners staying in my hotel since the rooms were cheap. All they wanted to do was buy as much hashish as possible and smoke it all day long. I didn't disturb them, they were less trouble that way. There were a few bad ones who tried to leave without paying but, if that happened, I threatened to tell the police that they were taking drugs.' He smiled ironically. 'They soon paid.'

'Kabul Radio is always telling us how bad it used to be, and how things are changing. They say new factories are being built and people have enough to eat. Perhaps for five per cent of the population that is true, but for the rest of us it is much, much worse. Even the most stupid people know it is propaganda. Before we were a poor country but at least we were free. Now the Shuravi have come; they take the natural gas from the north of the country and send it into Russia; they take children away from their parents to educate them into spying on their own families and friends; they bomb us and burn our crops and then they say we invited them to help us.'

He spat on the ground and shook his head.

'The Shuravi are liars. The truth is, they despise us. They call us "black bottoms" and it would make no difference to them if not a single Afghan remained in Afghanistan.'

I asked him what message he had for people in the West.

'Tell your people two things. First, we need ground-to-air missiles to protect our towns and villages. If the war was only on the ground we could win it in six months. The tanks are nothing. We have plenty of anti-tank rockets. But we cannot use them against aeroplanes and helicopters. Secondly, and most important, tell them that this war isn't only against the Shuravi, it is part of the great revolution of Islam.'

In the afternoon we returned to Ishkamesh where Qazi Islamuddin arranged for a man to ride my horse to Nahrin while we travelled there by jeep. It was a sturdy vehicle, the size of an Edwardian touring motor car, and travelling in it one experienced many of the same pleasures and discomforts as the first motorists, bowling along the mud-walled lanes. There were no other vehicles but our path was littered with mobile and unpredictable obstacles in the shape of hens, donkeys, sheep and children who dashed out towards us like flocks of tattered beetles and chased the clouds of dust behind us. Worst of all were the village dogs who ran alongside, snapping at any limbs that were visible, until a bang on the nose from the butt of a machine gun discouraged them. The nonchalant way the men handled their guns added a certain frisson: at best, their safety drill consisted of a thumb held firmly over the end of a barrel. More often the guns swung wildly towards one's nostrils or carotid artery as the jeep took yet another pot-hole at breakneck speed. Such carelessness irritated me but they were just as unconcerned for their own safety: slicing melons and pushing the wet chunks into their mouths on the point of a knife with the blade jerking erratically inches from their eyes and noses.

We ate supper at the house of a mullah and his family. Qazi Islamuddin impressed on me the privilege of the occasion.

'Our host is a very spiritual man. Ask him any question about the Qur'an, and he will answer you.'

I soon found myself in an abstruse conversation, the drift of which seemed to be that Jesus had in fact foretold the coming of a great prophet whose name was Ahmed, and this had been fulfilled in the person of Muhammad. I struggled to follow the saintly mullah's discourse with one ear while Qazi Islamuddin shouted an incomprehensible 'simplification' of his speech into the other. When at last we got up to leave the old man grasped my hand and kissed me on both cheeks, brushing my lips with his beard.

We set off again. In the darkness, the driver seemed to be tracing a huge game of noughts and crosses over the landscape, but at last I recognised one of the villages at which we had stopped on the journey north. We drew to a halt beside a mosque and bedding was spread out for us under the eaves. The others were performing their nemaz when suddenly the ground shuddered and the leaves of the trees rustled although the air was still. The shuddering grew more violent and a little boy shot out of the mosque, like a whipped mule into the courtyard. Other shadows followed him, and there were cries of '*Zelzeleh! Zelzeleh!*'.

It was different from earthquakes I had experienced in Japan which have a sharp, grinding tremor. Instead it was like standing on top of a huge jelly. People ran in all directions shouting in alarm – except Qazi Islamuddin, who remained in prayer. The tremors subsided after a couple of minutes. The mosque and houses had escaped damage, but the shock had put everyone into a frenzied excitement. A mujahed told me how, for the last year, there had been an unusual number of earthquakes which had filled people with superstitious fear. As he spoke a star trailing a long, powdery tail of light fell across the sky with apocalyptic brilliance.

It was market day in Nahrin and the streets were thronged with men and donkeys. Qazi Islamuddin and his followers went to look for Abdul Haq while I made my way to the chaikhane on the edge of the bazaar. I met Muhandis and we ate a hearty breakfast of skewered sheep's liver and glasses of sweet chai. As I lit a cigarette a man broke into a run in the street before us and soon there was a flurry of activity, with people hastily locking the fronts of their shops and hurrying towards the wooded hills above the town.

'They think the jets are coming,' said Muhandis with a grin. 'It often happens. Someone thinks they hear something, then everyone panics.'

A second or two later his expression changed.

'Come, come quickly. A bombardment will start very soon.'

He led me to a vegetable garden with a huge mulberry tree in the middle of it and a hen scratching around in a straggle of weeds. A minute later, Qazi Islamuddin appeared, sweating and out of breath, and the three of us crouched down along a shallow irrigation ditch, waiting for the attack to begin.

First the helicopters arrived, thudding over the town in a lazy circle while we pressed ourselves into a bank of crumbling earth under the boughs of the tree. Then the jets began their bombing runs with a thought-disintegrating roar rising to a mad pitch of noise as they swept over; then a massive thud, just audible through the thunder of the jets; then another. There was a lull of several minutes and some men sheltering with us in the garden broke cover, ignoring the others' shouts to stay where they were. Qazi Islamuddin sprang to his feet and aimed his gun at one of them.

'Move any further and I kill you.'

The men wavered in indecision.

'One more step and you're finished.'

Reluctantly, the men slunk back to their positions.

It had been a naked display of will but Qazi Islamuddin had

proved his mettle. I also saw how fragile leadership could be without a formal command structure.

The jets returned; several times when there were explosions the ground vibrated beneath my chest and the leaves above us quivered. I thought of aerial film of bombs exploding in the jungles of Vietnam, and the shockwaves radiating from the blast in swift shadows rippling through the forest. Unlike my companions, I was partially cocooned from the reality of the bombing by the memory of war films, in which the worst that happened was a loud bang and a sprinkling of stones and earth. To some extent the memory dulled the immediacy of fear. Even so, there were times when a plane swept directly overhead and we waited – one, two, three seconds for the bombs to explode, and everything contracted to a point of frozen terror. These moments passed quickly; then there was a breathing space until the next time. Muhandis scratched at the side of the ditch with a twig, a look of intense concentration in his eyes. Another man picked at the threads of his petou, and I changed into a cleaner shirt – anything to occupy one's mind until the waiting was over. For the next half hour the planes swung across the sky, the pitched thunder of their engines punctuated at intervals by the muffled boom of explosions. Almost certainly, the Soviets had chosen market day to maximise the effect of the raid.

At last the noise of the planes receded and an old man's face emerged from a clump of vetch on the other side of the mulberry tree. I had a sense of subdued relief bordering on hilarity, and it took several minutes for the light-headedness to disappear. Muhandis and I made our way to the bazaar. The air was thick with dust and smoke, and a dirty yellow cloud hung over us. Men hurried past. A woman in a blood-splattered veil rocked to and fro on the ground beside a bundle of clothes. We came to a house which had been hit; a group of people, gathered round a huge mound of rubble, were passing lumps of brick and mortar from hand to hand, while two men with sweating faces tore at the stones with their hands and hurled them to one side. There was nothing we could do to help. For several minutes we stood there, watching the pitiful drama, until I felt sickened by my own useless voyeurism and persuaded Muhandis that we should go back to the chaikhane. On the way we saw other clouds of smoke rising in between the houses, but the bazaar itself had escaped damage, apart from one line of stalls which had been cracked and splintered by the blast of a bomb falling in a stretch of open ground.

Later, in Moheb's vineyard, I wrote my diary. Suddenly I heard a sound, coming, as I thought, from the deserted house. I looked inside but it was empty. Then, through one of the windows at the back, I saw a boy's face peering at me from the mouth of a hollow in the hillside. Closer to, I found four children huddled in a cramped hole which had been dug into the dry gravel slope. Their eyes stared back at me unblinkingly from the shadow. Three boys and a girl crawled out and stood around me, screwing up their faces against the sunlight.

Although the attack had finished several hours before they were still afraid to come out in case the planes returned. Next door, some men were repairing a house and a heavy object, perhaps a large rock, was dropped on the ground with a dull thump, and the girl's eyes flickered momentarily in that direction. Her brothers soon disappeared but she remained hesitantly at my shoulder while I was writing, so that I felt obliged to talk to her.

Her name was Leilah, she said, and she was ten years old. Her father was dead, her mother was living with friends in Nahrin. In the autumn they were going to leave for Pakistan. I asked her if she wanted to go; for the first time, the ghost of a smile passed across her face.

'Yes, I want to go to Pakistan.'

'Why?'

'It is far away from the Shuravi. There are no bombs in that country.'

Looking into her brown eyes, I thought of her future in Pakistan; the dreary existence of refugees, months or years spent in squalid tents where the memory of the vineyard would fade into the distance.

The days passed and the songs on my tape cassette which had seemed so cheerful when I played them in Peshawar sounded sadder and sadder until I stopped listening to them altogether. In between raids, time had a jewel-like quality: the quintessence of summer. I talked with people in their gardens, in the shade of poplar trees and limes, watched haphazard butterflies flickering over beds of melons ripening in the sun and listened to the drone of hornets hovering over rotting mulberries. One family I stayed with had a particularly beautiful collection of pink, yellow, white and crimson roses, and I asked them to give me some seeds from the flowers in the hope that I could grow them in England.

'I will see the same colours in my garden and remember your kindness,' I said.

'*Insha'allah*,' they replied.

I spent an afternoon with two youths. One of them told me how his father had been sent to gaol for five years for helping the mujahedin while his elder brothers had sided with the State.

'They are no longer my brothers – they are *kafir*. If I ever see them again I will kill them. My religion tells me I should do so; it is stronger than blood.'

His friend listened to us without saying anything. In his hand was one of the fighting birds I had seen several days earlier, its claws tied together with a blue ribbon, and while his companion spoke with fire about the war he stroked the soft down on the bird's head. Then, in a pause in the conversation, he delicately untied the ribbon from the bird's legs and let it hop and flutter about the room.

'See how he beats his wings. He will be a good fighter.'

After the war he hoped to be a social worker, walking from village to village helping the people. He was unsure exactly how he would do this, but perhaps he would be a teacher, or a doctor. Almost as an afterthought he added what I now recognised as a stock formula in any discussion about the war.

'I will fight until the Shuravi leave my country – until I am *shahid* or my country is free.'

8

Nahrin

This is Nahrin: where the dogs lie in the dust in the middle of the street until the boys in the chaikhane throw slops of tea over them, where the smoke from the shish kebab brazier wafts across fly-blown strips of meat and over the shoulders of old men holding glasses of sweet green tea.

The sun is bright but the air is still cool after the night. A man drives a donkey, with a couple of squawking hens hanging from its shoulders, past the doorway of the shop where I am sitting. The walls are lined with bottles of medicine and boxes of pills, almost all of which contain vitamin supplements; I am breakfasting on warm nan, bread and jam with Abdul Kabir, a young man of twenty who is looking after the shop. He is well fed and his face has a meaty sensuality, capable of infinite degrees of suggestion. I ask him what kind of jam we are eating.

'*Alou* – Plum,' he replies, lingering over the sound of the word as if it were the name of some forbidden fruit.

'It's very good.'

He raises his eyebrows slowly, then narrows his eyes until they are trembling slits under his eyelashes and his tongue edges between his lips in a lazy smile.

'Mmm, delicious.'

The simple conversation hovers on the brink of ambiguity and goes too far as he inserts his finger into the syrup and deliberately licks it from the ring to fingertip.

'I am so tired, Abdul Baz. Look after the shop while I rest. I am sick . . .'

With a languorous wrinkling of his huge nose, his smudgy moustache bends in a spreading smile.

'I am sick here,' he lightly taps his hand over his heart and casts a hooded gaze in my direction.

Something about these innocent advances makes me want to burst out laughing and I find myself giggling uncontrollably, so that the town doctor, who is advising a customer, looks nervously in my direction.

Perhaps he is worried that I am mocking his professional opinion. I turn away in embarrassment and see a scrap of paper on the wall by my head that says: 'Stuff nose goes in secs' and the words revolve in my mind, while someone rolls an oil drum down the street. I sip at a glass of chai and spoon some sugar from a tin labelled 'Chloroquine Phosphate'. An old man comes in and asks for medicine.

'God – has it all gone already?' he says, shaking his head in sorrowful disbelief, then spends five minutes scanning the shelves and glancing furtively in my direction. At last he takes a strip of plastic from his waistcoat pocket and unfolds a grimy paper with an official Jamiat stamp on it which he shows to Abdul Kabir. But it makes no difference, Abdul Kabir is adamant:

'I am sorry, brother, truly we have none.'

The old man carefully folds the slip of paper once more, pushes the handful of notes he had ready back into his pocket and steps out into the sunlight.

Dr Habib is the senior doctor in Nahrin. He carries his equipment in an unbreakable plastic attaché case, the sort used by new clerks in insurance companies. He is acutely conscious of his inadequate medical qualifications – two years studying biology at a university in Kabul and a few weeks in the company of a medical student in a nearby province:

'If one or two foreign doctors could come here for six months and give us a basic training in first aid, hygiene and general medicine it would help save many lives. I do what I can but I have no training and only one assistant who knows even less than I do. After a raid there may be twenty or thirty casualties. At the moment we have no way to treat them: no painkillers, no blood bank, no penicillin. Ninety per cent of those with serious injuries are dead within a month, usually from gangrene. God forgive me when I say that it is better to be killed outright than wounded by a bomb.

'During the past year seventy people have been killed and about a hundred people have been wounded. We have no blood bank. Some of the wounded have fragments of metal in their bodies – these are invisible and cannot be removed. We have no cameras to take pictures which we could then show to experienced doctors who would be able to advise us. There is malaria. Before the war we used to receive anti-malarial medicine from the State, who also sprayed the mosquito-breeding grounds with DDT. Then the incidence of malaria was twenty per cent or so. Now the incidence is fifty per cent in many areas and where there is standing water it is as high as eighty per cent. Similarly, because there are no medical supplies, the incidence of tuberculosis has risen from ten per cent before the war to thirty per cent today.

'There are also skin diseases and fevers which we are unable to cure, why we don't know, but I think it is because of the Soviet bombing. They are using chemicals and most of the mujahedin are suffering from a skin disease which appears gradually over a period of six months to a year.

'Both the mujahedin and the townspeople lose their limbs from anti-personnel mines. We have no instruments for removing shattered bones. No facilities at all.

'The UNICEF representative does not come because of the Soviets. There may be no malaria in the Panjshir, but there is malaria in warmer places such as Khust, Andarab and Nahrin. Pneumonia and microbe-borne diseases are present. As well as bombing, biological weapons are being used against the Panjshir.

'Our children are suffering from bombing-related sickness and vomiting. The price of any medicine we can buy has doubled or trebled.

'Russia intends to conquer other countries, not only Afghanistan: they have been brought to their knees in the Panjshir. We are not only fighting for Afghanistan, we wish to help other countries, and we hope to God that we, the people of Afghanistan will be successful in this respect.

'When I heard there was a foreigner in the town I was happy because I thought you might be a doctor. I understand your work is different. Do what you can for us.'

The school teacher is insistent:

'Record these songs from my tape. The boys sing them in school.' He presses a button and an unbroken voice chants a ballad of the war calling the faithful to the *jehad*. Then the tempo changes and becomes a series of sharp, angry cries describing the crimes of the Shuravi and the bravery of the mujahedin backed by a chorus of older boys' voices intoning: '*Shuravi, dushman e ensaniat, Amrika, dushman e ensaniat* – Russia, the enemy of humanity, America, the enemy of humanity.' I ask him why the song describes America as the enemy of humanity and he smiles in a way which would have been disarming if it had not also shown a trace of unease.

'The Shuravi want to possess the world and so does America. The Shuravi have taken Afghanistan in their hand. You have seen what they do to our country, and America does nothing. Why? Because they do not understand that this war is a battle between men who believe in God, praise be to Allah, and men who believe in nothing but politics and land. The people of America are more interested in money than in God. They are both guilty.'

A small boy sits on a donkey picking his nose and staring into space. Muhammad, the keeper of the bath house, shuffles by, begging for money. He is an old man with a broken nose spread across a face of appalling dissipation and his clothes are in rags. The unworthy thought crosses my mind that he may be the anonymous denizen who laid such an unappealing booby-trap in the bathhouse. A man staggers past, bent double under a huge sack of grain. Next the town idiot, bare to the waist, with a pot belly and long matted hair, trots through the bazaar carrying a tin can full of water; he has a genial grin on his face. The word for 'mad' in Farsi is '*deiwaneh*', philologically related to the English word 'divine', and I wonder whether such a man is treated with the respect and kindness shown to holy men. Could he be a Sufi? Certainly he has the same confidence of step and brightness of eye that I noticed in certain Indian Sadhus. Then, incredibly, a woman in long green and white robes, wearing a *chador*, walks by leading a little dog on a lead. The sight is so extraordinary that, for a moment, I have the illusion of being somewhere completely different, where there are cars and cups of coffee. She vanishes into the passers-by and my surroundings close in on me once more.

I am inside one of the stalls in the bazaar. On the shelves are fist-sized crystals of salt, cubes of evil-looking soap the colour of congealed mutton fat, and boxes of State-manufactured matches and jars of naswar. I am drinking a glass of chai with the owner of the shop, Sa'id Mansour.

'It is getting harder to earn a living. Many things are two or three times the price they were before the war – that is, when I can get them – and then the people have no money to buy them. A few years ago the town was famous for its pistachio nuts – it was one of the main sources of the town's income. Now production is less than half, the men are away fighting, and the nuts fall from the trees unharvested. We can do nothing. We cannot buy to sell in the larger towns because the State controls them. Without buying and selling in the towns it is impossible for places like Nahrin to carry on indefinitely. Money has to flow from the towns into the country like water into the fields. The Shuravi are trying to stop the flow so that the country will wither. Men say this is a war of religion, a war of politics, a war of freedom. Maybe so. But I say this is also a war of money. Everyone needs money; to buy flour or rice, medicine or kerosene. The Shuravi know that without money we cannot survive. They bomb us, but that is only to make their real objective happen sooner. What is their real objective? I will tell you: they want to turn us into beggars. Then, when we have nothing to eat, they will offer us a handful of grain and tell the world how kind they are. They will mend the irrigation channels which they destroyed and say how they improved the primitive agriculture of backward peasants. They think they can treat us like dogs, starving us and beating us until we obey them. What fools they are. Our Muslim brothers all over the world know what is being done to us. They will not forget this war.

'Help from other countries? There was a time when I thought that Europe and America would help us. Several foreigners have visited the town since the war began. They stay for a week or so, take photographs of planes and smoke, and then they leave. I know that you can earn a lot of money from the pictures you have taken. But what will we receive? Nothing. Each time we ask such people for doctors and medicine, we wait and no doctors come. Only, perhaps, another journalist. Your people come and look at our suffering and sell it for money in their own countries.'

He asks how often there is news of Afghanistan in newspapers and on the television and when I tell him he is crushed with disbelief. I try to explain how Afghanistan is a distant country and the war is just another item occupying far less than one per cent of world news coverage.

The glass of tea has cooled and tastes, with a little imagination, like a cheap sherry. Sa'id splits a pistachio nut, offers me the kernel, then a whole handful. I sip the cold, sweet tea and munch pistachio nuts and try to piece together his words with my thoughts.

Dust Muhammad, the watchmaker, has two shirts. One is khaki-coloured, ex-army issue, given to him by a deserter from the State army; the other is of fine blue cotton embroidered with white silk. Today he is wearing the blue one. It reminds me of ones that used to flutter in multi-coloured rows in Portobello Road, or hung from the shoulders of summer holiday holy men with shoulder bags full of mysticism at $50 an ounce.

We are having breakfast together in one of the chaikhane by the bazaar or, to be more accurate, I am eating while Dust Muhammad watches me. He is poor and unwilling to accept hospitality which he cannot repay. There is a wireless playing in the background, the music is oddly familiar and suddenly I recognise the melody – 'Yesterday', by the Beatles. For a moment, the emaciated young man with a wispy beard sitting in front of me could be the ghost of a traveller on the hippy trail to Kathmandu.

But few hippies wore a shirt of such exquisite quality: innumerable threads, each meticulously sewn by hand into squares and lozenges, interpenetrating one another in a geometrical design of glorious complexity. It is a miraculous piece of work, and I say so. Dust Muhammad smiles: he is twenty-six but the lines of his face are those of a man ten or fifteen years older.

'My wife made it for me while I was in prison. She began to make it when she was sixteen; I was twenty-two and had just joined the mujahedin.'

We have talked several times before, but this is the first time Dust Muhammad has mentioned that he was in prison. I ask him whether I may tape the conversation and he invites me back to his room, over the stables of the caravanserai.

It is completely bare except for a cotton quilt and blanket in a corner and a table and chair beside the door. The table is scattered with cogs, hairsprings, screws, bits of wire and shells of transistor radios that are beyond repair. He spreads the blanket on the earth floor and I switch on the tape recorder. To begin with, his voice is taut with nerves and he stumbles over the words.

'At three o'clock in the morning in the month of Mizan, I was on my way to the *kargah* of my brother mujahedin when the Soviet occupational forces surrounded the party of men I was with, and captured us. We were kept in Khanageh for two nights and tortured. Then eleven Russian armoured cars and a Russian jeep took us in chains to the airport at Khunduz. We spent another three months there under Russian torture. Then we were taken to the town of Khunduz where I was for another twenty-one months. I was hung by the ankles and tortured with electricity and put in a cell which was so small that I could barely stand up.

'For eight months we were taken out of our cells three times a week and beaten and tortured. They questioned us about our weapons, and asked whether we had received them from America, but we answered, "We fight you with our faith." Our interrogators were Khad agents with two or three Russian supervisors. They even pulled the hairs from our beards.

'In another part of the prison, there were Muslim women: we could hear their voices. We had no books, no pens, no paper. I wanted very much to obtain a copy of the Qur'an. One day I noticed one of the guards: he looked a good man and I said to him 'You are a brother Muslim. Help me. Please bring me a copy of the Qur'an. He said nothing but later brought me the book, which I kept hidden from the authorities. I learnt it by heart.

'After twenty-one months I was put to work on a building project inside the gaol. One afternoon, when there was no one looking, some of us tied our turbans together, lowered ourselves over the walls and escaped. From there I made my way to Nahrin and have been living here for a year.'

Dust Muhammad pauses for a moment.

'Listen, helicopters.'

Sure enough, there is the faint clatter of helicopters in the distance.

'Do you want to continue?'

Dust Muhammad's voice is neutral but, even so, the question seems like a challenge and I have to restrain myself from responding like a schoolboy to a dare.

'I don't know. What do you want to do?'

'I have almost finished. I would like to give a message to the people of your country.'

We agree to complete the tape. While he speaks, I feel a growing tension in my chest; it is like waiting in line to buy a ticket at a station when the train is already on the platform. I look round the walls of the room, the low ceiling, the sunlight shafting down through the narrow window and know, with absolute certainty, that if there is a raid I have to be outside, under an open sky.

'*Tamam shod* – it is finished.'

I thank him and, as I pack the tape recorder away, the sound of a jet becomes audible. I try not to appear nervous but my hands and fingers fumble disobediently with the straps of my satchel. People are already running towards the hillside at the north of the town. Dust Muhammad is calm.

'You must go, but I will remain here.'

I try to persuade him to come with me but he is unmoved.

'Some places are safer than others, but nowhere is completely safe. I don't mind. I'm used to it.'

I say goodbye and hurry downstairs into the street below, but my relief to be out of the cramped room vanishes with the realisation that I have no idea where to go. I make for the garden with the mulberry tree.

The attack begins. The rollercoaster swing between relief and fear leads rapidly to a blankness of mind. An old man sitting next to me gazes expressionlessly at the ground. Each time there is an explosion he hunches his shoulders and, as the planes scream into the distance, he raises his head and his shoulders relax once more. One plane comes in low. The old man and I wait: we are both afraid of dying. There is a thunderous bang and the old man dips his head down further. But the sound of the explosion means we are both alive. Our neighbour's death is not our own.

The sound of the jets grows fainter and I get up to take some photographs; a chorus of voices tell me to wait. I ignore them and set off up the hill to get a view of the town which is partially obscured by thick smudges of rust-coloured smoke. From nowhere there is a sudden, terrifying roar and I run for cover, almost falling on top of someone huddled in a fox hole. I tumble in beside a young man and a few seconds later the bombs start falling again. From where I am I can watch the planes coming in over the ridge on their bombing runs, very low, no more than a couple of hundred feet. The explosions seem to be getting closer, and irrationally I imagine they are working methodically across the town towards where we are. A jet sweeps over the crest of the hill, less than a hundred yards away, and I watch two bombs falling diagonally from it. Then the stunning unreality of what is happening disintegrates in a massive double drumbeat which shakes the ground around us and another cloud of smoke rises above the trees.

The boy pulls at my shirt and shouts something: he is shuddering and gasping with fear and his words are unintelligible. I hear the word 'Allah' several times. Asking him something is like talking to a man pulled from a frozen lake. He jabs at the sky with his hand and buries his face in the earth again. Then, on the hillside above us, there is a burst of heavy gunfire. I curse at the invisible fool whose pointless heroics are almost certain to draw more bombing or rocket attacks in our direction. The gunfire goes on in bursts for several minutes, then finishes as abruptly as it began. From the edge of the foxhole I see a helicopter wheeling away. There is no sign of anyone else on the hillside and it takes several seconds for me to grasp that I have been cursing a helicopter gunship attack.

People begin to stir. The first to move are shouted back by those who are still under cover, but others follow them and emerge into the streets. A young man runs up to me.

'Come, come, there are *shahid*.'

I follow him without enthusiasm. We hurry through a maze of mud-walled streets and come to a mound of rubble across our path. Coming in the opposite direction a group of men is carrying a bed on which there is the inert form of a twelve-year-old boy. The blast has caught him below the waist, he is covered with dust and one of his feet is missing. My camera is ready. I check the light meter, adjust the focus and press the button. I am surprised by the methodical way I react, as if the mechanics of recording the reality are more important than the subject matter. Perhaps, by taking a photograph, I diminish the horror; I am hiding my eyes behind the camera. But only a moment is captured. The boy's suffering is not confined to the photograph. I have only one roll of film, and as the boy rocks and sways on the shoulders of the men and is borne out of sight, I take two further pictures.

'Come this way,' says my guide and, forcing myself not to think, I plod after him, my mind still juddering from the compression of time into seconds. What do the Soviet pilots think as they press the fire control button? Is there the same absence of emotion which I seek as I press the button of the camera? Do we both, for an instant, lose our humanity in machines?

There is a sound of crying, of a woman in high-pitched grief. The next moment a boy of five, wearing a turquoise blue shirt that comes down to his bare knees, races out of a doorway in tears. He might just have been bullied by a friend, or smacked by his father. Two old men are standing in the middle of the street and one of them calls out to the tearful boy:

'Child, is your mother lost?'

The little boy stops running in mid-stride and stands there, with his mouth open in a wordless cry. The nearest old man turns to his companion.

'His mother is lost.'

The words have no visible effect on the man's lined face, which gazes into space.

'Follow me over here,' calls my guide and we step across a carpet of leaves and torn off branches into the garden of a house. A small crowd has gathered round four bodies stretched out in the blasted remains of a melon patch, the heads and torsos covered with blankets. The feet are splayed slightly, like those of someone napping on the lawn under a newspaper on a hot Sunday afternoon. The legs are dusty and streaked with blood.

Some men are carefully placing the bodies on *charpoys*. I take two photographs: one of the men covering the bodies with blankets, another of someone's grieving face. I always wondered what sort of people took such photographs. My guide is waiting for me and we set off again. Just then there is the sound of helicopters and people begin running for open spaces, away from the houses. Someone shouts, 'Don't all go to the same place. Spread out,' and the young man and I lie down in a dry irrigation channel. But the helicopters only circle for a few minutes and then swerve away into the distance.

Perhaps they are taking photographs of the damage.

We walk across a field of baked earth and my guide tells me that he is the sole survivor of a family of seven, all killed in previous raids. He is not yet twenty.

In the sparse shade of a bush, there is a man lying on a *charpoy*. Half his leg has been blown off. Under a film of yellow dust and sweat his face is very pale. An old woman sits beside him and makes ineffectual efforts to cover her face with her *chador* as we approach. The man greets me courteously.

'*Jan e jour, khoub hasti, kheir amadi* – How are you, are you well, welcome.'

I ask him whether I may take his photograph. His face is open and smiling.

'Of course, I don't mind. Please, take as many as you wish.'

Once again I am surprised by my attention to focus, foreshortening and shutterspeed: I take two photographs. I thank him and he says something in reply but is unnaturally talkative and I cannot understand. I guess that at the moment he is in shock and not in too much pain. I manage to find a few, crumbling, Norvegin tablets at the bottom of my satchel which I tell him to take when the pain begins. Norvegin is about the same strength as Aspirin. I reach out to say goodbye and the blood on his hand and arm has dried in patches on his skin like an obscure map. '*Khoda hafiz*,' we say to one another, '*Khoda hafiz*'. As I walk away the old woman bends forward and helps him to drink from a glass of green tea in her hand.

I retrace my steps to the bazaar where my young guide bids me farewell. I have forgotten what I was doing before the raid but then a familiar voice calls out from a table by a kebab stall. It is Dust Muhammad, the watchmaker, who has been sitting there with the kebab seller throughout the raid. He offers me one of the kebabs which he has just ordered. Although I am not hungry I accept his hospitality. As I eat I realise that I have not washed my hands.

'The sun on a peach and a bird chirruping, for Heaven's sake, chirruping!' I was writing my diary on a hillside a short walk from the town. A brook swirled through the dappled shade of the tree under which I was sitting. My shirt and trousers were drying on a flat rock in the sun. I was enjoying a cigarette, listening to the wind in the willow trees that concealed a rushing river. Then, out of the tranquillity another sound infiltrated the landscape; a rumble in the hills that was not thunder. It only took a minute or so for the plane to vanish but the sound of its passing made me uneasy. I remembered a conversation with another traveller in Afghanistan who described a march with a group of mujahedin; how the man in front of him bent down to drink from a stream and had his hand and face blown away by a butterfly mine. The almost invisible strip of grey-green plastic among the leaves and grasses, the seismic mine in the dust of the road, the deeper reverberation emerging from the roar of the waterfall – wild places defiled by an alien present; everywhere the landscape was changed and made sinister by war.

Later I met Abdul Haq and a handful of mujahedin. They asked me how many people had been killed in the bombing. I told them of the dead and wounded that I had seen. They asked me to describe the location of the damaged houses and even as I answered, I realised the gulf that lay between us: the corpses I had seen were mere forms, covered in dust and blood, but they had been friends and neighbours of the men in front of me.

We waited in the shade of a tree for the sun to set behind the mountains. A mujahed with a sandy beard and humorous brown eyes, who introduced himself as a geography teacher, told me of his attitude towards death:

'For me it is not important. It is *qismet* – my portion of destiny – or *taqdir*. I do not fear death, for it is already decided. I do not know the place or time, but God knows. That is why I am not afraid, because it is God's will.'

I told him that the people of Europe and America admired the bravery of the mujahedin.

'Wouldn't they fight like us if the Shuravi invaded?'

'Perhaps it would be a different kind of war.'

While we were talking Abdul Haq's eyes were continually scanning the hills on the other side of the river. But he missed nothing of the conversation and explained that when people were killed their relatives were strengthened by the belief that the souls of the *shahid* would, without a shadow of doubt, enter Paradise.

As the sun disappeared into the mountains, Abdul Haq judged it safe to re-enter the town. He went straight to the bomb-damaged areas. The trees had been stripped bare by the violence of the blast and the leaves were already paper-dry and crackling underfoot. In an expanse of ground the size of a football pitch eight bombs had fallen, twelve people had been killed and eight injured. Three people had been sheltering in the cellar of a house which received a direct hit. The hole out of which they had taken their bodies seemed tiny – no more than four feet square. Some children and a dog were sitting on a pile of sun-dried bricks and timber. No one said anything to them. I wondered whether their parents had been killed and if, in years to come, they would remember the lilac evening when a group of men passed by.

Abdul Haq examined the wreckage of each house that had been damaged or destroyed. His face was expressionless, his thoughts indecipherable. Most of the people killed were known to him, at least by name. At the evening prayer he stood motionless in the twilight until a mujahed whispered something in his ear. But even after the gentle reminder he remained several minutes longer before rejoining his men.

Later we sat together by the light of a kerosene lamp while he wrote a letter for me to take to Shah Massoud in the Panjshir. Three golden lights came swaying towards us along the road and some shepherds, two men and a boy, appeared like refugees from another time to ask for payment for supplying meat to the mujahedin. A meteorite grazed the darkness like a stone cast across the frozen surface of a deep lake. It was time to say my final farewells, for the next morning it had been arranged for me to start the return journey through the Panjshir and Nuristan to Pakistan.

I regretted the timing, the day after a particularly heavy raid, but it meant that Amin'allah, who was returning to his village in the mountains, could accompany me to the next group of mujahedin. The Professor, Rahim and other companions were staying with their families and I sent them final messages of thanks and farewell. Nazim Khan reluctantly changed some money for me and then asked for a present by which he could remember me. I gave him my penknife, not without regrets. He accepted it like a tax collector and then, to my astonishment, asked for my water bottle as well, which I refused as pleasantly as I could. But I was sad to say goodbye to the others like Muhandis and Dust Muhammad. The best I could say was that I would not forget them.

About thirty of us settled down to sleep on the trestle benches of the chaikhane but my mind refused to let go of the day's images and I got up and walked along the street till I came to some shepherds gathered around a fire, their shadows dancing on an adobe wall and a chestnut tree. I did not approach them, but stood outside the ring of firelight and looked at them. Just so, I had glimpsed the life of the people but I was very little closer to knowing what it was to be one of them. Their past, present and future were contained in the fields and orchards, the streets and the bazaar of Nahrin. My time was different and in another place.

PART TWO

9

Khust

I had decided to call my horse Freckle. It seemed an appropriate name for a horse that could have trotted into the winner's enclosure of a Cotswold gymkhana, but Freckle had, I hoped, the blood of Genghis Khan's mongolian ponies in him and would make the journey with me through the Hindu Kush, over the 14,000-foot passes in Nuristan and back to Pakistan.

I took Freckle to be fitted with a new set of shoes while Amin' allah bargained for supplies of oats. We had been advised to buy as much fodder as the horse could carry since, in some areas, it would be unobtainable. When everything was ready we saddled up and set off, Amin'allah on a white donkey and me on Freckle.

We rode up into the hills above the town and a heavy shadow slipped from my chest; the bombing had weighed on my spirits. I looked forward to the journey ahead of me; if possible I would interview Shah Massoud in the Panjshir, then ride slowly back through Nuristan.

After several hours we entered a village steeped in warm dust and buzzing with flies. Rounding a corner Amin'allah told me to dismount. In a tumbledown ruin a small boy was tending a stove while nearby two men repaired a broken wall. They all greeted Amin'allah warmly, teasing him about the loss of his gun and exclaiming at his tanned face.

'God, you're almost black!'

While the boy prepared chai for us, his father and elder brother asked questions about the journey from Pakistan and marvelled at his description of the wonders of Peshawar. What news of people who had gone to Pakistan? Would they be returning? And what of Nahrin? We spent the next hour or so drinking chai with them until the hottest part of the day was over, then continued on our way.

The track followed the course of a river that was almost dry. On both banks there were tents and makeshift huts under the trees that housed refugees from the bombing of Nahrin. Stopping to buy some fruit from a man sitting behind a mound of grapes, I thought of people selling strawberries on the side of motorways. The man

complained to us as we ate grapes which were watery and bitter: the
bombing was getting worse, the people from Nahrin who came into
the village were a nuisance, there weren't enough eggs, why didn't
the mujahedin do anything? Amin'allah tried unsuccessfully to
soothe him and when we left the man gave us a grudging and
unfriendly farewell. In the late afternoon we came to a hunchback
with a chai stall who gave us tea and we talked to some men from the
Panjshir. I studied their faces for signs of battle and, indeed, they
looked more battle-worn than many I had met. Their questions
were ones that I often heard. Why wasn't help arriving? What did I
think of the war? Was it possible for them to win? They also told me
of the need for ground-to-air missiles.

That night we stayed with a friend of Abdul Haq's in the garden
of a house overlooking a deep valley. Our host was an educated man
who had travelled widely in Iran and Pakistan before the war. We
talked till late of our respective countries' customs and religions.
They were quietly appalled by the thought of abortion, but considered contraceptive pills a sensible method of birth control.
Meanwhile, our host's wife embroidered a waistcoat for me with a
design of orange and yellow birds. They were meant to be falcons, a
play on the meaning of my name, but they were unrecognisable.
Each creature had little red ears, a long sharp beak like a toucan,
two diminutive wings on its humped back and three claws at the end
of long, straight legs. The effect was Scythian.

We started off before sunrise and climbed into the mountains that
border on the land of Khust. Amin'allah kept falling behind and
several times I noticed him looking over his shoulder. I asked him
why.

'I am worried in case a dog is following us.'

It was an obvious lie and I felt my mouth go dry; his face was
troubled and I asked him what he was afraid of.

'In the last village we went through, two men said they liked your
horse and wanted to go with you to the Panjshir. I didn't trust
them.'

We continued to the top of the pass from where the valley of
Khust spread out before us. Several thousand feet below, an irregular thread of light running through silver-green fields marked the
course of a mountain stream and, farther in the distance, there was
the occasional flash of a larger river partially concealed beneath a
luminous mist.

An hour later, we stopped at a collection of tents to take some tea
where an Uzbeki admired Freckle, who was shining like a polished
nut, and told me of the good price he would fetch in the Panjshir. I

was pleased with him too. He was an amiable creature and mercifully free of vices, apart from a lurking mistrust of large grey
boulders. Approaching one, his ears semaphored wildly and his step
became cautious and measured.

In the afternoon we passed groups of men tossing bright clouds of
grain into the air against a backdrop of indigo mountains, with the
sun shining in their faces: ideal material for a Soviet propaganda
film, and I mentally supplied the commentary, 'Happy farmers
gathering a bumper harvest in the People's Republic of Afghanistan's autonomous region.'

We arrived at our destination. Amin'allah had accompanied me
many miles beyond his own village and wished to start back before
nightfall. We had come to know and like each other, and as we
parted I felt terribly bereft. I smoked my last cigarette and placed the
empty packet by a tree. Two boys of four and six rushed forward
and argued over its possession; the oldest claimed the cardboard
packet and the youngest got the silver paper.

The local mujahedin gave me a generous welcome. We had
supper in a room adjoining the mosque and I was shown great
kindness: my neighbour surreptitiously pushed fragments of
chicken towards me from his side of the communal dish, another
offered me a large pinch of naswar and a third produced a needle to
lance a boil on the sole of my foot.

They told me of bombings and people killed and how the village
school had been destroyed. I asked how they educated their
children.

'It is impossible. If we give them lessons in another house we are
afraid the Shuravi will discover it and bomb the place. We fear for
the lives of our children – we prefer them to live rather than to learn
to read and die. The Shuravi destroy our mosques and schools so
that they can call us ignorant people and teach our children communism. They want our children to be *kafir*.'

A mosquito landed on the commander's arm. He caught the
insect deftly by its wings, pulled it delicately from his skin and held it
between his fingers, then released it to hover once again in the light
of the lamp.

'We sell our corn, our horses, everything, to buy guns and ammunition,' he said, 'and still no help reaches us from Peshawar. It all
goes into the pockets of politicians and arms dealers. It must reach
the heart of the country. Here we help each other but even that is
dangerous. Three months ago the Shuravi came and took thirty
people away for helping the mujahedin. Some say they are in the
prison at Khunduz, but no one knows.'

The men spoke with the urgency of prisoners who wish to pass a message to the outside world.

The commander and my other hosts got up to go, leaving the two men who were to guide me to the next band of mujahedin to spend the night beside me. I raised myself to thank my hosts but a bearded man, older than the others, took my hand and pressed my arm down as we shook farewell.

'You are tired. Be seated. Tomorrow you will enter the mountains. *Khoda hafiz*.'

My foot was being shaken and I took several seconds to re-emerge from sleep fathoms deep, back into the darkness of the room. It was time to be off. I splashed water from the stream on to my face and saddled Freckle. The saddle-bags containing oats were unevenly balanced and I juggled like an enchanted sorcerer's apprentice with handfuls of oats until one of my companions rescued me from my drowsy travail by putting a small boulder into one of the saddle-bags.

The sun climbed bright and yellow into the sky above the mountains. The way led through terraced fields threaded with bubbling springs. Stepping over little streams, our shadows frightened twinkling shoals of minnows.

In my diary I wrote:

'Something rather grand about riding along with two armed men as escort, through fields starred with cornflowers – and in places where water has collected, their colours merge in the reflected sky.'

My mood of lyricism was politely interrupted by one of the mujahedin.

'With permission I would like to ask you a question.'

With tiresome wit I replied that he didn't need permission to ask a question but I might not give an answer. He ignored my childishness and persisted.

'In your country, after a man and a woman are in one place, you understand, does the man wash afterwards?'

My answer merely stimulated his curiosity, unlocking a torrent of questions, and the conversation flowed over the fertile ground of 'the way of a man with a maid'. I learned that an Afghan farmer, in good spirits, will make love to his wife three times a week, though rarely more than twice on one occasion. This usually happens in the evening. Both the man and the woman undress before making love. Prowess in bed and on the battlefield go hand in hand in the quality of spirit known as *javanmardi*, which can roughly be translated as 'manliness'.

'And if I come to England, would it be easy for me to find a wife?'

He was thirty years old. He had a high forehead, lively black eyebrows and brown eyes that were direct but not intrusive. His nose and lips were well set in a thick moustache and beard that covered the collar of his shirt.

'And this is a friend of mine – from Afghanistan.' What would be the reaction? How would an English girl adapt to the position of a Muslim bride?

'It would depend on the woman,' I said.

'It's the same here,' he replied, the look on his face, with its hint of resignation, conveying an experience of life that I recognised, and we both laughed.

In the villages children seemed less curious about my appearance, either because they were used to foreigners, which was unlikely, or I was moving towards a region whose inhabitants I more closely resembled. We unsaddled at a simple, two-storey house with a walled garden enclosing an orchard of peach trees. In an upstairs room I was introduced to Abdul Ahad, the commander of the area that adjoined Abdul Haq's. He was a young man with a limp and a face made gentle by suffering. As a boy his leg had been injured, and it had mended badly. We drank chai together and he showed me the pistol he had just bought from a poet. He asked me if I could tell him where it came from: it had been made in Spain in a town called Guernica.

Several other mujahedin were present, including a large man with a nineteenth-century weightlifter's moustache and a man who had written a poem about the war. When he read it out to the others, they doubled up with laughter at its leadenly unpoetic metre, clichéd sentiments and sumptuous hyperbole. But the poet was unabashed by his critics' scorn.

'Perhaps the BBC would like to broadcast it?'

I told him I was a fellow poet and made what I hoped was a neutral but encouraging comment on the work's literary merits.

'If you're ever in Afghanistan again, please contact me and we will discuss poetry again.'

'*Insha'allah.*'

'*Insha'allah.*' We echoed each other's thoughts.

The poet's companion was a solemn-looking individual with a wool hat balanced on his head like a muffin man's cap. He did not ridicule his friend's poetry and said nothing to me until he was about to go.

'Could you take me with you to your country?'

I watched hope die in his eyes when I told him that without a passport he would be unable to leave Pakistan, let alone enter England.

Two men appeared to argue their case before the commander. One of them had an ascetic profile with a pointed grey beard which he wore with a look of unconvincing piety. The other had a squint, a thick black beard and naswar-ravaged teeth. They were neighbours. Blackbeard had gone into his neighbour's land to retrieve a sheep which had strayed. Smugface's dog, 'a strong-spirited creature, brave and faithful', had surprised Blackbeard, assumed the worst, and attacked him. Blackbeard had then shot the faithful hound with a hunting rifle. The treatment for Blackbeard's wounds had been long and expensive, and he was now claiming the cost of the medicine. Smugface gave a smooth reply, explaining that, although he was happy to pay for his neighbour's medical expenses, unfortunately they were more than offset by the price of the slain dog. Matters were deadlocked.

Blackbeard slowly removed a vast grimy bandage from his leg. As he unwound the coils of material the tension mounted. The last discoloured patch was removed revealing an unimpressive wound and the room mocked him for his faint-heartedness. Blackbeard defended his case stoutly:

'It may not look much, but the brute's teeth went in deeply. Besides, you can't see my worst injuries. They're further up. Just here,' he said, sweeping his hand across his backside.

'You needn't show us those injuries, brother – we'll trust you.' The commander turned to Smugface. 'And how old was the dog?'

Smugface looked down the length of his long nose and gave a cloying smile.

'He was a clever dog, he knew the ways of sheep . . .'

'What price for such a dog?'

'It all depends. He was obedient, he had experience . . .' He named a price which was more than the cost of the medicine, and Blackbeard exploded in disbelief.

'Thief! Liar! You had that dog for years. It was old and deaf. A cur. I've seen it run away from sheep.'

'But not from you, brother?' interrupted the commander mischievously and the room subsided into happy chaos while Blackbeard and Smugface continued to hurl personal insults at one another.

The dispute wrangled on for the next hour or so, and I went outside to find some peace in the garden where a neatly dug stream was flowing at the base of a line of poplars. There were horses tethered beside a little house and a man was loading an ass in the yard; in the background a group of women were sitting in the shade of a chestnut tree. It was as if a Persian miniature had come to life. I sat on the grass and for several minutes contemplated a moving picture of the past; the greens and pinks and dusty yellows, the flick of a horse's tail and the flight of a bird into the branches of a tree. The sound of a distant jet rumbled across the sky. The man stopped loading the ass, ran round to the front of the house and stared up above him. The women rose from where they were sitting and moved uncertainly into the sunlight, and someone appeared at an upstairs window holding a Kalashnikov. But the plane was far away and in a few seconds the sky was silent once again. The Persian miniature had vanished and in its place I saw a village whose people lived in daily fear; for whom the sound of an aeroplane was a reminder of a foreign and hostile power.

Freckle's hooves scraped and knocked on the baked earth of the yard. White butterflies flickered in the trees like wayward flashes of sunlight and a child was calling across the fields. The pendulum-like swing from past to present – here the garden and there the bombing – was too vast to encompass in a single thought.

A voice called my name from the house, inviting me in for more chai. The dispute about the dog had been settled, to the disgruntled satisfaction of both parties, and the talk had turned to religion. While a shambling youth with a sore on his lip gave a masterly performance of slothful unconcern as he prepared the tea, we discussed the Creation. They told me how the universe came into being with the glorious words: '*Kun fa yakun* – Be and it was', and I translated the first four verses of Genesis and the first four verses of St John's Gospel for them.

At midday I ate a meal in the tent of a family from the Panjshir. The grandfather was called Haji, having performed the haj pilgrimage to Mecca before the war.

'By the grace of Allah I was able to perform the haj. Nowadays very few men go to Mecca. The money they could have spent on the haj goes to the mujahedin for the cause of *jehad*.'

They had been living the life of internal refugees for four years and they told me how literacy, which before the invasion had been comparatively high, was plummeting among the young.

'We are *mohajer*. We move from place to place. If our children are lucky they attend school for a few months, but then the school is bombed or we have to move to another place. How can they learn anything?'

The walls of the tent were hung with strips of material, decorated with a repeating design of roses which had been made with a woodblock dipped in red dye and pressed repeatedly into a simple pattern. After the meal Haji apologised for the lack of sweets to serve with chai, but his son searched diligently in a pile of saddle-bags and managed to produce two sand-encrusted specimens. He offered one to me and gave the other to his youngest son who was hiding behind his mother's skirts. Watched by the small boy's older brother, I sucked at the gritty sugar while the drone of a spotter plane echoed over the mountains.

In the afternoon the commander led me to his own house further up the valley. As I rounded a bend in the track, there was a boom of falling water. I must have started noticeably for, without a word on my part, Abdul Ahad understood.

'Don't worry — it's only the river.'

We came to the impressively carved gates of a large farmhouse and Abdul Ahad waved a welcoming gesture towards a veranda that was almost invisible in a shifting haze of mosquitoes. Inside, the plaster walls had been painted with roses and lilies; the effect was somewhere between a Minoan fresco and William Morris wall-paper. A month before Soviet paratroops had passed through the valley and left their mark — across the painted birds and flowers the numerals 'XXIX' had been hacked into the plaster.

'By the grace of God this house remains standing,' said Abdul Ahad. 'Others were set on fire.'

Later we were joined by Abdul Ahad's father and several other older men, and ate a supper of rice and bread. My neighbour's face was muffled in his turban, which he had wound under his nose. The effect was so comical that I had difficulty maintaining an expression of solemn concern as he complained at length about a pain in his foot. When I told him I had no medicine his conversation lang-uished. One of the company was a mullah who told me about the death and resurrection of Hazerat Issah. His version was as follows: Jesus was in a house with some of his disciples when a Roman soldier entered to arrest him. Only Jesus had vanished. The soldier rushed out to tell his companions, but his face had been transformed into the likeness of Jesus and his fellow soldiers killed him. Jesus himself escaped and continued to prophesy thereafter: thus, the legend of Jesus' death and resurrection.

There is a fund of mutual ignorance between the West and Afghanistan. We know little about Afghanistan's recent history — just as little as they know of ours. For many of them the Second World War was a great battle in which the Shuravi were on one side and Hitler on the other. Nevertheless, I was startled by one guest's pronouncement that Hitler was a great man. 'Why?' I asked.

'Because he fought against the Shuravi.'

He was dumbfounded when I told him that America and Soviet Russia had been allies and it was several minutes before I was able to persuade him that Hitler was anything but a courageous champion of freedom. I also told him of the millions who had died in the concentration camps; but he was unimpressed.

'When the Shuravi invaded there were seventeen million people living in this country. One million people have died because of the war. Three or four million have fled to Pakistan and Iran. Numbers are meaningless; the suffering is real. I will tell you in one word the name of our suffering: *zolm* – oppression.'

Before dawn I was woken by inner rumblings and plodded outside, to be challenged by the doorkeeper who asked me sleepily what I was doing. I explained. He grinned sympathetically and selected a handful of pebbles from the side of a field. 'Take these for your comfort,' he said, dropping them into my hand.

Later, after a breakfast of nan and yoghurt, I sat on the sheep-cropped grass of an orchard under an apple tree and composed another hypothetical piece of Soviet propaganda:

'When the bandits and counter-revolutionary forces were finally stamped out in the People's Republic of Afghanistan, the literacy rate in areas which they had terrorised was found to be appallingly low. But new education schemes have been introduced and the numbers of literate adults and children are showing a healthy increase.'

Two boys came hesitantly towards me. The taller wore grey cotton trousers and a dark jacket that had once been a school blazer; on the breast pocket a shield had been woven with the name 'Ashcombe School'.

His younger brother wore nothing but an orange shirt. They stood watching me writing for several minutes then, at a brusque command from his brother to 'offer the guest an apple', the half-naked child lobbed a fist-sized rock into the branches above our heads and three apples obligingly dropped to earth. We each munched away and stared at one another.

Freckle, who was grazing nearby, suddenly raised his head and whinnied as a figure rode up to the edge of the orchard on a black horse. The man dismounted and a small crowd gathered to admire his steed. It was a superb animal with a scarlet palfrey embroidered with flowering suns thrown across its shining flanks.

'Such a horse would cost two lakhs, two hundred thousand

afghanis,' whispered a man beside me in a voice hushed with wonder.

The horse's owner was seeking news of his brother but his enquiries were ignored: all attention focused on the horse. How much had it cost? Who sold it? What part of the country was it from? Was it strong enough to cross the higher passes? Was it experienced on rocky ground? The man tolerated the questions like the owner of a luxurious motor car surrounded by a group of schoolboys, but eventually his patience began to fray.

'I'm looking for my brother, not selling this horse. If none of you know where my brother is . . .'

Instantly, several of the onlookers remembered seeing a traveller pass through the village: he was on a mule, or was he on foot? He was alone. No, surely he was in the company of a man with a gun. He was young. Or was he old? The rest of us patted the horse's flanks and examined its teeth. The animal seemed to have a miraculous effect on people's memories, unlocking long and detailed descriptions, all of them different, of the man's brother until at last the rider recognised the futility of further questions.

'Enough!' he shouted, twisting the reins around the pommel. 'The sun is getting hotter.' Raising his leg above shoulder height he put his foot into the stirrup and swung into the saddle. The horse, feeling his weight, snorted.

'My greetings to Abdul Ahad – *Khoda hafiz*,' he called over his shoulder, and he cantered away between the apple trees.

At midday I set off up the valley with an escort provided by Abdul Ahad. His name was Shir Muhammad and he was to be my guide over the 14,000-foot pass into the Panjshir. At first he had been extremely unwilling; Abdul Ahad's taunts of laziness and cowardice had had no effect and he was only persuaded to go with me by the loan of a pistol.

We passed several houses which had been burnt by the Soviets. Others looked as if they had been bombed, but Shir Muhammad told me that they were damaged in the earthquake a few weeks earlier. The path narrowed; Shir Muhammad walked in front of me while I ambled along on Freckle who snatched mischievously at the grass on either side of the path. We met several people coming the other way. Some were driving asses laden with sacks of grain, others were bent double under huge bundles of hay which they had gathered in the higher pastures. Occasionally we passed women clothed from head to foot in long *chador* who, when they saw us, crouched down at the side of the track with their faces turned away from us.

We rested on the banks of a river and two village boys playing in the shallows stopped splashing one another to stare at us with wide brown eyes and hands clasped like fig leaves over their soaking cotton shorts. Nearby a herd of cows cooled their udders in the water.

We climbed higher and the willows, poplars and apricot trees gave way to thorn trees and fields of corn. The harvest was well advanced; lines of three or four horses tethered together, with an ox on the inside, trod the threshing floor in dusty circles while men pitch-forked sheaves of corn under their hooves. The mountains shut out the afternoon sun and the floor of the valley was already in shadow. I was stirred from a reverie by the sight of a brown paper bag lying on the path. It seemed faintly incongruous but I thought no more about it until, a mile or so further on, Shir Muhammad pointed to a collection of tins scattered by the side of the path.

'Shuravi. Several thousand of them came this way a month ago. Some walked from Khust, others came down from aeroplanes and helicopters.'

The numbers were obviously exaggerated, but where had they gone?

'They stayed here for ten days, then they went in that direction,' he said, pointing up the valley towards the pass.

'Where are they now?'

He shrugged with unconvincing nonchalance.

'In the Panjshir, or perhaps they are camped near the top of the pass. Who knows? Don't worry, Abdul Baz, I have a pistol. If I see any I will kill them.'

The air was noticeably cooler; we had reached the final plateau of cultivated fields and above us was an unworkable terrain of scrub and boulders. The valley was already in twilight and a new moon hung over the mountains to the west. It was time to find a place to sleep. Someone had lit a fire and we made for the light of the flames to find three men who worked the land belonging to Abdul Ahad's father. They spread a blanket for us against the side of a mound of corn and offered us bowls of icy yoghurt and handfuls of dry nan bread. The cold air from the mountains was pouring down into the valley and I burrowed into the corn for warmth, while a huge ram, with threads of sperm hanging from it, pushed and nuzzled at my feet for scraps of bread. A tin can full of sweet chai was passed among us, then the five of us bedded down for the night, wrapped in our petous and covered with cotton quilts. The two men on either side of me giggled together like naughty schoolboys.

'Is the foreigner warm?'

'What are you saying, brother?'

'Is he *warm*?'

High up in the shadow of the mountains was a solitary point of light from a shepherd's fire. I watched it, like the glowing wick of a burnt-out candle, until it vanished in the dark.

We saddled Freckle by starlight and continued our journey. The ground was strewn with invisible rocks and here and there the path was crossed by splashing streams. The noise made Freckle nervous; several times Shir Muhammad cursed him and threw stones at his flanks to make him enter the water. The sky paled, the peaks caught the light of the sun and the colours of the rock shifted from grey to lilac. I had seen the landscape before; the green turf, the weathered boulders rising in massive cliffs towards the sky, and mountains piled on top of mountains. It was the world of Moghul hunting illustrations, out of which the black horse and its rider had fleetingly appeared.

The drone of a spotter plane circled over the valley as we passed an unexploded bomb half-buried in the ground, but there were several craters in the area where other bombs had exploded, though why they had been dropped in such a deserted place was unclear, unless they had been intended for mujahedin who were harassing Soviet paratroops.

We came to a huge wall of boulders. Leaving Shir Muhammad to lead Freckle, I clambered over the rocks by another route. On the other side, a glassy pool glinted in the sunlight surrounded by a margin of frosted turf. The cold of the water was sharp as a razor and its edge glittered with crystals of ice. Shir Muhammad took an age to join me and I called out to him impatiently. Close to, I saw that his eyes were wide with fear.

'There are six men hiding among the rocks. They had guns. I asked them what they were doing and they said they were afraid of the plane. But their faces were evil and I think they were lying. We must not stay here. Perhaps they heard your voice and know that you are a foreigner. We must go at once.'

Walking away over the bright grass I thought of the men resting their guns on the rocks and it was difficult not to turn round. The back of my head felt exposed, like an eye staring into darkness, and my skull listened for the sound of a rifle shot. At last we were out of range and the path climbed steeply. More tins and wrappers of Korean Flavormint chewing gum littered the ground, and I wondered what had passed through the Soviet paratroopers' minds as they stomped along the same path, laden with tins of food and bullets. It was a desolate place. In front of us the mountain tops converged like jaws of broken teeth and the path disintegrated into a scrabble of frost-shattered stones. A group of figures was making its way down across a scree of black shale. Shir Muhammad unbuttoned the pistol from its holster and hid it in the folds of his petou.

'Say nothing to them,' he said, 'they are wearing army uniforms.'

But when they got closer it was clear they were deserters; their clothes were in rags and their boots were flapping at the toes. One of them was barefoot. Shir Muhammad hailed them and engaged them in conversation: I rode past without greeting and stopped a hundred yards further up the mountain. When he rejoined me, Shir Muhammad told me their story. They had deserted from a garrison of State troops in the Panjshir, escaping across a minefield, and were making their way back to their homes in Mazar, a journey of several hundred miles. They had neither food, money, nor weapons.

'God protects the faithful,' was Shir Muhammad's only comment.

Higher up, patches of discoloured snow still lay in the shadow of the cliff and we caught up with a family of refugees beside a pool of meltwater. The father led a mule on which a veiled woman sat. They had four children: the eldest was a girl of about twelve, with matted hair, carrying a small child on her back; a boy of ten was holding a squawking hen under his arm and leading his younger sister, who had a huge blackened sore on one side of her face. We placed the two youngest children on Freckle and, in return, the father gave us a handful of dry, salty cheese.

'Eat this. It will give you strength to climb the mountain.'

I needed it; my stomach trouble had got worse and every hour or so I had to prop myself behind an outcrop for another session of quiet despair. A thousand feet from the summit we stopped at a natural platform to rest. My knees were quivering and my conversation was rambling and confused. I found some shelter from the wind with the sun on my face and prepared myself for a final effort which I hoped would take me over the pass into the Panjshir.

I woke to find Shir Muhammad talking with two brothers. Freckle, another horse and a mule were tethered nearby. The family had disappeared. I was too weak to lead Freckle so Shir Muhammad took him up the remaining stretch of the pass, followed by the two brothers, while I brought up the rear. The mule collapsed repeatedly and each time the men kicked and cursed it to its feet.

'The brute is a son of Iblis,' said one of them. 'If it lies down too long it will never get up.' Sure enough, a few hundred feet from the top, we found a donkey that had recently been abandoned. It was still alive, but unconscious. I considered putting the creature out of its misery with a large rock but lacked the strength to make a decent job of it; besides, it was unlikely to survive another freezing night.

The final stages of the pass were the worst: the effects of altitude and exhaustion made our progress slow and dream-like. I set myself targets; a ledge, a steep zig-zag of the path, and a rest; across a scree of crumbling stones, a patch of snow and then another rest.

Shir Muhammad was at the top of the pass waiting for me. The Panjshir stretched out below us, its hills and valleys already merged in shadow, and in the distance the peaks of the Hindu Kush glowed in the rays of the setting sun. We descended under a darkening sky into a fierce wind which swept across the bare ridges, cutting through our petous and cotton clothes. Stars were glittering through scudding clouds by the time we arrived at a sheepfold, where we found some shepherds warming themselves at a fire of thorns and dried dung. They invited us to share their meal of bread and sheep's milk which they heated on the fire. The talk, once again, was of war and religion. They told us how the Shuravi had suddenly appeared over the pass, of sheep slaughtered by the soldiers, and of villagers fleeing their homes to spend days and nights without shelter. Planes 'so high they seemed like sparrows in the sky' dropped bombs destroying several houses as well as the village mosque.

The eldest of the shepherds, a man of fifty wearing a wool skull cap and a goatskin coat, asked how many Muslims lived in England. Hearing how few there were, he shook his head in sorrow:

'Religion is the water of life; without it the earth is a desert.'

They stood up to pray in the circle of boulders, facing Mecca with gusts of wind fanning the embers at their feet. On the other side of the valley the skyline trembled with intermittent flashes of light, but I heard no thunder. We lay down to sleep under a thick covering of blankets that smelled of sheep's wool and woodsmoke. One of the shepherds wrapped my turban round a smooth stone for a pillow and I closed my eyes, dimly sensing the tremor of the ground as Freckle shifted his weight and his hooves knocked against rocks outside the fold.

Panjshir

The sky was grey when Shir Muhammad woke me, and the wind had the touch of winter. We followed a sheep track further down into the valley and, as the early morning sun pierced the clouds, we came to the white crested waters of the river. The wind whipped at the waves and carried the spray into our faces. I was only half-awake and the noise of the river sounded like a rain-drenched London street full of buses. I leaned forward in the saddle to massage some warmth back into Freckle's ears but after a minute or so my hands were numb with cold. The wind was impossible. It tore the petou from my shoulders and stung water from the corners of my eyes. Meanwhile, to keep my spirits up, I had a spitting competition with myself: on the wings of a freezing hurricane, one gob of spit sailed a satisfying fifty feet or more.

At last we arrived at Khawak; a collection of squat houses huddled in a side valley. A young boy directed us to the local mujahedin headquarters, a one-storey building of mud bricks with a splashing stream flowing past the door. The room was in darkness except for a faint glow from two small apertures set high up in the wall. Then, as my sight adjusted to the shadows, I saw the motionless shapes of a dozen men stretched out on the floor, like prisoners in a dusty dungeon. Shir Muhammad knelt down beside the man nearest the door and talked to him in a low voice. I found a space in the corner of the room, leaned my head on my knapsack and listened to the wind thundering outside.

The biggest strawberry I had ever seen rested on a silver plate. From nowhere a waiter appeared who raised it for my inspection; then, he winked at me and pretended to drop it. Bendix buttermints and plums followed in quick succession. When I woke, Shir Muhammad was gone.

The shutters of a window had been half-opened and I looked around me once again. Some men in combat jackets were sitting around a pot of tea in the centre of a square of sunlight. Bandoliers of bullets and machine guns hung from the walls. In another corner of the room a man was sleeping under a pile of torn blankets with his head pillowed on a saddle. Under a thick reddish beard his face was drawn, the skin very pale, the colour of ivory, and there were dark shadows under his eyes.

One of the men noticed me stirring:

'*Ay baradar* – brother. *Kheir amadi* – welcome! Will you drink some chai?'

It was lukewarm and a single glass of the bitter brew was enough.

'I'm sorry the water isn't hotter but the weather is cold and we have very little firewood,' said my neighbour. 'But you're lucky to be here now. In winter the snow is chest high and the streams and rivers are covered with ice. Six months ago the Shuravi came, no one was allowed out of their houses and three people froze to death. Here, take some naswar.'

The next few hours were spent in conversation with various members of the group.

There was Muhammad Rahman, a handsome man of twenty-five with a trim black beard. He was the village doctor, and like Dr Habib in Nahrin, had studied biology at a technical college. He showed me a bundle of handwritten lecture notes.

'This is the only medical training I have. We have no medical supplies. A month ago when they bombed the villages further up the valley, I was the only doctor. People were wounded . . .' he paused, and I saw the effort in his face, '. . . several amputations were necessary. We had nothing, no painkillers, no medicine, only knives and hot water. It was terrible.'

I asked him about the gaunt figure sleeping in the corner but he shrugged.

'He has been ill for several weeks. He cannot keep food in his stomach. Four or five days ago he stopped eating and for the last two days he has not woken from sleep. There is nothing more I can do for him.'

Iqbal was a broad-shouldered giant of a man with grey eyes and a beard that reached over his chest. He was in his late thirties, older than most of the others, who treated him with respect mixed with a certain degree of fear. He helped himself to generous quantities of my naswar and bragged about the number of Russian soldiers he had killed.

'When the Shuravi came we were waiting for them. We covered ourselves with our petous and hid behind rocks. There was a battle. Many of them died and the others ran away. I myself killed four or five.'

The others said nothing.

Whenever the mujahedin wanted any errands done they shouted

to a young man with stooping shoulders and a hesitant manner, who silently carried out their requests. His name was Qusud and during the afternoon, while the others were outside, he came and told me his story. He was a stranger to the village. His father was a seller of antique carpets in Kabul; shortly after the invasion he and the rest of the family fled to Pakistan, but Qusud remained behind.

'I was ashamed of my brothers for running away so I came here to the Panjshir to fight. Now one of my brothers is in America, another is in Peshawar.' He sighed. 'And I am here. Sometimes it is difficult; the other mujahedin resent my book-learning, they laugh at the way I talk and always give me the dirtiest work to do. If I refuse they say I am proud. I have no choice.'

Later he accompanied me to the house of a man who was said to be one hundred and twenty years old. It was a simple, two-room dwelling with a cleanly swept earth floor. A cooking pot simmered over a smouldering fire of dried dung and beside it sat the old man himself, wrapped in blankets. He grasped my hand firmly but he was almost blind and his conversation wandered from time to time. I asked him what his earliest memory was and he told me how, at the age of ten, he had met Amir Abdul Rahman. The past was good: corn and oats were cheap and plentiful, it was peaceful and men were kind to one another. The secret of longevity was plenty of fruit and the avoidance of bad meat. His advice for life was just as simple: pray to God five times a day.

As I was about to go, he stroked my beard, kissed his hand and then he blessed me. 'Wherever you go may your way lead you among good men.'

So I took my leave into the windy sunlight, and almost fell into a mound of horse droppings outside the door.

We returned to the mujahedin's headquarters and found the bloody remains of a goat stretched out across the threshold.

'Supper,' said Iqbal, 'very good, strength for your journey.'

Apart from some bread and a handful of dry cheese it was the first solid food I had eaten for three or four days and the effects were disastrous. In the middle of the night I woke feeling as if a bayonet had been planted in my stomach, and barely had time to pull on my boots and lurch into the howling darkness. It was only the beginning. The second or third time I managed to find a low wall which gave some shelter from the winds storming directly off the peaks of the Hindu Kush. When I got back I found Qusud had lit a lamp beside my blanket. He said nothing but remained awake for the next few hours while I came and went like a man with a guilty conscience. Usually I had five or ten minutes' warning: 'Like going into a Greek lesson unprepared,' I wrote in my diary, 'the same sense of certain and impending misery.'

The next day I decided to travel on, down the valley, in the hope of meeting up with Shah Massoud, the commander of the Panjshir. Qusud kindly volunteered to go with me. We had already saddled Freckle when the local commander made a belated appearance. Seeing Freckle, he was full of admiration and insisted on showing me his own horse. It was a grotesque-looking beast with a thick grey coat and a head like a violin. The mujahedin gathered round and the commander looked me in the eye.

'Well, Abdul Baz. What do you think of him?'

'Strong and very ugly,' I replied.

'It's the sort of horse you need to cross the passes in Nuristan.'

'Perhaps.'

'Look at his muscles! Good thick legs! He doesn't need oats to climb a mountain.'

'Extraordinary.'

'You can take him anywhere: rocks, snow, ice, he doesn't care.'

It soon became apparent that, as a special act of kindness, he was willing to exchange horses. If any horse was made for the rugged journey into Nuristan, his was the one. It was built like a tank and had a hard, thuggish look in its eye. I was tempted, but I had grown fond of Freckle and the smirking faces of our onlookers finally convinced me. I thanked him for his kind offer and refused. The commander laughed and slapped me on the shoulder.

'Good, very good, Abdul Baz. *Khoda hafiz* – God protect you.'

We set off down the river valley towards the village of Safir Chir. As we descended, the sun came out, the wind dropped and my spirits lifted: the northern gorge of the Panjshir is a magnificent sight and well worth the trouble of a visit.

We stopped beside a solitary tumulus. Several hundred feet below us the turquoise river meandered between walls of bone-coloured rock. Just discernible, on the other side of the valley, were the paths taken by Nuristani merchants trading with the Panjshir: faint lines traversing an almost vertical cliff-face like the tracks of snails. Except for the sound of Freckle tearing at the tussocks of dry grass, there was utter silence. Qusud sat crosslegged in the dust a few yards away. Neither of us spoke. Time vanished in the stillness of mountains. Then, without a word, we stood up, shook the dust from our clothes and continued on our way, passing a stretch of sandstone where travellers had written in the dry, disintegrating surface. The words read like the fragments of a lost papyrus: Sa'id

. . . Ali . . . the men of Khunduz . . . Victory.

The track climbed once more and in the distance I saw the sunlit green of trees and the shapes of houses. After the barren landscape of the past few days it surprised me with the same wonder and delight as my first glimpse, years before, of the domed roofs and minarets of Isfahan.

But as we got closer the vision revealed another, terrible reality. Every single house had been gutted by fire and only the shells of the buildings remained. The groves of mulberries were stricken where the irrigation channels had been deliberately destroyed and their leaves were already turning brown. The streets were empty and the gardens overgrown. Doorways opened into mounds of rubble and windows were empty squares of sky. There were no ghosts in the afternoon sunlight but Freckle's pace altered and his ears twitched nervously.

The bomb damage I had seen previously had an arbitrary element, but the smoke-blackened ruins of the town were evidence of a conscious and sustained act of destruction. In Ishkamesh and Nahrin the spirit of the town somehow survived; here, it had been obliterated as if it had never been.

It took another hour to reach the next village. This was Safir Chir which was still inhabited. Four or five mujahedin came out from a house to greet us and one of them asked me whether I knew the two foreigners who were staying in the village. I replied that I had just come from Khust and knew of no other foreigners in the area; he seemed surprised.

'Why don't you know? You are also from England.'

'England is a big country.'

'So is Afghanistan.'

'Where are the Englishmen?'

'I don't know.'

'Why don't you know?'

'I am an Afghan.'

Chance encounters with fellow countrymen are one of the hazards of travelling. If one happens to be English the risks are considerable. On this occasion curiosity and the need for some kind of medicine were decisive factors and so, after some delays, I eventually managed to find the house where they were and I knocked on the door.

'What is it?'

The reply strengthened my misgivings but by then it was too late: I opened the door and stepped inside. Two foreigners were sitting on the floor with a map spread out in front of them: Peter Jouvenal and

Julian Gearing, freelance reporters working for CBS.

We ate with the mujahedin and, over a meal of goat's meat and rice, they talked with the diffidence of men more interested in others than themselves. Both had made several previous trips inside. They had just finished filming an interview with Massoud and were planning to return to Pakistan in a few days' time.

'If you want to interview Massoud you'd better get cracking,' said Peter. 'He's already two or three days' march from here and moving south every day. He travels pretty fast. But I wouldn't take the valley road; the Soviets are holding the next village down, about four hours away.'

They told me that to reach Massoud I would have to use the paths through the side valleys which were impassable to horses. Even then, there was no guarantee of finding him unless I was prepared to spend a long time waiting.

My illness had weakened me and it was unlikely that in my present condition I would be able to catch up with Massoud. However, if I rested for one or two days, and managed to find some medicine, it might be possible. I decided to postpone my plans till the morning; for the moment I was glad to have arrived in the Panjshir.

When we had finished eating, I went with them to an upstairs room in a derelict building and they showed me their supplies and equipment. They were well-prepared. Besides a large medicine chest, they had a mouthwatering selection of food: boxes of instant meals, including sausage and mash; beef in gravy; paella; curry; packets of soup and vitamin drinks; tins of steak and kidney pie and baked beans; porridge and honey and bars of chocolate. I read the labels and my stomach rumbled with longing. In addition they had a tent, sleeping bags, foam rubber mattresses and inflatable pillows.

We settled down for the night and listened to the World Service on the radio.

'Always the same boring old stuff,' said Peter, switching off the presenter of a current affairs programme in mid-sentence. 'Talk till the cows come home – they never get round to doing anything.'

'Who don't?'

'Nobody. If people in Britain got off their backsides a bit more the world would be a better place.'

'There'll always be someone who thinks they know better,' said Julian, 'it just depends how many people agree.'

I was tired and had some difficulty following the conversation. Julian put out the lamp and we lay back to sleep. But my thoughts refused to settle; I had almost forgotten the world of trade figures and percentage-point increases in inflation, mortgages and tube fares. I thought of starting work in the City. Then I remembered Ali and Rahim, Moheb and Amin'allah.

The sound of the river carried on the wind blowing through the bombed out windows. At my shoulder, the light from the mujahedin's lamp showed through the cracks in the wall and I listened to their muffled voices until I fell asleep.

The next morning we had breakfast with the mujahedin. Peter ladled out dollops of jam for them while Julian filled their tea with powdered milk, as we sat in the bright sunlight under an apricot tree. There were ten or twelve men in all including a tall, turbanned youth with long, black hair dressed in dramatic white robes.

'You don't see so many like him any more,' Peter nodded in the young man's direction. 'In the beginning there were a lot of them. In Pakhtia they used to wear bright red turbans as well. They don't seem to think it's worth it nowadays; they've learned about camouflage the hard way.'

The helpings of jam had created a picnic atmosphere among the mujahedin and they had begun teasing Peter to give them some more when a man shouted out that a jet was approaching. It was high up and no one paid it much attention but their smiles had vanished. We continued drinking our tea then, suddenly, a jet thundered towards us along the valley and ten seconds later there was an explosion on the other side of the river. There was a mad rush for the nearest cave with men scrambling over each other to get through its narrow entrance. Another jet was beginning its bombing sweep and I glimpsed the white-robed mujahed leaning behind a rock looking up through the trees. There was another explosion, much closer: earth and pebbles pattered on the leaves like hailstones. Peter pushed at my shoulder.

'I'm not staying out here any longer. Let's get in quick.'

We bundled into the cave mouth in a welter of boots and elbows, and landed in a circle of men. A heated discussion was already in progress between the group's quartermaster and a shepherd over the price of a sheep. Outside there was another explosion and the white-robed youth tumbled in on top of me. He grinned at me nervously.

'Are you afraid?' he said.

'Sometimes.'

His forehead cleared and he threw back his shoulders. 'The mujahedin are never afraid; we believe in God.' I knew what was coming next and prepared myself for yet another catechism about my beliefs. Sure enough, the inevitable question followed.

'Do you believe in God?'

'I'm a Christian.'

'Ah yes, Hazerat Issah. A good man, a very spiritual man, and a great prophet,' he smiled at me with an expression of benevolent condescension. 'But Muhammad, blessed be his name, is the best and the wisest of all the prophets. He is the Seal of the Prophets; after him there is no other.'

Yet again I was being lectured. My nerves were frayed. I'd had enough. It was time to answer back. I ransacked my memory for whatever remained of my lessons in Muslim theology and remembered the prophet Khezr; Khezr the green-robed, Khezr the immortal, sent to wander the earth until the day of Resurrection, initiating holy men into the mysteries of the hidden world.

A mischievous impulse prompted me and I found myself asking the sort of question a bored student asks in a Bible class.

'If the prophet Khezr is immortal, how can Muhammad be the last of the prophets?'

Instantly, half a dozen voices were raised in explanation and the price of sheep was forgotten in a passionate debate over Khezr's prophetic status.

The quartermaster, who had been on the point of losing the argument with the shepherd, quickly assumed the tones of authority. Khezr had been alive before Muhammad's birth: it necessarily followed that Muhammad came after him and was the later, therefore the final prophet. He made a clear distinction between immortality and finality. Then he told me the following story:

'A long time ago there was a man who wished to learn the secret of life. He searched for it in books and he searched for it in the hearts of men. One day a stranger dressed in green came to him. "You who have journeyed for so long on the path of truth, what is your heart's desire?" And the man replied, "I wish to find the secret of life." "*Khoub bash* – may it be well," said Khezr. "Come with me and I will show you the secret of life." And the man went with him.

'They travelled through many countries and at last they came to a garden. There was a young prince writing a letter to his beloved, a beautiful princess. Then a thief who was hiding in the bushes ran up behind the young prince and killed him and ran away. Khezr did nothing. The man was astonished and asked Khezr the meaning of what they had seen. Khezr said nothing.

'They came to the sea where a ship was floating on the waves. It was a great ship loaded with jewels and gold. The man followed Khezr on board and they set sail. After a while the sky darkened, there was a great storm and the ship sank to the bottom of the sea, leaving the man and Khezr clinging to a piece of wood. They were cast on dry land and the man asked Khezr the meaning of what had happened. Once again Khezr said nothing.

'They arrived at a palace where the sultan was giving a banquet in a room full of courtiers. Suddenly there was a terrible earthquake which destroyed the palace, killing everyone except for the man and Khezr. "What is the meaning of all we have seen and done?" the man cried, "It is all suffering!" "Patience," said Khezr. "What you have seen are not misfortunes but the miracles of God. The sultan was an evil man who was plotting against a saint who lived in a village nearby. After the banquet, he and his courtiers were going to kill the holy man. But God is great and the earthquake destroyed them."

' "What of the ship full of gold and jewels?" said the man. "Such riches would have put bread in the mouths of the poor." "No," said Khezr, "you are wrong. It was the payment for an army. If they had received it many good lives would have been lost."

' "And what of the young prince who was killed in the garden?" asked the man. "And the beautiful princess?" Khezr replied: "If they had married, their son would have grown up to be a cruel conqueror of cities and an unbeliever. By the young prince's death, he and the beautiful princess were saved the shame of an evil son and the world did not suffer his sword." '

The quartermaster threw a pinch of naswar under his tongue and gazed into my eyes to see whether I had understood the story. I felt I had missed certain things: what happened to the thief?: how did Khezr know all these things? And what was the secret of life? I was about to clarify these details when Peter asked me for a translation.

The talk turned to the subject of food and a shifty-eyed Uzbeki told us of tins of Russian food which he had found, left by the Russians.

'There isn't much food in Nuristan,' said Peter. 'It might be worth getting some for the journey back. A lot of the mujahedin won't touch the stuff but it's not too bad; I've eaten stacks of it myself. Gets a bit boring after a while.'

The Uzbeki promised to bring us some tins. The raid continued and, while we waited for the bombing to finish, the conversation faltered to a halt.

Half an hour later, we climbed out of the cave into the daylight. The local commander arrived and advised us to take our kit with us to the caves on the other side of the river in case there was another attack. We followed him across a rickety wooden bridge to the mouth of a torrent flowing down through a tall gorge into the Panjshir from a side valley. There were several rock overhangs faced with walls of piled stones and a glade of willows under which a family was encamped.

We had just unpacked our paperbacks and Walkman sets when the bombing began again. When the bombs exploded the shockwaves sounded like huge tents flapping in a storm and once, when a bomb detonated nearby, the sides of the gorge rang like struck metal. As the jets swept over there were innocent-looking little clouds of smoke from the flares which they dropped to confuse heat-guided missiles. Several times, the shadows of the planes flashed momentarily across the cliff wall in front of us. I was looking up at the sky as a swallow flew over and for several seconds the blood pounded in my heart. One of the jets came in very low, a couple of hundred feet or so, and dropped its bombs nearby – but they were duds. Whenever a bomb exploded the men called out from one shelter to another – Where did it fall? Were any houses hit? What was the damage?

A couple of hours later the jets were still making their bombing sweeps along the valley; clearly it was no ordinary raid.

'That's all we need!' said Julian. 'Another bloody offensive.'

It was a depressing thought: I had been looking forward to washing my clothes and smoking a cigarette in the shade of an apricot tree.

During a lull in the bombing we were joined by a small party of mujahedin. Two of them were markedly different from the others in appearance: one had sandy brown hair and blue eyes, the other's hair and moustache were blond. They were Russian prisoners or, more accurately, deserters who, since their conversion to Islam, answered to their Muslim names. The one with blond hair was called Tawfiq and had learned a little Dari, but his companion, Ali, could only manage a few elementary words.

They had left their patrol and fallen into the hands of the mujahedin. Luckily for them, one of their captors spoke Russian and they were able to communicate enough to save their lives. They had converted to Islam and had been living with the mujahedin for the past six months. They were not allowed to carry weapons and had to remain in the company of the mujahedin at all times, but apart from these restrictions they were more or less free to come and go as they pleased. They were both twenty and came from Georgia, in southern Russia – that was all they would say about themselves, fearing that if their true identities were known, their relatives might suffer reprisals.

Their quasi-captivity had affected them both in very different ways. Ali was silent and unsmiling. He seemed deeply withdrawn and I thought he was probably on the edge of a nervous breakdown. Tawfiq, on the other hand, spoke semi-comprehensible gibberish to anyone who would listen and walked about with a devil-may-care nonchalance when the bombs were falling. Perhaps he was already a little mad. It seemed a curious irony that he should be bombed by his own countrymen. When I asked him, he merely cursed the war.

'It's mad. If bombs kill me I'm dead. Russian bomb, Afghan bomb, American bomb. It's all the same I'm dead.' Glancing round at the mujahedin, he shouted, '*Insha'allah*,' in a loud voice. He turned to look at us, winked and smiled. 'Everyone is happy.' For a moment he let his head fall abruptly, then raised it with an expression of false jollity. 'Everyone is happy. I live. You live. They live. Everyone is happy.'

The bombing lasted for over six hours in all, and when we left the rock shelters the sides of the gorge were already in shadow.

I washed myself and rinsed some of my clothes in the torrent but made a cursory job of it for the water had the chill of melting snow. Then I joined the others in the derelict house where we ate a meal of gritty rice, with the mujahedin in the room nextdoor. The lamp flickered in the wind gusting through the broken window while the men told us of their families in Pakistan and the beauty of the valley before it was ravaged by the war.

'Now everything is "*kherab*" – ruined. But one day, *Insha'allah*, the people will return to the valley and the gardens will bloom once again. Then you can come and visit us and we will discuss poetry together.'

Their faces were caught in the golden light of the lamp; their features were stark with hardship. Unlike the people of Nahrin, the life of their towns and villages had already been totally devastated, and their livelihood destroyed. But still they remained. Their continued presence was, itself, a powerful testimony to the strength of their beliefs.

'At the beginning of the war there were some people, perhaps, who were fighting to protect their families and land, their crops and houses. Not any more. Their families have gone to Pakistan and the land is ruined. We are fighting because we believe in God. If all the country is burnt, all the trees dead and all the rivers dry, we will still fight. Afghanistan is a battlefield in a war between God and Satan. Every mujahed is a soldier in the army of God. We are the hands and fingernails of the Muslim world, of the *Ummah*.'

If they were the hands and fingernails of the Muslim world, where, I wondered, was its heart? Not only their words, but their actions revealed a depth of religious feeling the West has not known for more than five hundred years. I thought of the poetry of Jalal Uddin Balkhi Rumi, its images of the moth-like soul extinguishing itself by *faná* in the fire of God, and remembered the lines:

I died as mineral and became vegetable
I died as a vegetable and became animal
I died as animal and became man
When was I less by dying?

Perhaps it was this sense of life itself reaching towards God which imbued Islam with such strength and made most forms of Christianity look weak and sickly by comparison.

I slept raggedly and was already half-awake when the mujahedin got up to perform their nemaz. After they had done, they told us to go with them to the gorge. Another raid was likely and would start as soon as it grew light. We tried to persuade them to wait for us while we made some tea but they were adamant: there was no time to lose.

Crouching in a narrow passage of rocks and stones for hours at a time had been uncomfortable so Peter and Julian decided to take their foam mattresses along with their cameras and sound equipment. We arrived at the caves before dawn and settled down to wait, still grumbling about the lack of breakfast. A quarter of an hour later the first of the jets entered the valley and dropped its bombs a little distance from where we were.

The attack went on for several hours without a halt. Peter and Julian moved to the edge of the cliffs from where they could film the bombing of the village more easily. I watched the upturned faces of the mujahedin scanning the northern peaks as the jets dived over and into the valley. Their profiles would have made dramatic photographs: 'Mujahedin under attack, Panjshir Valley, autumn, 1984', but I did not want the bother of taking out my camera.

Besides, using a camera would set a gulf between us: they would become the subject matter of a photograph, items of news, objects of visual information, and I would become a stranger pointing an expensive and irrelevant machine at them.

A photograph of a man who is afraid is more intrusive than a photograph of one who is beside himself with suffering. Both are forms of nakedness: pain and grief strip everything away, down to the creature of blood and flesh and tears; but fear shows the weakness of a man's spirit.

There was a lull in the bombing and for a few minutes we were able to relax. Naswar was passed round and the mujahed who had quoted Sa'adi to me the previous evening pressed a gift into my hands. It was a small, dry gourd which had been hollowed out and a wad of scarlet thread inserted at one end. The surface was stained and polished with use and its curves fitted comfortably into my hand.

When an Afghan makes an offer of a gift it should be refused at least three times. To accept sooner is grasping and ill-mannered. My friend was insistent.

'Take it, Abdul Baz, take it,' he repeated. 'It contains naswar which is difficult to find in Nuristan; it will help you climb the passes. In England you can use it and remember our time together.'

A rhythmic thud echoed overhead and a Mi 8 helicopter appeared travelling up the valley in the direction of Dastri-Wat. Two or three minutes later another went over, then two more together.

My thoughts were still disorientated by the bombing and it took several minutes to piece together the significance of what was happening. Our route out of the valley lay to the north of the Panjshir, then east into Nuristan. The Soviets were only a few kilometres south of where we were. Now they were moving north of our position as well. We were being cut off.

The helicopters continued to pass over; so far I had counted twelve. If there were twenty to twenty-five troops in each of them, there was already a sizeable force blocking off our escape route to the north. The mujahedin had picked up their guns and were checking their ammunition clips. There were no more than thirty of us scattered between the cliff shelters; some of us were unarmed.

From the north of the valley some villagers appeared, running: several men with rifles and two women holding their veils tightly to their faces, then an older man pulling a cow by a rope that led through its nose. Peter and Julian scrambled round the mouth of the gorge to join us.

To attack us the Soviets would have to cross the torrent and a boulder-strewn patch of ground. We had the protection of stone walls at the top of a small scree. To our left a torrent flowed into the main river of the Panjshir; to our right a gorge led up into a side valley.

Some villagers who were sharing our shelter made the first move by gathering their bundles and hurrying down towards the torrent's edge. They waded across and ran up the gorge to our right. It was the trigger we had been waiting for. A few mujahedin stayed behind, the rest of us shouldered our belongings and broke cover. There were about twenty of us in the gorge when another helicopter went over. A door in its side was open and a machine-gunner started firing down on us. Peter and I threw ourselves behind a boulder. There was no time to be frightened. The temptation to look over the top of the boulder was irresistible. Two hundred feet above us the gunner stood at the door of the helicopter swivelling his gun wildly at some men running along the bank. One man was up to his waist in midstream lurching towards the shelter of some rocks on the other side. The sunlight was bright. The helicopter disappeared over the top of the gorge. We stumbled into the torrent and, on the other side, we found a path which led up into a side valley. A few minutes later we caught up with Julian and the three of us left the mujahedin to set off up the side valley, away from the threatened village.

My feet slipped around inside my sodden boots as we jogged uphill. Breathing hurt and I cursed my folly for smoking as my lungs strained for more oxygen. It was like a cross-country run with no prizes at the end and only the fear of losing kept us going. The path was steep, and a quarter of an hour later our pace had slowed to a brisk walk.

We stopped for a brief rest. I had counted more than thirty helicopters going over: seven hundred men to the north.

We had reached a plateau from where we could see down the valley, but the gorge itself was hidden from view. Behind us the mountains rose up dramatically towards a blue sky and white, luminous clouds. Some men called out to us from the doorway of a hut and invited us to share a meal of yoghurt and bread. One of them, a plump mujahed with nervous eyes, spoke some German and told us that the nearest village was six hours away on the other side of the mountains; he did not know its name, and few people went that way.

There was no chance of retrieving our horses and equipment, at least for the time being. We had no food either. Quite possibly the Soviets would try to seal off the valley by dropping paratroops at the top of the pass. We decided to aim for the village on the other side of the mountains where we could wait until the situation was clearer. We sent a message to the local commander to this effect, and set off.

The path climbed continuously. Spotter planes circled the valley: at the sound of their engines we covered ourselves with our petous for camouflage. Below us the bombing continued intermittently. In the late afternoon we met a boy of seventeen and his two sisters coming down the path towards us. How far was it to the next village? Ten hours, perhaps more. They had started before dawn and had had no rest since then. If we decided to cross the pass we should be careful: there were mines.

'Look out where you place your foot. Most of the path is clear, but sometimes a goat will move a stone and a mine will fall onto the path. In the dark it is dangerous.'

We thanked him for his warning and had a hurried consultation. Whether we went forward or back, we would have to spend a night out on the mountain. We decided to keep to our original plan and try to reach as far up the valley as possible before dark.

The peaks above us gradually changed from orange to lilac and their shadows lengthened across our path. Peter spotted the first mine. From then on, we shouted out the location of a mine whenever we passed one. I thought of jelly-fish and sea-urchins. At one point I saw Peter bend down and carefully pick something up. 'See, this one's already inactive – the pin's gone,' he said holding the olive-green plastic object between his fingers like a dead rat. 'They won't kill you at once. Just blow your foot off. That's what they're made for; someone wounded by one of these needs another man to look after him. It's bad for morale. It slows a group down. If the wound goes gangrenous, it's worse. Not a nice way to die.' He tossed the thing away: as it landed there was the sharp crack of an explosion. Peter grinned at me sheepishly: 'That's lucky. I'd thought of lobbing it at you for a joke.'

The next mile or so was littered with the olive-green objects and several times my concentration wavered in what seemed like a game of hopscotch over a jumble of irregular rocks and boulders. We kept to the path, but when that disappeared we chose a route across flat stones. Wherever possible, we avoided boggy ground and streams.

Eventually we came to the diagonal silhouette of a massive wall of boulders. I was for staying put but Julian and Peter wanted to press on and reluctantly I followed them. It was twilight by the time we halted on a bare plateau. We had a sleeping bag, a ground sheet and two blankets. We made a roofless igloo of rocks and huddled inside it. I still had my Walkman and put on a tape of Bob Dylan but it was a mournful sound, made worse by the fading batteries. After spreading out the groundsheet, Julian and I wrapped ourselves in our petous and lay down enviously beside Peter in his sleeping bag. Then we pulled the remainder of the groundsheet over us and tried to sleep, but whenever one of us moved a freezing draught struck the other's neck and shoulders. It was a comfortless night and we argued and complained at each other's selfishness till dawn.

For breakfast we shared a packet of Batchelor's soup stirred into a bottle of melt-water. We climbed another wall of massive boulders and came to a desolate expanse of rock and ice pools enclosed by tall, jagged cliffs. The way over to the next valley lay in front of us, but where it was among the silent peaks surrounding us, we had no idea.

The sun had risen high in the sky and we lay down and pillowed ourselves against some boulders. A spotter plane flew over. We drew the petous over our heads while it described a slow circle overhead and I blinked at the sun through the threads of the blanket. Then the drone softened in the distance and we pulled back our petous once more.

The altitude was slowing us down. We were tired and Peter was ill. Although he said nothing it was clear that the strength had gone out of him. There seemed to be two possible-looking routes: to the left or to the right. We tossed a coin and started to climb the cliffs to our right. None of us said anything. I listened to the sound of my breath and watched my knees bend and straighten as I moved from boulder to boulder. My legs seemed to belong to someone else. The rocks were different colours in the sunlight: dark brown, pale yellow and dusty white, like the colours of the faces of men. Shale and pebbles cascaded down the cliff face. Several hundred feet below, Julian was sitting on a rock and further down I could just see Peter's figure slumped against a bank of stones.

The last part of the climb was the easiest. At the top of the cliff was a sharp ridge of stone, steep as the roof of a house. I flattened myself against the rock and looked over: on the other side was a sheer drop into a sunless abyss, littered with patches of ice and snow. We had chosen the wrong route.

We retraced our way down the cliff and back to the side of a shallow pool which glittered in our faces. The wind blowing across its surface made it look bitter and unfriendly. A bird called and its cry accentuated the wilderness around us.

We were exhausted and for an hour or so we rested by the edge of the pool. The landscape was elemental: rock, wind, water and light. The sun was warm on our faces but the wind was cold. We had no food or maps. Peter was ill. The next village was six or seven hours away and it was already past midday. If we failed to find the way over the mountains we would have to spend another freezing night in the open. On the other hand, by now the Soviets would have entered the village we had come from. Peter was for trying again to cross the pass; Julian and I were for returning.

Our conversation was interrupted by two Su 17 jets, barely visible in the radiance of the sun, tearing apart the silence of the mountains. War in the sky, war in the towns and villages, war in a remote mountain pass: where we were was yet another battlefield in a war that was ancient before the rise and fall of Babylon. Like particles of dust on a vast irregular chessboard extending into the past and future our presence was infinitesimal.

But we were hungry, and eventually we agreed to go back to try to find some food and a guide: we would not get far without them.

The descent was less arduous, but it was demoralising to retrace the paths which we had slogged up the previous day. As we went through the minefield, the afternoon sun struck the towering cliffs on our right and cast gigantic shadows across the crumbling pinnacles of red rock. A luminous sky with light-filled clouds stretched across the tops of the mountains. I remembered the Tarot card portraying the Fool and looked at the ground at my feet.

We descended to the treeline and further on we saw horse droppings on the path. Then at twilight we came to a small forest of birch trees beside a torrent. Out of the dusk a voice called a greeting to us.

'*Manda nabashi.*'

The man was unarmed, about thirty years old with a thin, gentle face. When he heard of our failure to cross the pass and our lack of food, he reached down into his waistcoat pocket and drew out handfuls of dried mulberries and walnuts for us to eat.

Then he took us to a cave where he gave us bread and glasses of hot chai. Some other, older men joined us and we asked them about the situation in the village – but no one knew. We talked for a short while longer and then lay down under blankets which the men provided for us. During the night other members of their families arrived, including some women, and we moved to a shelter of loosely-piled stones carpeted with leaves and roofed with the branches of trees. For once there were no fleas and we slept soundly.

The next morning we found another cave across the torrent. There was still no news from further down the valley and in the afternoon Julian and I set off to contact the local commander. Peter remained in the cave since by now he was too ill to walk. On the way down we passed several families living in caves. Near the *kargah* itself the boulders along the path were covered with the dust from explosions and an unexploded bomb had embedded itself in the bank of the river. Some mujahedin told us what had happened; how the Soviet troops had attacked the village and taken the tops of the hills overlooking the mouth of the valley. Fighting was still going on.

Peter and Julian's equipment had been hidden but it was inaccessible on the other side of the river which was already occupied by the Soviets. There was no news of Freckle.

As it grew dark other mujahedin arrived. Some had been fighting in the village, others hiding in the mountains. The situation was confused. By most accounts the Soviets had been defeated, many had been killed and the rest had retreated, but then when we asked for Commander Kohzad we were told that he was still fighting in the village.

A fire was lit under the branches of a great walnut tree. A cauldron full of water from the torrent was placed on top of the flames and a goat was slaughtered. Meat and handfuls of salt were thrown in and while it cooked we warmed ourselves beside the blazing logs.

The firelight shone on the faces of the men and the sparks leapt up into the branches of the tree. The mujahedin teased the two Russians about the bombing: 'Are you afraid of those *kafirs*?' 'Why not tell them to stop the bombing?' 'Do you prefer living in the Panjshir to living in Russia? It must be an unpleasant country!' Tawfiq responded by tussling good-naturedly with a mujahed. They were both in their early twenties and as I watched them wrestling the actions of armies and politicians seemed meaningless. But I could not relax. The light of the fire was an easy target for a mortar bomb and there were no sentries posted against a surprise attack.

At last the meat was cooked and we each received hunks of scalding goat on nan loaves. The men ate quickly and slipped away into the night, but Julian and I remained by the embers to wait for the Commander.

The fire subsided into ashes and Kohzad had still not returned from the village, so I wrote a message for him explaining our situation and gave it to a mujahed to deliver. Then the group's quartermaster gave us some supplies which we tied in my petou-knapsack and we started back up the valley. There was no moon and it took several hours to reach the cave. We found Peter listening to the radio by the light of a borrowed hurricane lamp. He had covered the floor with dry leaves and the lamp cast a comforting glow over the inside of the cave. It was good to be back.

11

Nuristan

The cave was our home for the next few days. There were two or three families in the vicinity and the men used to visit us. Yaqub, the man who had given us handfuls of nuts and berries when we first arrived, visited us every day and once his elderly father accompanied him. There was also a lapis trader on his way to Pakistan and a middle-aged man who, it was said, had two beautiful wives in a cave on the other side of the river and a Kalashnikov to protect them.

The days were bright and clear but autumn was already in the air and the leaves of a nearby spinney of beech trees were turning gold. From eight or nine o'clock in the morning till six o'clock in the evening the jets attacked in waves; the sound of bombs exploding reverberated up the valley and every few hours spotter planes flew over.

'Bombing and spotter planes getting a bit oppressive,' I wrote in my diary. 'Cold days being in cave, but dangerous to be outside. Makes men feel like mice under the unpredictable eye of savage birds of prey. Washing socks and hearing the sounds of jets sweeping through the roar of the water and the wind through the booming rocks. The scene like a Shell calendar but everything somehow discoloured.'

The syntax reflects my state of mind when I wrote the passage: time was fractured and suspended in a vacuum, events were isolated and had no connection with one another. It required a considerable mental effort to think beyond our immediate situation and we were struggling to ignore an undermining sense of fatalism. I wrote my diary. Julian listened to Bob Marley tapes. In desperation we took turns reading my pocket Bible.

Peter was very quiet. He spent most of the time in his sleeping bag at the back of the cave and I noticed that the whites of his eyes had a yellowish tinge, suggesting hepatitis. Every evening we tuned in to the World Service but there was no mention of any new offensive in the Panjshir valley.

It was disturbingly unreal to be caught in the middle of a forgotten war. At times it was like being in the grip of a massive

hallucination: living on nuts and berries in a cave, being bombed by
Soviet jets. The outside world acquired another meaning.

Early in the morning, when the mountains were still dark against
the dawn, I used to go to the torrent, splash its icy water on my face,
then watch the sunlight gradually cover the peaks high above the
cave. But before the chill of the night had faded from the rocks, the
bombing began once more and I returned to the gloom of the cave.

The uncertainty was weighing on our minds and our tempers
began to fray: Julian complained bitterly when I lit a cigarette in the
cave; I accused him of wasting the batteries of my Walkman; Peter
sulked in his sleeping bag. There were long silences between one
conversation and the next. To stop our morale deteriorating
further, we tried once more to find a guide, but most of the men we
asked were ignorant of the way or unwilling to go with us. Once it
seemed as if we had succeeded when Yaqub reluctantly agreed to
take us; but he qualified his promise with '*Insha'allah*' in a wilting
tone of voice and I realised we would not be able to rely on him.

We also needed food for the journey into Nuristan, and spent
hours negotiating with two shepherds to buy a sheep. One of them
was a slow-witted youth of seventeen with a sun-darkened face and
clumsy movements, wrapped in the folds of a torn petou. His
companion was the owner of the sheep, a small, wizened man with
a shrewd eye for business. Unfortunately, a speech impediment
rendered him virtually dumb and the bargain was pursued through
a bewildering sequence of gestures, sharp inarticulate moans and
shaking of heads, while the simpleton made dismal attempts to
mediate. In the end, several days and numerous meetings later, the
deal fell through.

Without food, we could not rely on the kindness of our neighbours indefinitely. Entries in my diary got shorter and I could not
conceal my misgivings about our future: 'Our situation in a nut-
shell: we only have one escape route, we don't have much time or
strength – and we don't have a reliable guide. We have to get the trip
right. If not we will be too weak to do it a third time.'

I decided to go down the valley once more to find a guide. On the
way down I made enquiries of groups of villagers camped under
rock overhangs or in the shelter of sheepfolds, but none of them
knew of a guide to take us over the pass. I arrived at the *kargah* at
twilight; there was heavy fighting in the village and there were only
a few mujahedin present. I wrote another letter to Commander
Kohzad outlining our probable route into Nuristan and gave it to
one of the mujahedin. He was against our departure.

'Wait another few days. The Shuravi will go and then it will be easy. We will find your horses and equipment and there will be no problem.' But his optimism seemed misplaced and did nothing to reassure me. Once he realised we were determined to go his manner changed.

'If you go now, you go without the permission of Commander Kohzad. Your safety is no longer his responsibility. If you meet with bad men that is your affair.' He warned me of the unreliable character of the Nuristanis. 'Some say they are not true Muslims, but *kafir*. They are a stupid and lazy people: the women work in the fields and the men do nothing but drink chai. If they want something they steal it from travellers. Only a fool travels in Nuristan without a gun.'

He went on to describe notorious acts of brigandage, each more bloodthirsty than the last, until he was in a more cheerful mood. 'But if you must go it is God's will, *Mosafer aziz khodast* – the traveller is beloved of God. I will give you some food for your journey; you'll be lucky if you can buy an egg in Nuristan.' We tied bundles of sugar, tea, bread and meat into my petou and said goodbye to one another. It was now dark and I still had no guide.

I descended a path and came to a shadowy collection of buildings; closer to I saw that most of the houses lacked roofs and tarpaulins had been stretched across the walls. Here and there the gleam of a lamp shone in the darkness. I went from one to the next in search of a guide. Once again I was unsuccessful, but several times the name 'Mustapha Khan' was mentioned as a man who might help me. A group of men invited me to join them for a glass of chai and one of them set off in search of the elusive Mustapha Khan.

It was almost like a homecoming to be alone once more among Afghans and for the first time in several days my spirits lifted. But the conversation was solemn. 'Tell your people what is happening here. Tell them what you have seen with your own eyes,' were the constant refrains. 'If your people believe the Shuravi we are lost.'

Half an hour later Mustapha Khan stepped into the circle. He was older than I had expected, a man of sixty or so with a slight stoop.

'Who is seeking Mustapha Khan the hunter?' he called out. 'I know every pathway, every stream and every cave in this valley. I can guide a man anywhere, for a price.'

We shook hands and studied each other's faces in the lamplight. His eyes were quick and knowing and when he smiled I saw his two lower front teeth were missing. He looked a rogue, but I liked his confident lack of modesty and we quickly agreed a price.

We set off back to the cave with Mustapha Khan leading the way, staff in hand. He moved over the rough stones at a good steady pace, and only an occasional rattle of loose pebbles marked his passing. The moon rose, bathing the rocks and trees in still, shining light. We climbed without a rest until we came to an icy spring hidden in the shadow of the cliffs.

As we moved through the crystalline night air the subdued roar of water tumbling in the darkness beneath us, the war was unimaginably distant. Mustapha Khan beckoned to me to leave the path and I followed him down to the torrent's edge. He knelt down and removed a small tin box from underneath a boulder and poured its contents on to a flat rock. From a waistcoat pocket he produced another packet of powder and carefully measured out some of it on to the rock beside the first mound. He mixed the mounds together in a practised rhythm, several times dipping his hand into the stream and shaking sparkling drops of water over the darkened surface. Then he chose a smooth pebble from the water's edge and ground the mixture in a swift circular motion until it was spread in a thin layer. Up till then he had said nothing, but after patting the substance and sprinkling it with a few more drops of water from the river he turned to me. 'Take some, Abdul,' he said, 'it will do you no harm.' By now I had guessed that the mysterious substance was naswar and I put a pinch under my tongue. A satisfying heat radiated under my tongue, my pulse quickened and the heaviness vanished from my legs.

We had just begun to cross the river when there was the sharp whistling sound of a mortar to our right and we glimpsed a bright light disintegrate with a bang a few hundred feet below us. Mustapha Khan muttered something and launched himself across a makeshift bridge of branches paved with stones. Half-way across he stumbled, dislodging two large rocks which slipped into the hissing water with a heavy splash, and he only just managed to scramble to the other side. The branches were still in place and I teetered across them towards the staff which Mustapha Khan held out towards me. There were no more mortars and we continued on in silence. But the spell of the moonlight was broken.

When we reached the cave it was in darkness and Peter and Julian were asleep: I lit the lamp and introduced them to Mustapha Khan. We talked briefly of the journey and decided to climb the pass the following day. Mustapha seemed completely unperturbed by our company and when we arranged our blankets for the night he lay down between Julian and myself as if spending the night with three Englishmen was the most natural thing in the world for him.

It was still dark when Mustapha Khan woke us and for the next few hours we climbed without a break, except for pauses when jets or spotter planes passed over. By mid-morning we had crossed the minefield and reached the edge of the plateau where we had camped previously. We stopped for a rest and shared our meat and bread with Mustapha Khan who in turn produced generous supplies of dried mulberries and *qu'rut* and told us of his exploits as a hunter. One of his closest companions, a skilful hunter like himself, lived in the village over the mountains. On arrival we should ask for a man whose name sounded like 'Muddy Sore' who would surely help us.

We reached the top of the pass by mid-afternoon: Mustapha Khan pointed down into the neighbouring valley several thousand feet below at some dark specks at the foot of a grey mountain.

He was eager to return before nightfall so we paid him at once and thanked him for his help. Then we shook hands and he kissed us farewell.

The way down led across a scree of jagged black boulders. It was one of the most uncomfortable and desolate stretches of country I have encountered. Scott's description of the Antarctic – 'God this is an awful place!' – fitted it perfectly and when the first flecks of sleet began to sting through the air, my misery was complete.

We found a herd of goats sheltering in a fold of the hills and some villagers watching over them. The men had dispiriting news for us: a few hours earlier Soviet troops had attacked and overrun the village and surrounded the mujahedin in their *kargah*. The people had fled to the north of the village and taken refuge in caves and sheepfolds. The men were slow-witted with the cold and the shock of the past few hours, and were unable to help us further. To our right, a cloud of smoke was rising over the crest of a hill. It seemed unwise to spend any more time in conversation so we took the path to our left which the men assured us led towards Nuristan. Half an hour later we came to a huddle of buildings and a boy led us to a small, windowless hut where we slumped down on a straw-covered floor. After a few minutes he returned with some blankets and a lamp which he set in a niche in the wall.

'You are safe here,' he said; 'the Shuravi are two or three miles away and will not be here before morning, *Insha'allah*. Now I will try to find you something to eat. But we have very little food. Most of our possessions are in the village. We only live here in the summer, when the sheep are in the higher pastures – or when the Shuravi come.'

The boy vanished into the night and we settled down to wait. The warmth of the little room and the gentle light of the lamp were deeply soothing. Peter lay down and went to sleep immediately, while Julian and I sat in silence, listening to the wind rustling in the roof of thorns and leaves. There was nothing to be said.

I was woken by the arrival of an old man bringing a plate of eggs and bread which he placed on the floor in front of us. He had the slanting eyes and wispy beard of an Uzbek. He introduced himself as the village headman; his son was the local mullah and the building we were staying in was the village mosque. The boy was his grandson and would guide us over the next pass into Nuristan.

While eating we heard the sound of a plane circling overhead and the old man became agitated, wringing his hands and moaning softly to himself.

'Taking infra-red photographs,' said Peter. 'The muj still haven't got used to them. Even if they're under cover, heat concentrations reveal their position. Nothing much they can do about it, except stop lighting fires.'

We gave the old man some money for the meal, turned down the lamp and settled down to sleep. I considered briefly what might happen if we were captured, but I was too tired to give it much thought. For the moment it was good to be wrapped in a blanket listening to the wind buffeting outside the door.

'Quickly! Quickly! Get up! Get up!' The lamp was lit and the old man was standing over us, wrapped in a coat and wearing thick leather boots. In his anxiety, he lapsed from Dari into another dialect which I could not understand, but it was clear from his shaking hands and voice that there was no time to lose. We threw our things together, pulled on our boots and followed the swaying lamp into the darkness.

Outside the boy was waiting for us. The old man handed him the lamp then bent down to hoist a huge bundle of clothes and blankets on to his shoulders; he extinguished the lamp and tied it to the old man's pack, then we set off. At first the old man went ahead, but after a quarter of an hour the path rose more steeply and he began to fall behind. Several times he stopped to ease the pack on his shoulders and finally he came to a halt by the side of the path and unhitched the pack on to a boulder. I offered to take it but when I put my arms through the carrying cords and took the weight of the pack on my back I could hardly stand. My weakness shocked me but there was nothing I could do: it was too heavy for me. The old man tied a few items into a blanket and hid the remainder of the pack under a thorn bush.

We stumbled on through the darkness. Now and again flares shot up over the village behind us, and mortars and artillery reverberated in the hills around us. '*Ay khoda, khoda,*' the old man groaned. 'The Shuravi are terrible, terrible, terrible.' Half an hour later he left us. We stood in silence and watched the dawn filter into the east: mist and clouds hung suspended against the mountain walls. A thick column of smoke was drifting up from the floor of the valley and the morning air was bitter with the smell of ash. A wind blew across the rocky slope, rattling the branches of some thorn bushes and, in between gusts, there was the sound of a small child crying. The boy was telling me to wait until his grandfather returned when he clutched at his stomach and slipped away behind some boulders. Some time later he staggered into view, still adjusting the cord of his trousers, and mumbled '*mariz* – sick'.

The sun cast a pale yellow light from behind a bank of grey cloud and the high-pitched wailing of the child echoed across the wet stones. The old man reappeared with a bundle of dried mulberries and bread which he pressed into Julian's pack. We gave him as much money as we could afford, and set off after the boy who had already starting walking up the pass.

The path was still in shadow and the ground was frozen hard beneath our feet. The boy stopped repeatedly to relieve himself. Eventually he sat down on a rock and called out that he could go no further. We tried to persuade him to go on but it was hopeless: his cheeks were hollow and his eyes were half-closed with exhaustion. We waited for him to recover his strength and the sun grew hot on our shoulders. The boy was lying on a rock: his clothes were in rags and his feet were encased in thin brown plastic shoes, split at the heels, crudely patched with strips of green plastic and tied together with strips of torn cloth. He turned his back to the wind which twitched the loosely-wrapped petou from his body, displaying a shirt tail and trousers, streaked with blood and faeces.

We ate a few handfuls of mulberries and I bent down to drink at a glistening rivulet of water running between narrow margins of close-cropped grass. It was numbingly cold and the grass and weeds at the water's edge were encased in shining beads of ice.

A helicopter flew over the mountains further down the valley. For a minute or two it hovered on the edge of the cloud of smoke from the burning village, then an explosion erupted beneath it and, as it wheeled away, another darker cloud of smoke and dust climbed into the sky.

'Must have been a big one,' said Peter, 'probably a thousand-pound bomb.'

The boy was still asleep on the rock and I had to shake him by the shoulder to wake him. We had no idea where the pass crossed over into Nuristan: only the boy knew where it was. He was on the verge of unconsciousness and for a quarter of an hour I had to shout and bully him into giving us directions. His mouth was thick with saliva and several times I had to ask him to repeat himself. At last I understood enough to have a reasonable idea of the direction we needed to take. His eyes had closed again and when I put some money into his hand his fingers remained motionless.

Our progress up the pass was heartbreakingly slow. Peter was very weak and we stopped every fifteen minutes. I kept looking back at the place where we had left the boy and finally, to my relief, I saw that he had disappeared from the rock.

The peaks seemed to grow sharper in the bright frosty air and the sky was a cloudless blue. In the middle of the morning several Mig 27s and Su 17s howled overhead in a plunging attack and began bombing the valley below. The attacks went on, intermittently, for the next two hours. But we reached the top of the pass and sat watching the planes race over the mountains, listening to the monstrous thumping of their bombs. The roaring of demons in the sky and the mountains trembling, fire and terror: how could the people who lived in these remote hills and valleys possibly begin to understand what was happening to them?

From where we were, safe on the heights overlooking the valley, the bombing was so much noise and smoke: just as the battlefields of Troy must have appeared to the inhabitants of Mount Olympus. For a few minutes I ignored the dangers of hubris and considered the similarities between those all-too-human deities and ourselves. Observers from another world, we had passed among the people, seen their suffering and heard their prayers, received their kindness and momentarily known the turbulence of war. But all the while we had been wearing an invisible armour: the knowledge of another life to which we could eventually return.

In front of us, the desolate beauty of Nuristan stretched out towards the majestic range of the Hindu Kush and freedom. Behind us were the mountains and valleys and plains of Afghanistan, and a people who remained captives in their own country. As we began the descent into Nuristan I felt like an escaped prisoner: relief and exhilaration, mixed with guilt and regret for those who could not come with me. We crossed another, mine-strewn plateau and descended into a barren valley where an icy river tumbled past a few, abandoned shelters made of stones and timber. It was late afternoon, the sun had dropped below the mountains and a sharp wind was picking up. The boy had told us of a village an hour's journey over the pass into Nuristan, but we had been walking for three or four hours already and there was still no sign of it. We briefly considered spending the night in one of the shelters but then decided to press on.

An hour later we rounded a bend in the river and saw a thread of smoke drifting from between some large rocks at the bottom of a cliff. The fire belonged to a family from Khunduz who assured us that there was, indeed, a village another hour's walk down the river.

We walked until it grew dark. A figure on horseback approached us out of the twilight. Again we asked how far it was to the next village and again the reply was an hour, or even a little longer. The journey had become unreal and I toyed with the whimsical idea that travellers in search of Shangri-La might well have received the same answer, always the same answer, 'Yes, keep on, it isn't far from here, only another hour, another day, you may get there by candle-light . . .' spurring them on towards an unknown end.

The moon was high in the sky by the time we came to the glow of a lamp hanging inside a tent. Some men, refugees from the Panjshir, invited us inside to share their meal and stay the night. We accepted gratefully: we had been travelling almost continuously for more than eighteen hours and were glad to be able to rest at last. As we sat drinking chai I asked one of them, out of idle interest, how far he thought it might be to the next village. I had already guessed the answer and I was not disappointed.

'With a good horse – maybe an hour. *Insha'allah.*'

12

Pushal

The next morning, when we told our hosts of our plans, their brows furrowed with concern. 'The men of Nuristan are not like us – you cannot trust them. Without a guide it is dangerous and without a gun it is madness,' said one of them. 'It is better to travel in a group,' said another. 'As many men as possible. Even then it is not completely safe: often caravans are ambushed by Nuristani's who take all the arms and ammunition. They say they need the weapons for themselves but often they are sold again in Pakistan.' 'Better trust a thief than a man from Nuristan,' added a third.

When Peter heard what they said he snorted with disbelief.

'It's a lot of balls. The only reason they're going on like that is because they're Panjshiris. In fact, the rest of Afghanistan has always looked down on the Nuristanis in the same way as some English think of the Irish.

'For years the Nuristanis felt they had a raw deal and some time back they declared themselves independent from the rest of the country. It would be a joke except it gives them the excuse to take taxes from people travelling through, in other words, robbing the arms convoys. But they're hardly likely to bother us.'

I did not share Peter's confidence. Nevertheless, I told the men we intended going on, with or without a guide. The eldest of them insisted we should stay. The impasse was finally resolved by one of the men agreeing to go with us in return for a sum of money, on condition that the others supplied him with a gun. He settled for a hand-held automatic. His name was Abdul Latif; he was a handsome man, about thirty years old with a ruddy face and neatly trimmed beard. As added protection for his return journey he persuaded a youth of eighteen called Shukur to accompany us. Shukur had curly dark hair, amused brown eyes and skin the colour of copper, except for his hands and fingers which were stained black with walnut juice. It was clear by his clothes – filthy cotton trousers and disintegrating quilted jacket – that he was poorer than Abdul Latif. They packed a small bundle which Shukur carried and after thanking the remaining three men for their hospitality we set off.

We plodded along a switchback-like path, up and down the cliffs of a deep gorge, for several hours until we saw signs of cultivation: carefully dug ditches and terraced fields of maize and corn. A little further on we came to a village and stopped for some chai in the shade of a walnut tree. A crowd of curious Nuristanis gathered round to stare at us and I, just as curious, stared back at them. My first impressions kindled no affection for them: they looked at us with small brown eyes set at the top of vast noses, and when I smiled in their direction they gave no signs of having noticed, but continued gazing with unwavering attention, until I began to feel like a piece of wood or an oddly shaped stone.

It was difficult to believe that any of the people standing around us were descendants of Alexander's army, as Nuristanis and others have claimed: but it was equally difficult to see any other clear racial antecedent. Their bone structure was stronger than that of Pakistanis, but they lacked the aquiline features of Iranians. Neither did they have the almost Mediterranean looks of the Tadjiks nor the Mongolian characteristics of the Uzbeks.

Abdul Latif must have intuited my thoughts for he summed them up exactly: 'Nuristan is different: Nuristanis are different. Nobody understands them, and they don't understand anyone else. Do you, brother?' he said, turning to a villager standing a few feet away and speaking in rapid Dari. 'You're a lazy lot of men who don't even know how to harvest corn.' The man's eyebrows twitched but he said nothing in reply. 'You see, Abdul Baz? They don't understand anything.'

I thought it was an unwise assumption; Abdul Latif's condescending attitude towards the Nuristanis made me uncomfortable and I was glad when we left the village. But we had underestimated the effect of the past few days and our packs grew heavier and heavier; another couple of hours further on, when we reached the next village, we decided to go no further. We had eaten very little nourishing food for a while and it seemed better to gather strength for the journey ahead of us.

We made our way along sloping streets which led through a maze of wooden houses until we arrived at a simple one-roomed building perched on the side of a hill. Inside there were two small windows, high up in the wall facing the valley and a few, colourless remnants of carpet on the floor. This was the village mosque; the surrounding houses belonged to the mullah and his family.

We spent the afternoon in protracted negotiations for food. Hunger and fatigue shortened my temper and after a few hours my view of the Nuristanis had become decidedly uncomplimentary:

'The distressing effects of inbreeding all too obvious,' I wrote in my diary, '. . . low foreheads and a flickering vulpine light to their eyes.'

The mullah seemed particularly untrustworthy, but at last we managed to persuade him to sell us a chicken – at an exorbitant price. His son volunteered to prepare the meal and as he murmured a prayer to God and drew a knife across the chicken's throat I noticed the mullah watching the proceedings with a look of seraphic happiness. Later I saw his infant grandson, with bits of dried dung hanging from his locks, playing with the bloody chicken's head in the dust.

Eggs, after long discussion, proved to be unobtainable and our hopes of milk were dashed when we were told that the cow was lost in the mountains. Vegetables were also difficult to come by. On the way we had seen pods of maize drying on the roofs of houses, and the alleyways of the village were green with the tendrils of marrows, but in the end we could only obtain a handful of bullet-like tomatoes and a few onions. Even though we supplied our ingredients, a pot of chai took several hours to arrive.

It was difficult to assess whether our hosts were mean or simply poor, stupid or unable to understand us, lazy or disorientated by our sudden appearance, unfriendly to outsiders or just shy.

However, the situation became clearer when a Panjshiri, who happened to be living in the village, came to the mosque. He had been in the village for almost a year, but the distant way he was treated by the mullah and his family showed they still considered him an outsider. He asked eagerly for news of the Panjshir and his face grew solemn when he heard of the new offensive. That was why he had left the Panjshir, he told me. He couldn't bear the fighting any longer, otherwise he would return at once. It was a lonely life in the village; it was difficult to talk to his neighbours and their customs were different. But it was better than living in one of the refugee camps in Pakistan.

He was a sad, ineffectual fellow. Even though our two Panjshiri companions did their best to avoid talking with him, he was determined to attach himself to our little group, for the evening at least, and he took over the cooking of the chicken from the mullah's son. It took two hours of continuous boiling to cook the chicken and when it finally arrived in a bowl of boiling broth it was tough and stringy. We shared the meat with Abdul Latif and Shukur, while the gravy was appropriated by the mullah's son and the Panjshiri who mopped it up with handfuls of maize bread. Once or twice I caught the Panjshiri gazing at us with a look that was both passive and accusing and I thought guiltily of the division of the meat and the gravy, until I remembered the journey still to come.

As the evening wore on, the fleas began to bite and we persuaded the mullah to let us sleep outside on the flat roof of his house. The moon was a watery sphere of light and the silver shadows of the hills were drenched in stillness, but the beauty of the night was lost on us as we rubbed and scratched ourselves to sleep.

The following morning we made a late start and only travelled for an hour or so before we stopped for breakfast. The mosque where we drank chai was altogether more impressive than that of the previous village: it was a large wooden building with a portico of intricately carved pillars leading into a spacious room with large windows looking out over the mists of the valley. Somehow, Abdul Latif succeeded in getting a villager to bring us some milk to have with our tea and our morale soared. But when the time came for us to pay, a man with a brutal face and a tangle of creases between his eyes demanded two hundred afghanis for his services. Abdul Latif launched into a furious tirade:

'Such a price is robbery: ten times more than the price it should be. Even twenty afghanis is too expensive for what you have given us.' The Nuristani's shaggy upper lip curled:

'You have drunk and you must pay.'

'Your people call yourselves Muslims? You should be ashamed!'

The final price was settled at seventy afghanis, much to Abdul Latif's disgust, and on the way out of the village he talked contemptuously of the man's greed and impoliteness.

For the rest of the morning we travelled through a dramatic landscape of steep-wooded gorges: hand over hand down giddy cliffs and along precarious walkways made of slabs of stone, balanced on the branches of trees which had been wedged into the cracks between boulders on the edge of the river. Almost every bridge we came to was in a state of dangerous disrepair, and Abdul Latif shook his head disapprovingly:

'These Nuristanis are very lazy, they wait for travellers to mend their bridges rather than do the work themselves.'

Inwardly, I wondered whether their apparent laziness was more a disregard for strangers bordering on dislike. The few people we passed rarely spoke with us. Instead, they kept their stride and only acknowledged our presence with a sidelong glance. Although they seemed a somewhat morose people, their clothes were more colourful than those I had seen in other parts: the men wore shirts and trousers of pink or yellow or blue under dark, loosely fitting waistcoats and the women were dressed in dark red or purple veils, blouses and trousers of green or brown cotton. I wondered whether Nuristanis were naturally more fond of colour or whether, as Peter suggested, there had been only minor bombing in Nuristan, and the people had not experienced the need for less obtrusive colours.

The sun was blazingly hot. Peter was in sorry straits and each time we stopped to wait for him he took longer to catch up with us. We came into a broad valley with lush meadows on either side of a foaming grey river. A man was wading through the torrent with the waves up to his waist, peering down into the water around him. Then he raised his hands and cast a circlet of net weighted at the edges, tugged a string and hauled up a big, struggling fish. It looked so simple.

We lay down on the grass and watched him work his way to and fro upstream. Every seven or eight casts of the net he was successful. Whenever he caught a fish he would raise it to his mouth, bite it, then lob it with a fine, overarm throw, thirty or forty feet on to the further bank. I thought of the freezing water and the slippery surface of the rocks under his feet and remembered a haiku:

In the upper reaches of the Galaxy
a fisherman casts his net.

When he noticed us he waved and the next fish he caught was hurled, tumbling through the air, on to the grass beside us. In all, he caught over a dozen fish. Then he forded the river to where we were and stood smiling and dripping in front of us. By sign language Julian managed to congratulate the fisherman on his skill and he smiled with pleasure; then, after motioning us to stay, he waded back into the river. Once safely across, he walked along the bank picking up the fish and entered a small, two-storied, wood and mud-brick house. Twenty minutes later he reappeared carrying a cloth bundle and stepped once more into the water. In mid-stream he placed the bundle on his head, holding it in place with one hand, leaving the other hand free to maintain his balance.

He reached our side of the river safely and unwrapped the neatly folded bundle to reveal seven grilled trout and a handful of walnuts. It was a memorable meal and he brushed aside our attempts to pay him. We thanked him and continued on our way feeling far better disposed towards the people of Nuristan than we had been a few hours earlier.

Our journey took us through a series of picturesque valleys, which reminded me of Brecon, but I was rapidly losing interest in my surroundings. I had begun to run a fever: my legs seemed oddly disconnected from the rest of my body and I was panting in quick, shallow breaths. Even though it was late in the afternoon my skin was burning and rivulets of sweat stung the corners of my eyes. It occurred to me that I might have a mild form of sunstroke or even malaria. An hour later, the evening breeze began to cool my face and for a while I was more comfortable. But the wind had a deceptive chill to it: I felt colder and colder until my teeth started chattering and I had to wrap my petou closely around me. I thought of snow on the passes and decided to buy warmer clothing as soon as possible.

We arrived in the village of Gardwal at dusk. It was one of the larger villages in the area and even had a shop selling a surprisingly wide selection of goods. As well as the more usual items such as tea, sugar, salt, soap and matches, it also had other scarce, and useful, things such as powdered milk, bales of cloth, pots and pans, knives and axes and, best of all, a pile of third-hand clothes. We were running short of money so restricted ourselves to the absolute essentials. Peter and I bought a jumper, and Julian bought a petou. Each of us now had a pullover and a petou as protection from the cold of the 14,000 foot passes that lay ahead of us.

The village headman invited us to spend the night and took us to a house surrounded by trees. After laborious negotiations we succeeded in buying a chicken. However, the chicken had no intention of becoming soup and struggled free from the hands of its owner. We sat down in an adjoining room and tried to conduct a conversation with the headman while his son chased the squawking chicken round the kitchen. Outraged screeches rent the air followed by crashes, curses and alarmed cackling.

The headman placed a pinch of naswar under his tongue and feigned a dignified unawareness of the pandemonium going on between the rooms. The uproar increased to a terrible pitch: a sustained cacophony of force flinging itself against hard, physical objects, and blood-curdling screams of animal terror. An expression of mild annoyance flitted across the headman's face, but he did nothing, contenting himself with another pinch of naswar. Other members of the family joined the chase, and an anarchic dance of destruction went on in the kitchen until a horrible climax of shrill cries and a last despairing cluck. It had been a brave performance and would have taken the edge off our appetite – but for the three-hour wait which followed. When 'dinner' finally arrived we attacked the steaming rubbery chicken with a hungry vengeance.

After supper the headman left us and Abdul Latif and Shukur began whispering together in a corner. I could not understand what they were saying but their eyes were anxious and I saw them shake their heads in doubt or perplexity.

I asked Abdul Latif what the matter was. He leaned towards me and lowered his voice. 'I do not trust these people. While you were buying clothes some men asked us questions about the three foreigners. Did you have money? Did you have guns? I said it wasn't necessary for them to know such things. I thought they were bad men.'

I was disturbed by this news but Peter and Julian's unconcern reassured me.

'He's just nervous about being in a Nuristani village,' said Julian. 'I wouldn't worry about it. Anyway, even if he's right, there's nothing we can do.'

Some time later the village headman returned and we settled down for the night with the moonlight and the sound of the river at the open window. Almost immediately, the fleas began their night shift, but by now we had got used to them and we were soon asleep.

The sound of gunfire woke us: several rifle shots, followed by a burst of semi-automatic machine-gun fire. The village headman scrambled from his blankets, lit a lamp, took his rifle off a hook on the door and hurried outside. My heart was thumping and my tongue was dry.

Abdul Latif unclipped his pistol and sat on his bedding with his back against the wall. Peter and Julian displayed an admirable degree of sangfroid, not even bothering to raise their heads from their pillows. Shukur and I looked at one another nervously across the lamplight. For a quarter of an hour we waited but nothing further happened, and eventually Abdul Latif reached over and put out the lamp.

We made a late start the next morning. Shukur had decided to return to his family and we teased him about going back on his own. 'Careful where you sleep!' 'Don't travel after dark!' 'Don't let anyone know you're alone!'

Shukur smiled in a bemused way and mumbled something about having to help his brothers harvest more walnuts. We could only give him a modest sum of money for his labours but his eyes lit up with happy surprise, and he was still smiling when we bid him goodbye.

We took a path which led through orchards of apple trees. Abdul Latif and Julian set a good pace which Peter and I could not match: the effort to keep on walking showed in Peter's face, while I found even the gentlest climb made me pour with sweat. Our burdens were comparatively light, nevertheless they were too much for us, and as soon as we caught up with the others we decided to hire a donkey.

Abdul Latif shook his head gloomily: 'The Nuristanis do not have much use for horses or donkeys, and anyone who owns one is sure to charge a high price.' I told him that, in our present condition, we would not be able to reach the next village unless we had an animal to carry our kit. Resignedly, Abdul Latif made the necessary enquiries at a nearby house while we lay down on a sunny slope to watch some women in a meadow, cutting the long grass with sickles.

Just below us, a little stream ran through an orchard of apple trees: an old man was leading a pony along a path beside the water. A sharp, unintelligible scream rang out. The old man halted in mid-stride and raised his head to look in the direction of the sudden noise. In the middle of a cliff a window had been cut and an old woman was leaning out of it, her lined face ugly with rage. With another scream she launched into a shrill arpeggio of abuse, directed at the old man who gestured dismissively and shouted back at her until he coughed.

The old woman had more lung power, but she hurled her words with such venom that her voice kept disappearing in malevolent whistles. Her face vanished from the window and the next instant she was standing on the other side of the stream from the old man, waving her arms and shouting toothless cries. The old man shook in a tantrum of inarticulate rage. Other women came through the trees and stood on the same side of the river as the spitting crone, watching the drama. The violence of their emotions choked the couple completely and for a couple of minutes they could only click their tongues, hiss and yelp at one another. The argument ended as abruptly as it began: the crone suddenly rushed out of sight among the trees leaving the old man leaning against his pony, panting with exertion.

Meanwhile, Abdul Latif had managed to find a donkey whose owner agreed to our hiring it, provided that his son went with us. The owner was a hungry-looking brigand, sporting a thick beard and armed with an ineffectual-looking axe. I had noticed many Nuristanis carrying such axes, with long hafts and axe heads similar to Bronze Age types. Apart from stripping small things from branches and knocking people on the head from behind, it was difficult to see a purpose to them, other than as minor status symbols.

We agreed to the owner's son accompanying us, in spite of his outlandish looks. Dressed in a voluminous outfit of salmon-pink and orange, and wearing a dark red cap embroidered with gold threads, he looked like a pop star crossed with an ice-cream sundae. He had a soft, beardless face and his eyes were heavily streaked with *kohl*, not an unusual custom in Nuristan but, in his particular case, one which lent an additional frisson to his appearance. Abdul Latif regarded our new travelling companion with barely concealed distaste and pointedly avoided helping him saddle the donkey with our belongings.

Without the weight of our kit we made better progress and walked for several hours through hills forested with gnarled holly oak trees. There were many more women working in the fields than I had seen in other parts of Afghanistan. One group screamed like a busload of schoolgirls as we went past but we did not stop to find out whether their cries were welcoming or threatening; however, I noticed that our Nuristani guide had puffed out his chest and was grinning to himself. The cries faded into the maize fields on the edge of another village and we stopped for a rest in the cool interior of a mosque. Its tall ceiling was supported by well-finished wooden pillars, the walls had large windows set with panes of glass and, unlike many of the other mosques I had visited, the atmosphere was light and airy. I had not seen glass in a window for some time and I imagined the impression of wealth and splendour such a building would create in the mind of a shepherd from one of the more remote villages.

We ate some maize bread and drank some chai in a corner of the mosque while an old man instructed three small boys in the reading of the Qur'an: a labour of love, since it entailed teaching them the holy language of Arabic.

The old man read the *suras* to the three boys kneeling in a line in front of him. I watched one of them following the text with his finger but as the rhythmical tones of the old man's voice continued, the little boy's finger seemed to lose the rhythm of the sound of the words and began to trace a hesitant meander across the page.

Our departure was delayed for some time by the disappearance of our donkey. Our flamboyantly dressed guide, whom we had nick-named Pauline, was unconcerned, knowing that the animal would eventually find its way back home. Luckily we had removed our kit, but it was annoying and Peter mustered his energies for an argument. Pauline stood with a sulky expression while Abdul Latif did his best to communicate our feelings of displeasure; but something was lost in the translation and our threats to inform the local mujahedin commander had no effect. However, I managed to hint that, if he was an exemplary guide, we might show our gratitude by money in addition to the sum we had agreed with his father. Pauline smirked and shambled off into a field of maize. Half an hour later he re-emerged, leading the donkey, with an even broader grin on his face and I felt my earlier instincts towards the Nuristanis reawakening.

As we followed the bends of the river the rugged hills in front of us unfolded in a series of valleys of idyllic beauty. 'Nice countryside,' commented Peter. 'Pity about the people.'

Ever since the incident of the mule, Peter and Pauline had been engaged in a silent war of attrition: so far, Pauline was holding the upper hand. Difficulties occurred whenever the path narrowed and we had to walk in single file: immediately Pauline would lash at the donkey with a thick stick, driving it round the side of the path until he had overtaken the rest of us, then relax again to a leisurely ambling gait so that we had to shorten our paces to avoid bumping into him.

A few minutes later Peter and Pauline actually came to blows when Peter tried to reverse these tactics on the sulky youth, only to receive a smart prod in the back from Pauline's stick. Abdul Latif hurried between them and an uneasy truce ensued but Peter's thunderous looks and Pauline's camel-like expression cast a pall over the rest of the afternoon.

We were making for the village where we hoped to find an acquaintance of Peter's called Doctor Abdul Haq. For some time he had acted as Shah Massoud's second-in-command in the Panjshir and Peter had met him on several occasions. 'He's all right – speaks reasonable English considering he's learned most of it from books. Not so much of a military man, more of an intellectual. Likes talking about philosophy: a bit of a Qur'an-basher.'

The shadows of the mountains slipped into the valley, the evening breeze blew more coolly and my teeth began to chatter like castanets. The fever had returned and, by the time we entered the village of Pushal, I was quite ready to wrap myself in a petou and lie down on the nearest bit of open ground. We found a small group of mujahedin from the Panjshir who told us that Doctor Abdul Haq was expected to return the next day. It was welcome news for it meant that we might at least be able to get some medicine for Peter, since by now it was almost certain that he had contracted hepatitis. My illness was less easily recognisable, but the fever's cyclical nature suggested malaria.

Pauline sloped off to stay with a friend of his father's. The rest of us spent the night in the small upstairs room where the Panjshiris

were staying. On one of the walls someone had painted a painstakingly detailed picture of roses and tulips spilling in complicated
arabesques from a tiny vase. Next to it, a clumsily-drawn aeroplane
like a large ugly butterfly had been added with a shower of bombs
falling from its belly like misshapen pupae.

The next morning we met Dr Abdul Haq. He had fine features
and grey eyes and, dressed in a jersey, corduroy trousers and a tweed
jacket, he would have looked like a slightly absent-minded post-
graduate reader in philosophy or astrophysics. Instead he wore the
characteristic wool hat of the mujahedin and a combat jacket over a
cotton shirt and trousers. A twist of wool was pinned to the front of
his jacket.

Doctor Abdul Haq was a Sufi, although he did not specify which
order of Sufis he belonged to. His knowledge of western philosophy
was extensive and I had difficulty following his exegesis of Sufi
thought, which he illustrated with examples from Santayana and
Hegel.

He had recently married and was staying in a small house with his
young wife while he waited for further instructions from the Jamiat
Islami political headquarters in Peshawar. The middle of Nuristan
seemed an odd place for him to live, and the hunger with which he
asked us about politics and philosophy made me wonder whether
his Nuristani neighbours provided him with all the intellectual
stimulus that he required.

He looked sorrowfully down his nose at the fragments of maize
bread which we had eaten for breakfast.

'It is not the place I would choose to be: between the political
office in Peshawar and the battlefields of the Panjshir; but it is God's
will that I should be here – a man may follow the way of truth
anywhere.

'The inhabitants of Nuristan are mostly simple people who do not
understand the war in Afghanistan. All they see of the war are
groups of mujahedin travelling through, who demand food and
shelter and give almost nothing in return. Most of them wish to have
no part in the war and the Shuravi treat them as if they were neutral,
although they employ Khad agents among the local population. In
this valley there are several such men.'

We told him of the loss of our horses and equipment and he
advised us to wait in the village while he sent a messenger back to
the Panjshir to locate our belongings, adding that the journey there
and back would take at least a week.

'I would offer you horses and equipment if I could, but it is
impossible,' he apologised. 'I myself am waiting for money from

Peshawar. But I will find a room for you and you can stay there for a while. However, you must be careful: the Shuravi will know of your presence sooner than you think.'

After promising to bring us some medicine he got up and silently closed the door behind him. His presence had cast an indefinable melancholy on us and it was several minutes before one of us spoke.

'Bit of an odd fish,' said Julian. 'Difficult to see what he's really doing here.'

At midday we said goodbye to Abdul Latif and Pauline. We gave Abdul Latif a penknife in addition to the money we had promised him, in gratitude for all the bargaining he had done with the Nuristanis along the way. Pauline received a very modest bonus from Julian and myself, which he took with a shifty smile. Peter steadfastly refused to give him anything at all.

The room which Doctor Abdul Haq provided for us had a rammed earth floor, crumbling mud walls and two square windows just below the ceiling. Two Panjshiris were deputed to look after us: both were burly men with buccaneers' beards who seemed to be perpetually embracing one another. Their names were Mustapha and Rahman but almost immediately we renamed them Tweedledum and Tweedledee.

In the afternoon we were visited by a man of sixty in a grubby but expensive white turban, who was the owner of the room where we were staying. He had Uzbeki features and was always in a relentlessly good humour. He nodded enthusiastically when we asked whether we could buy eggs and cobs of maize and assured us they were both in plentiful supply. Hours later he told us, still with a sunny smile, that there were no eggs and the maize was not yet ripe.

'Tell him he's lying,' said Julian. 'There are fields of maize all over the place. As for eggs, knowing the Nuristanis, they probably can't find them.'

Tweedledum interrupted the discussion to tell us that he and Tweedledee were happy to organise meals for us.

'It is easier if you let us buy the food. Otherwise the Nuristanis will ask you for too much money. Even so, it is difficult to get many things: there isn't much meat – the Nuristanis will wait until an animal is almost dead before they kill it; no fish – they are too lazy to go fishing; and very few vegetables or cereals except maize bread. But you can eat as much maize bread as you like.' He turned to our host and explained our requests once more in slow and careful sentences. Once more he beamed his assent. Once more nothing happened. In the days that followed, the same sequence of hope, patience and despair occurred with such regularity that it became a ritual without which the day would have been somehow incomplete.

In the evening other villagers visited us, and sat watching us while we ate a meal of soup and maize bread. They said nothing during the entire time that they were with us. At times it seemed as if we were actors in a three-part play: Act I – three strangely dressed men eat a meal, one of them complains about his share of the soup, no dialogue; Act II – the same three men drink tea and one of them smokes a cigarette, some dialogue: Act III – a wireless is switched on and the men listen to it, no dialogue.

When the last of the Nuristanis was gone, Tweedledum showed us how to lock the door, by looping a piece of wire over a bent nail. As an extra precaution he suggested we should lean a large block of wood against the door.

'It won't stop anyone who wants to come in, but the sound will give you some warning.'

We thanked him for his kindness and turned out the lamp, but the blood lust of the Pushal fleas was so insatiable that we woke the next morning unrested, with blotchy, bad-tempered faces. After that we slept outside.

We began to slip into a state of near-catatonic boredom, enlivened at intervals by bouts of fever or expeditions to the nearby privy where a family of chickens looked up expectantly through the hole in the floor. The thought of chicken for supper began to lose its attraction.

Both Peter and I were too weakened to walk very far and most of the time we remained inside. The days passed uneventfully.

Sept. 12th Listened to the BBC World Service. Haunted by spectral menus and the prospect of a *bath*. The Nuristanis are appallingly lazy. Only women and children work in the fields: the men stroll around with their tiny axes like fasces which they tap against their legs and twirl like ungainly walking sticks. Apart from that they do nothing – except lie in an unconvincing way about money and distances. Perhaps the time it takes to sort out the truth of the situation fills the otherwise tedious vacuum of their lives. Talked with Julian about a journey he'd made with the salt traders of the Niger – glimpses of another world: a relief from the grimy claustrophobia of the room where we are staying.

Sept. 13th Fever cleared today. The women are harvesting the maize. The sun is still strong although there is an invisible shadow presaging the coming of autumn. No meat, just beans and potatoes. However, since we're not doing very much it probably doesn't matter. Doctor Abdul Haq comes in and talks of '*yaqin*' – Al Ghazali's doctrine of direct mystical knowledge, intuition, and the deficiencies of western ideologies. He also asks about our view of muj. strategy. Nuristanis watch us with mouths half-open.

Sept.14th Today I should have started work in the City. Deloused clothes in the morning.

Sept. 15th Fever again. Maize harvesting continues. Still negotiating for corn-on-the-cob. A Nuristani came in, a spectre of impoverished humanity: ignorance and unintelligence written deeply into a face frozen in an expression of horrified incomprehension-at-life. He watched us for half an hour without a word. Like energy-vampires, they take the charge off one's presence and then leave.

Sept. 16th The maize is almost harvested. Shadows shift across the mountains on the other side of the valley. Sounds of dinner (?) being chased and slaughtered. A child being swung in a hammock under the green shade of trees by the river. Helped Tweedledum and Tweedledee thresh corn.

Sept.17th Fever again. Apples cooked in gravy and maize bread for supper.

Sept.19th Day started with an argument over one teaspoonful of sugar. Peter: It's no good being some kind of Madonna with a bleeding heart. Self: Nor an Action-Man with a video camera. Julian: (*silence*). We are like sulky and voracious fetishes in a mud hut being placated with food offerings. Tweedledum and Tweedledee hugging and giggling like fourteen-year-old girls. 'He is my wife,' said Tweedledum with disarming openness. Listening to the Brandenburgs and watching a bright crescent moon rising over the mountains; a moment between East and West.

The next day Muhammad, Peter and Julian's interpreter, arrived. He was twenty-eight years old and the sun had bleached his hair, giving him a European appearance. He had acted as guide for Peter and Julian on their way into Afghanistan and they greeted each other warmly. We drank chai and he told us of his experiences during the previous weeks. He had been visiting his family when the offensive started but had managed to make his way back through the bombing to Safir Chir where he learned from Commander Kohzad of our departure. He had found some of Peter and Julian's equipment which he had transported by persuading some lapis traders to lend him their horses as far as Pushal. He had also brought a number of tins of Russian food which the Uzbeki had promised us. Our morale rose, although he brought sad news of my horse. During their stay in the village, the Soviets had shot all the livestock and horses they could find, including Freckle.

There was no reason for us to remain any longer in Pushal and we decided to set off the following day. As we travelled from village to village, through the valleys with their bright streams, fields of golden maize and orchards of apricot trees it was possible to imagine that one had stumbled into a wild garden of Eden whose people were miraculously preserved from the vileness of the twentieth century. Staying in a village for any length of time, one was drawn into another world of slow and subtle change, measurable by the colours of the corn and the height of the river, the rising of the sun and the setting of the moon; a different universe whose inhabitants welcomed us with fear and kindness. But gradually the poverty, the primitive conditions and the drab monotony of an existence with nothing but the basic necessities had become oppressive. I felt like a traveller from the future, imprisoned in a present that was also the past remembered from a previous life.

The night before we left I went outside and sat on the flat roof beside our room. The air was still and the trees and mountains seemed a shadowy picture of eternity; the very substance of a dream. It had been my dream too. God's fingerprints are everywhere.

13

Parun

The next morning, we spent several hours negotiating for more horses and drivers since the men who had brought Peter and Julian's equipment from Safir Chir were not prepared to make the journey to Pakistan. At last Doctor Abdul Haq located two men with horses who were willing to offer us their services as far as the border. One was a Nuristani called Hamid'allah, a tall, thin man with a sorrowful face who understood some Dari. His infant daughter was gravely ill, but he agreed to hire us his diminutive pony for the journey: he would wait for a couple more days until his daughter was out of danger, then he would start out after us. Surely, we said, he would have difficulty in catching up with us? Hamid'allah shook his head in disagreement.

'A pass that takes a foreigner twelve hours, an Afghan can do in six hours. A pass that takes an Afghan six hours, a man from Nuristan can do in three.'

Hearing Hamid'allah's speech, the other driver, who was a Tajik, scowled inscrutably. He was about fifty, with a foolish, weather-beaten face on top of a squat, wiry body. He was introduced as a mullah, although his appearance suggested it was merely a courtesy title. His name sounded something like 'Tarzan' and that is what we called him. His horse was a poor creature with sores on its belly, but apart from Hamid'allah's it was the only other one available.

We saddled the animals watched by Tweedledum, Tweedledee and an impassive crowd of villagers including Haji who at the last moment relented and sold us two chickens which we tied to one of the horses. Then, after thanking Doctor Abdul Haq for his kindness, we made our farewells and set off. We had made a late departure and so we travelled through the afternoon without a break until nightfall when we came to a cave, with a stone hut nearby. Inside it an old woman was splitting matchstick-sized splinters from a log, all of which she carefully placed, one by one, in a small, glowing nest of flames to boil some water for a pot of chai. Later I sat, wrapped in my petou, with a hot glass of chai in my hand, looking at her face in the light from the dying embers. It was impossible to guess her age;

the years had obliterated whatever beauty she may once have had. All that remained was the spirit in her eyes and the life in her gaunt, wrinkled limbs.

A man came in with a bundle of sticks which he placed by the fire. Instantly, the old woman began yammering and shrieking like a macaw. Her toothless gabbling was impossible to understand but she was clearly in an extremely bad temper. The man tried to stand his ground, but the violence of her attack was too much for him and he soon made a hasty retreat.

Later, lying in the cave, I listened to another interminable argument about meat and money in which I could hear the old woman taking a loud and prominent role. I had hardly got to sleep before I was woken by Muhammad telling me it was time to go. We loaded the horses in darkness and stumbled our way for several hours until the moon rose above the mountains and we stopped for a rest in a circle of open ground. Moonlight glittered in the crystals of frost covering the rocks and there was the sound of a stream trickling in the shadows.

We set off again and continued climbing as the sky paled. The mountains became distinct and we scanned their contours for the path that would lead us over the pass but a light sprinkling of snow had fallen and the track was invisible. However, Muhammad knew the way and we climbed up and up in the shadow of the mountains through a cold, lifeless terrain of boulders and pools of still, dark water. It was hard going: however deeply I inhaled my lungs seemed to need more and more air and I could feel the thudding of my heart in my chest. On the way we passed the stiff, frozen carcases of horses which had been abandoned; Tarzan's horse stumbled repeatedly, cutting its shins, and soon it was leaving a trail of blood on the stones of the path. Two men overtook us driving horses laden with lapis and we heard their curses and shouts echoing in the silence above us as they whipped and cajoled their animals up the pass.

Near the summit one of their horses missed its footing at the edge of the path and tumbled down a steep slope with a clatter of rocks and pebbles until it crashed against a boulder. It was still alive but too badly injured to get to its feet again. One of the lapis traders removed the saddle-bags full of the precious stones, placed them across his shoulders and staggered back up to the summit where he strapped the burden on to the remaining horse.

Tarzan and I were climbing the last few hundred feet of the pass when his horse also tripped and slid down a scree for twenty or thirty feet. We scrambled down after it and discovered, to our relief, that the wretched creature was not seriously injured. Once we had removed the baggage, Tarzan was able to coax the animal to its feet. Then we repositioned the load and a little later we reached the summit.

As we rested at the top my fever returned with a vengeance. Even though the sun was shining I was cold and shivering like a dog, so that Muhammad had to hold my arms steady in order to fit them into the sleeves of his combat jacket.

Hours later I began to sweat and, ignoring the others' warnings, I drank deeply whenever I found a pool or rivulet of water. The day clouded over and it began to snow in soft white flakes which drifted against my face and melted on my cheeks and forehead. My thoughts cleared and my pace grew firmer. Further down the pass we took shelter from the storm in a shepherd's hut and watched the mountains, framed in the doorway, vanish into a mass of grey snow clouds. Two shepherds appeared out of the snow and joined us in the little hut. They were both old men and their trousers were made of sacking. One of them was wearing spectacles.

Julian extracted some solid fuel tablets from the baggage and we cooked a few tins of Russian food. The contents were an unappetising mixture of barley and fragments of meat in congealed dripping. I used two twigs as chopsticks to push the stuff into my mouth, sluicing it down with mouthfuls of tepid tea, and gazed out at the winter landscape. The border was still more than a hundred miles away. If one of us became too sick to go on, we all knew the others could not wait for him. England seemed a long way away.

An hour later the clouds rolled back revealing the mountains transformed by newly fallen snow, sparkling in the sunlight. We set off again, down into a deep valley. On the way we met a group of several hundred mujahedin climbing the pass on their way back to Khunduz.

In England, if one accidentally catches the eye of a passer-by, there is usually an exchange of nervous glances: the first look ends abruptly as soon as eye contact is established, then there may be another, confirmatory look, to check whether the other has turned his gaze away; if he hasn't, it is only the third look which is directed to assessing the person's character. However, in Afghanistan, when two men pass one another, each will look into the other's eyes without embarrassment, and I studied the men's faces as they trudged past. Most of them were in their twenties, their expressions clear and I saw no trace of the false manliness which obscures and diminishes the character of young men in the West. The gruelling climb was written in the lines of fatigue on their faces and their teeth were bared with effort. Several of them were wearing rubber plimsolls and none had any waterproof clothing. The shepherd's hut was the only shelter for thirty or forty miles and, except for their petous, they would have no protection if they spent the night on the snow-covered pass. '*Manda nabashi* – May you not be tired,' they called out to us; '*Zenda bashi* – May you live,' we replied.

The path descended across a series of treeless ridges until it levelled out beside a broad shallow river. There was still several hours' journey to go until we reached the next village, the sun was already low over the mountains and so when we came to the ruins of a stone-built sheepfold we decided to stay the night there. After lighting a fire with the branches of some dead thorn bushes, we killed one of the two chickens which we had brought with us from Pushal. Unfortunately, there was not enough fuel to cook it properly and even jokes about smoked chicken could not disguise the taste of blood and the texture of raw, stringy sinews.

The next morning we made a leisurely start, since the horses were tired after crossing the pass, and we planned to go only as far as the next village of Kantiwar. At midday we encountered another, much larger group of mujahedin: two thousand Badakhshanis laden with guns and ammunition on their way into Afghanistan. Once again I noticed the effects of the journey in many of their faces but my attention was caught by one man in particular. He was on horse-back but, because he was too weak to hold on to the reins, his bony wrists had been tied to the pommel of the saddle. His face was skull-like and hollow with sickness and exhaustion, like a fasting Buddha. An aura of death surrounded him and, as the horse and its scarecrow burden swayed past, I superstitiously stepped back to avoid the wraithlike rider's shadow.

The path descended below the treeline and the air was sharp and fragrant with the smell of pines. Further down we came to fields of maize and corn, and arrived in Kantiwar by late afternoon. The houses were larger and more solidly built than others we had seen in Nuristan, and the inhabitants were better dressed. We sat down on a bench carved from the trunk of an enormous tree and waited while a small boy ran off to announce our arrival to the local mujahedin. Sometime later he returned with a youth of fifteen carrying a Kalashnikov, who led us to the mujahedin headquarters. He took us to an upstairs room and, after lighting a lamp and spreading out some rugs and pillows for us to sit down, hurried off to prepare a meal.

The room was bizarrely furnished: in one corner there was a chest with a selection of corroded torch batteries neatly arranged on top of it; a reproduction antique clock hung in silence above the chest.

By the door was a poster showing a mujahed kneeling with outstretched arms offering his bleeding head on a dish towards the word '*jehad*'.

Three older mujahedin joined us, and we shared a meal of bread dipped in a cheese broth. Peter had difficulty eating anything and I could feel my fever returning: I watched the others drinking chai and felt as if I was looking at them from a great distance through a powerful telescope. The scene was slipping out of focus into a blur of light and voices when suddenly the door was opened, the flame of the lamp leapt and flickered in a freezing gust of wind, and Hamid' allah stepped into the room. The cold air brought me to my senses and I heard the grief in his voice as he told us of the death of his daughter. She had died the day after our departure and the following day he had set out after us. I thought of him walking alone over the frozen pass and saw how sadness and the cold wind had pinched his features into a tragic caricature.

All night long I dreamed of climbing mountains and woke to find my clothes and blankets sodden with icy sweat. But a breakfast of milky tea with sugar and warm bread restored my spirits and I looked forward to the day's journey as we saddled the horses under a bright blue sky scattered with golden clouds.

Two burly mujahedin called Selim and Karim joined our party. Just as we were leaving the village they called out to us to wait while they visited a friend. We followed them inside and, at the far end of the room, we saw a young man lying on a couch.

'They want to say goodbye to him,' whispered Muhammad. 'He is very sick and they do not know if he will be alive when they return.' I asked him what kind of illness the man was suffering from and Muhammad gestured between his legs.

'His flesh is poisoned. Perhaps he will not be able to have children.'

While Selim teased his sick friend into a wan humour, Karim sewed a primitive loincloth from strips of a torn sheet. When it was complete, he presented it to the young man.

'There you are brother,' he said. 'Now you can be a bit more comfortable.'

Then the two of them clasped his hand and Muhammad beckoned us to leave.

A couple of hours later I was stricken by another bout of fever. The sky filled with clouds and it began to rain. Tarzan shook his head and muttered that unless his horse had some oats in the next village it would have to rest for several days to gather its strength. However, when we arrived in the next village of dripping adobe houses, we were told that there were no oats for sale. It was too wet to continue travelling, so we made our way to the village chaikhane. We opened the door and a familiar face greeted us: Massoud Khaleli, one of Jamiat Islami's political officers whom I had met in Peshawar, was sitting propped against a mound of cushions with a glass of chai in his hand. We sat down beside him, a fresh pot of chai was brought and we talked about our respective journeys. He was already expecting us: the day before a man had come with news of three foreigners on their way from the Panjshir. We also learned that two days after our departure helicopters had landed in Pushal and troops had asked the inhabitants whether they knew of any foreigners in the area.

'You've had an exciting trip!' he grinned. 'You're lucky, often nothing happens. Go in, take photographs, do interviews, make films, come out again. Simple. Anyway, from now on you have a nice easy walk back to Pakistan. I would like to be going with you, but I must go to the Panjshir to see Shah Massoud.'

I mentioned my suspicion that I might have contracted malaria and he gave me some tablets: 'What are you doing asking me for medicine?' he laughed. 'You've become like an Afghan!'

We talked while the water clattered down outside the open window and more pots of steaming chai were placed beside us. At last the rain stopped and, after arranging for a supply of oats for our horses, Massoud Khaleli bade us farewell. As we walked away I heard him call out to Muhammad: 'Don't let the foreigners argue with each other; they can be worse than old women!'

The meeting had boosted our morale considerably and we were in better spirits as we set off up the valley towards the next pass. We climbed for several hours through a forest of massive pines until we entered a layer of cloud. A fine drizzle drifted through the branches of the trees, deadening the sound of our voices, and I allowed myself to fall further behind the others until I lost touch with them completely. Towards sunset the path led out of the forest and on to a plateau of grassy hillocks and neatly cultivated fields on the edge of a village. It could almost have been a scene somewhere in the Swiss Alps, with the wide, shallow-eaved houses set against the backdrop of snow-covered peaks. I was fondly imagining the sound of cowbells when two vicious-looking dogs bounded out of some bushes at the side of the road, baring their fangs and growling at my approach. The mujahedin had taught me one thing at least: see a dog and pick up a stone, preferably a large one. With one eye on the dogs, I bent down and chose several stones. One of the dogs edged back but the other, a strangely coloured cur with wolfish features and a coat like a hearthrug, growled even more fiercely and with such loathing that it sounded almost human.

Seconds before I had been tottering along at the speed of a geriatric: suddenly I found new reserves of energy. The first stone missed, but it sent the nearest dog scurrying away to a less threatening distance. The second hit the wolf-like animal in the chest, knocking the air out of it in mid-growl, but the effect was only momentary. The next moment it turned on the missile, biting and snapping at the lump of rock as it rolled into a ditch. While it savaged the stone I slipped past, shaking with adrenalin, and a few minutes later I reached the comparative safety of the village.

A man led me to a room adjoining the village mosque where the others were already warming themselves beside a large wood-burning stove. Our Nuristani hosts were kind and generous. They knew little about the war and less about the outside world, asking me which part of Afghanistan I was from and exclaiming with surprise on hearing that I was from the same country as Peter and Julian. They provided us with pots of chai and rounds of maize bread. Later, when the meal was over, they brought in mounds of blankets and quilts for us to sleep on.

The next morning we woke early and, after a hurried cup of chai, we continued up the pass, arriving at the summit just in time to watch the sun unravel the threads of clouds from the surrounding peaks. We rested at the top for half an hour, then set off down the other side of the pass at such a good pace that we were well below the treeline by midday and within another couple of hours the path had levelled out beside a wide river flashing in the sunlight. But as the afternoon wore on the sky darkened, the mountains took on the colour of wet slate and it began to rain again. The first village we came upon was a sad collection of semi-derelict houses whose inhabitants would not, or could not, offer us shelter, but they told us of another village an hour's journey along the valley where there was a large mosque in which we would probably be able to stay the night.

We arrived at the next village as the light was fading and, after many frustrating enquiries, we were finally shown to the mosque. It was a large, gloomy building: the floor was covered with damp straw and the only light came from a solitary lamp hanging from a pillar in the antechamber to the main part of the mosque. A weird, twittering shadow of a man, who seemed to be the self-appointed guardian of the mosque, materialised and gestured towards a corner of the hall where we laid out our kit.

Our supplies of food were almost finished and so we decided to buy a sheep. The animal was slaughtered and skinned by the light of a fire while a crowd of small boys stood by entranced, with dreamy expressions on their faces, as if they were watching a display of magic. Selim and Karim took charge of the preparation and cooking while the rest of us retired to the mosque.

I could feel another bout of fever coming on, but the medicine which Massoud Khaleli had given me seemed to have had some effect and the temperature swing was less extreme than before. By now it was dusk and the interior of the mosque was like a Piranesi print, with massive pillars and archways vanishing into a dark ceiling. The only other person visible was the guardian of the mosque, pacing backwards and forwards in the dim light of the open door. At odd intervals he uttered a sharp cry, stopped in mid-stride and stood in statue-like silence, with his head tilted back on his shoulders and his arms stretched out in front of him. After a minute or so his arms dropped to his sides, his shoulders slumped and he walked rapidly to the nearest wall where he started whispering, gradually raising his voice until fragments of the prayer he was chanting became audible. Sometimes it was all over in a matter of minutes, but on several occasions he continued for quarter of an hour or more.

The man's agitated devotions became oppressive and taking one of Julian's tape cassettes at random, I switched on my Walkman, hoping to insulate myself from my surroundings. The sound of 'Frankie goes to Hollywood' began pounding in my head:

'When two tribes go to war, a point is all that you can score,
When two tribes go to war, a point is all that you can score.'

Silhouettes of men appeared at the doorway. The guardian of the mosque unhooked the lamp from the wall and went to greet them. They were carrying guns and anti-tank rockets, their clothes were sodden and they seemed to be in the last stages of exhaustion. The guardian hung the lamp by the door and I watched the men's faces pass through the light as they entered the mosque.

Most of them were young but as they blinked in the radiance of the lamp, they looked like children suddenly woken from a night-entangled chaos of sleep. The guardian greeted each of them in turn and motioned them towards the inner hall of the mosque. They obeyed him without question and stepped through the uneven glow into the shadows.

They came in twos and threes, and in groups of twenty or more. Some were stoop-shouldered and had deep hollows under their eyes; others carried themselves with confidence and their eyes were bright and alert. Some were laughing but many were haggard and unsmiling: the coward, the clown, the hero and the saint, all appeared in the light and vanished into the darkness. The seemingly endless flow of different faces was hypnotic; a dream-like procession of souls through the gates of existence into the shadow of God. The men with their rain-drenched turbans and petous were fruit-sellers, tailors, goat herds and shopkeepers but as mujahedin they had entered a realm of the spirit where belief engenders reality, where there is no other God but God and submission to the will of Allah is the acceptance of eternal life. In a holy war the warrior and the holy man are no longer entirely distinct: the holy man becomes war-like, the warrior becomes holy. The *jehad* is a continuous act of prayer and each mujahed is a man of God.

In all, over two hundred mujahedin took shelter in the mosque. Other lamps were lit and it was as if we were camping in a forest under a thick roof of branches through which no stars could penetrate. I switched off the tape and unhooked the earphones, expecting to hear a loud hubbub of voices; but there was only a low murmur. Then the guardian of the mosque resumed his prayers: the continuous urgent chirruping of his voice was at once pathetic and annoying. I decided to see how supper was coming along.

I found Selim and Karim in a room adjoining the mosque sitting beside a steaming cauldron. When I asked how long it would be before the meal was ready they replied with the calm unconcern of men who had already eaten their fill: Selim's face was glistening with fat and had a glassy expression of uncomfortable repletion. His movements were slow and laboured, and I noticed him loosening the cord of his trousers. Karim made a half-hearted show of urgency and managed to toss a few handfuls of sticks onto the fire before lapsing back against a pile of saddle-bags. 'Patience Abdul Baz, patience. It is almost cooked,' Karim lifted the lid of the cauldron and a cloud of meaty fragrance swirled into the room. 'Another half hour, Abdul Baz, and it will be ready.'

Karim noticed the look of disappointment on my face and, picking up a large spoon beside the fire, he dipped it into the seething pot. A few seconds later he lifted it from the steam, grumbling at the heat on his hands, and held it before me.

'*Bekhor! Bekhor!*' I was still entranced by the smell of mutton soup. '*Bekhor* – drink some, Abdul Baz!' Karim blew on the liquid to cool it and slowly handed me the spoon, careful not to spill any of its contents. It was hot and salty and after a few more spoonfuls I could feel the fat congealing on my lips and lining the inside of my stomach.

After what seemed an age, Karim finally decided the meat was cooked: there was enough for all the members of our group to eat well, and the meat that remained was tied into a square of cloth and pushed into our saddle-bags.

No one made any suggestion that we should share the food with the other men in the mosque, nor did our neighbours show any sign of envy or mutter among themselves about our selfishness. Whenever different companies of mujahedin met one another, the unwritten rule was that each group looked after itself. Only after the group's needs had been attended to would its members turn their attention to other groups or individuals.

But war and religion also created another, deeper fellowship. The men in our party and all the others in the mosque were brothers in the cause of Islam, under a sacred duty to protect the true religion from destruction at the hands of unbelievers. In this respect, differences of tribe and race were immaterial.

Then I recalled a clip of film, taken during the Great War, of turbanned soldiers conscripted from one of the corners of the British Empire. They had looked homesick and unsmiling, and at the time I wondered whether they could possibly have understood the conflict in which they were taking part: Muslims in a Christian war, Asiatic warriors on the battlefields of Europe. Had it all been a monstrous dream to them or had they somehow seen beyond the chaos and glimpsed the shadow of a reason why they were there? Had they been accepted by their fellow soldiers: men from the Gorbals of Glasgow and the plains of Arkansas, Welsh hill farmers and mechanics from Pittsburgh? Had they received the same kindness as I received from the mujahedin?

I asked Muhammad how he thought the mujahedin regarded the foreigners who came to report on the war. At first he gave the standard answer: 'Any man who helps us in the war against the Shuravi is our brother.'

'But is he a mujahed?'

'If he is a Muslim he is a mujahed. If he believes in God he is like a mujahed. If it is more important for him to fight the Shuravi than to fight for our religion, he is a friend. Those who come to this war because they can earn money from films and photographs may help us, but they do not interest us. Shah Massoud has been visited by many such reporters and does not wish to see any more of them.'

'What do the men here think of us?'

Muhammad looked into my eyes and laughed. 'Perhaps they think you are strange men who have a lot of money to buy a sheep.'

'Are they jealous?'

'No, but probably they are hungry.'

Karim and Selim had boiled some water on the embers of the fire and we sat in silence sipping hot, sweet chai. The fever had subsided but my thoughts were still careering from one image to another. Some of the men had stood up to perform their nemaz and as I watched them I felt as if I had tumbled into another person's body and was looking through the eyes of a stranger. I was tired of dirt and discomfort. 'I prefer the future, or whatever it is we love, to the past,' I wrote in my diary, '. . . withering of a romantic dream . . . six days to go to Pakistan.'

14

Papruk

The next morning we journeyed only for three or four hours, as far as the next village. We were approaching the Mom pass and did not wish to spend the night out on the mountain. We were welcomed by a party of villagers with faces like smiling, pink potatoes. The village mosque was a sizeable building, fronted with wooden panels which were embellished with lozenges and circles. A porch ran along the front of the mosque, supported by pillars of wood sculpted at top and bottom with what looked like rudimentary Ionic capitals. Whether the decoration was a survival of ancient Hellenistic influences or an independent style of Nuristani mosque architecture was impossible to tell. However, I preferred to think of the unevenly carved scrollwork as an artistic form which had indeed been transmitted from generation to generation for two thousand years, surviving the ebb and flow of Greece and Rome and the tide of Islam, preserved in a remote mountain village.

It was a grey, dreary day and to pass the time I read one of the few books we had with us: Le Carré's *A Small Town in Germany*. The sight of me reading intrigued my Nuristani neighbour who assumed I was studying a religious text and asked me to tell him of its contents. I translated the title for him. Then he asked me to place the book in his hands and for several minutes he sat in silence, slowly turning the pages from the end of the book to the beginning, and as I watched him I remembered the mysterious fascination of an unknown alphabet seen for the first time.

Towards evening another band of mujahedin arrived, on their way back from Pakistan. They were in good spirits and several of them tried to talk with us, but we had been asked the same questions too many times, and our answers were short and uncommunicative.

We woke while it was still dark and started towards the Mom pass. Gradually our party separated into single file and after a while I was walking alone. The colour of the sky turned from dark blue to grey and I felt icy twinges in my backbone which I had come to recognise as the first signs of the fever. For the next two hours I stomped along in a light-headed daze, almost unaware of my surroundings, until I came to a village where I found Muhammad and Julian sitting outside a chaikhane. One by one the others arrived and we had breakfast of nan and chai, but it was another half an hour before Peter appeared.

The track led on up a broad valley along the banks of a river. The sun was high in the sky over our shoulders and in front of us the snow-capped mountains of the Hindu Kush gathered themselves in the distance. In the early afternoon we arrived at the foot of the pass and we stopped for a meal, but when Julian undid the saddle-bags to take out the cloth-wrapped bundles of meat it was clear that some-one had tampered with them. It would have been pointless to challenge our travelling companions: no one would have admitted stealing the meat and suggestions of theft would only have caused unnecessary bad feeling.

When we set off again, we had not gone very far when Tarzan who was already some way behind called out to us that his horse could go no further.

'The horse is not well, it has not eaten enough food and its legs are cut and bruised. The pass will kill it,' he said, lashing at the creature's rump with a short whip. A brief tremor shook the horse's flank, but otherwise the animal did not move. Selim took a turn at whipping it, but with no more effect until Tarzan stopped him, and told us that neither he nor his horse would go any further. We had no choice but to remove the baggage and, after paying Tarzan for his services so far, we bade him farewell. Without another word, he shambled back down the hillside with his horse hobbling behind him and as we watched him disappear from sight Selim shook his head in disapproval.

'He is not a good man. This morning I found him eating meat. I know he had none of his own and I asked him where it was from. At first he said he bought it in one of the villages we passed through, but yesterday he told me he had no money. When I reminded him he changed his story and said that he had been given it.'

Selim called out to Hamid'allah to wait so that the baggage on the ground could be transferred to his horse. To our dismay, Hamid'allah refused. When Dr Abdul Haq had asked him to take Peter and Julian's equipment he had agreed, provided that the load was divided between two horses. Now he was being asked to take two loads for the same price. It was unfair. Besides, the double weight would be too much for his horse. Selim and Karim began to harangue him loudly: the horse was not carrying a large load, in fact it was less than originally agreed, and therefore he was being paid too much. Hamid'allah said nothing.

'The horse is not carrying enough, you fool!' shouted Karim. 'If you do not take the Englishmen's load you are cheating them. To refuse is dishonest.'

A look of anger entered Hamid'allah's eyes but still he said nothing.

'You don't understand, do you?' Selim bellowed into his face. 'How could you? All Nuristanis are dishonest!'

Without a word Hamid'allah turned away from them and began untying the ropes which attached the baggage to his horse. Seeing this, Selim and Karim launched into another tirade against the stupidity of all Nuristanis, and Hamid'allah in particular.

Muhammad and I managed to separate the knot of shouting men and the next quarter of an hour was spent smoothing Hamid'allah's ruffled pride, in between appeals for him to help us. For the love of Allah would he not agree to take some of the extra load at least? Surely he had a religious duty to help the traveller? Was not the traveller the beloved of God? As we were talking two men with a horse approached us. They were from the Panjshir, on their way back to Pakistan. Selim and Karim quickly set about persuading them to take some of the load. After a certain amount of bargaining they agreed. Hamid'allah eventually gave way to our entreaties and within another quarter of an hour the baggage had been divided between the two horses, loaded up and we were on our way again.

The pass rose steeply and we soon emerged above the treeline and came to a barren waste of boulders. The air was colder and the landscape filled me with a sense of impotent despair. The feeling was quite irrational but I gave way to it and every step I climbed my spirits sank lower and lower. My eyes were following the path at my feet when a noise further along the path in front of me made me raise my head. An old man with a staff was walking towards me. There was a large dog at his side. The old man was bent with age and the dog at his heels moved stiffly and its muzzle was covered with white hairs. Master and dog approached me with unconcern. I caught the old man's eye and we nodded to one another. I asked him whether there was any shelter further up the valley and he gestured up into the mountains like an amiable Old Testament prophet. Then we bade each other farewell. The meeting had dispelled my gloom and for the next hour or so I climbed steadily.

The sky was grey and the mountains on either side had a dark, sullen colour like frozen thunder clouds. I stopped beside a large boulder out of the reach of the wind to look back down the scree: Hamid'allah was a few hundred feet below me and I waited for him to catch up with me. If I was going to spend the night out on the pass

I preferred to have a companion. But instead of pausing to rest he continued up the pass and reluctantly I tagged on behind him: I had already resigned myself to a freezing night in the open when he shouted and pointed up the mountain; a thin thread of smoke was curling into the sky and coming closer we saw a herd of cattle and flocks of goats.

A small group of herdsmen had set up camp among several stone shelters which had been built under overhanging rocks or between groups of boulders. We searched around until we found a vacant shelter and then, while Hamid'allah unsaddled his pony, I went off to gather some firewood from a nearby thicket of stunted thorn-bushes. By the time I returned the others had arrived and we set about preparing supper from some of the few remaining tins of Russian food.

The surrounding cliffs dimmed in the twilight and an icy wind began to blow, tossing flecks of snow into the fire at the entrance to our shelter. We were joined by a Nuristani with a murderous-looking face, carrying a carbine on each shoulder. He had an air of careless cruelty and when the conversation turned to war he talked dismissively of the mujahedin.

'How can they win against the Shuravi? They don't even have enough food. If they don't sell their guns what will they eat?' He waved his hand towards the guns which he had placed against the wall. 'Guns are good business: I bought these from some men who were passing through my village; now I will take them to Doulat and sell them at a profit.'

I left our new companion talking to Hamid'allah and walked over towards the herdsmen who were gathered around a blazing fire. Across the flames I noticed the old man whom I had met earlier and when he saw me he beckoned to a boy who brought me a wooden bucket of yoghurt. As I raised it to my lips I heard the rustle of ice and felt a mouthful of watery crystals dissolve on my tongue.

There were no women, only men and boys. Some of them were busy milking cows, others stood beside the fire: small boys capered among them shouting at the cold or holding their hands into the flames and laughing at one another's bravery. Beside me a man squatted down to milk a cow with his head resting against its flank, stopping now and again to blow on his fingers. When he had finished he offered the milk to me: it was already half-chilled, and as I returned the empty bowl to him a young calf nuzzled against my petou.

I went back to the others and found Peter huddled in his sleeping bag suffering from a migraine; while Julian cursed and swore at the elements as he tried to cook supper over a few disintegrating embers. I mumbled something about too many cooks spoiling the broth and guiltily slipped away, back to the warmth of the shelter.

A small fire had been lit and I wrote my diary by the light of the flames while sparks and smoke leapt up through a hole in the roof into the stars. 'Decor v. Neolithic: one standing stone supporting an igloo arrangement of huge stone slabs. The uneasy thought that a small misalignment could send several tons crashing down on to one's cranium.' As I wrote the words, a stray sheep or goat wandered over the top of the shelter, dislodging thin trickles of dust and sand. A startled expression flitted across Hamid'allah's face and we laughed nervously at one another.

In all, seven of us packed ourselves into the shelter and did our best to sleep, Selim and Karim particularly showing a magnificent disregard for everyone else's comfort, thrusting their boots into people's faces and elbowing their neighbours away from the warmth of the fire. In the middle of the night another sprinkling of sand on my face woke me. A handful of embers was glowing faintly in the dark. Then a voice called my name and there was the sound of a match being struck. The nose and bared teeth of the Nuristani arms trader appeared: his eyes were in shadow.

'It is difficult to sleep,' he whispered. 'It is so cold.' The light dropped from his fingers and a black curtain of silence descended between us. I disliked the man and had no desire to talk to him.

'I will light the fire again,' he said. There was a crack as a stick broke and he placed a handful of twigs on the embers. He began to blow on the ghost of the hearth, a few soft points of light appeared, and I glimpsed the dim outlines of his face in the glow. At each breath the points of light coalesced and grew stronger until the twigs burst into flame. With his eyes screwed up against the smoke and his lips parted in a grimace of effort, he looked like a pantomime devil. But as the flames grew higher, the muscles of his face relaxed and his expression became less brutal so that I was sorry for my earlier churlish refusal to talk with him. He looked into the flames and I gazed at his face, trying to interpret the character starkly uncovered by the brightness of the fire. Was it a cruel face, or simply friendless? Or an ugly mask concealing an unimaginably different soul?

'Are you warmer now, Abdul Baz?' he said, raising his head slightly to look across the flames to where I was sitting. 'Would you like some chai?'

While we waited for the small, blackened teapot to boil, he told me in clumsy Dari how he would sell the two guns in Doulat. It was the third time in as many months that he had made the journey: on each occasion he traded guns or ammunition for goods which he took back to sell in his village. With luck he would be able to make one more journey before the snows covered the passes. It was easier than working in the fields and he earned more money. The Shuravi were unimportant. The people of Nuristan were free; since they had declared their independence the Shuravi no longer dared to interfere with them. The war in other parts of Afghanistan did not concern him sooner or later it would come to an end. In the meantime he was going to make as much money as he could.

One of the figures lying beside him turned over and muttered: 'Ask him where the guns come from.' The man gave no sign of having heard and I said nothing. Whether he had acquired the guns honestly or not was irrelevant. I no longer cared: the tin can of chai was warm in my fingers, it was enough.

The flames died down, the fire fell into a small heap of smoking embers and I pulled a flat stone from the side of the hearth to press against my stomach for warmth. Somewhere in the dark there was the reassuring sound of a man snoring. I was already half asleep.

A light sprinkling of snow had fallen during the night and the mountains were the colour of iron under a drab, sunless sky. There was no wind and the horses' breath pumped into the freezing air, coiling around the men as they fastened the baggage.

Just as we were about to go, one of the herdsmen hurried towards us with a wooden bucket of milk in his hands, which he offered to each of us in turn. Then we set off.

The track climbed abruptly and we came to patches of ice and snow. The sun was still hidden by the mountains and it was too cold to rest for more than a couple of minutes at a time; we were making reasonable progress towards the summit, but as we got higher our breathing became shallower and our steps grew shorter and shorter. The last few hundred feet were the worst. In places the path was almost non-existent, so that the drivers had to lash and kick their animals over boulders and outcrops of bare rock. Several times the horses slipped on the frost-covered surfaces and once, with a scraping and clattering of hooves, a horse fell to its knees, cutting itself badly. While the owner dragged the creature's head up, two of us did our best to lift the weight of its load and somehow the horse managed to stagger to its feet again. At last we reached the top of the pass, and the sun shone in our faces, but there was a cold wind blowing and we had to huddle in the shelter of a large rock to eat a few handfuls of bread and mulberries. The slopes on the other side of the pass had already been in sunlight for several hours and most of the snow had melted. The surrounding peaks were sharp and bright under a clear sky.

Already the war seemed far away. Each pass we crossed was like a vast door opening and closing behind us: on the other side, hidden by the mountains, the destruction of towns and villages and the bloody business of war continued.

But our thoughts were turning towards Pakistan and England.

'A cream tea,' said Julian. 'That's the first thing I'm going to have when I get back. A massive cream tea. Strawberry jam and dairy cakes and buttered scones and cream all over everything.'

Peter gave him a jaundiced look: 'You'll be lucky if you get that in Peshawar.'

'Then, when I've eaten that, I'll go out and have a Chinese meal.'

'For God's sake, Julian!'

'And a nice hot bath.'

'And a bed with clean sheets,' I added.

'Forget about the clean sheets,' muttered Peter. 'Just a bed would do me.'

'We ought to reach another village this evening,' said Julian. 'If you're lucky you might get a bed at the Nuristani Intercontinental.'

Peter's expression brightened: 'Yes, I'd forgotten about the Nuristan Intercontinental.'

I listened incredulously. An hotel! Immediately an improbable-looking building was taking shape in my imagination: a large two- or three-storey structure, a Nuristani imitation of a motel, built by some villager who had emigrated to the United States, earned his fortune and returned to create a monument to his wealth and culture. Perhaps, originally he had hoped to attract the richer, more adventurous tourists: hunters who wished to shoot the wild ibex or the wolf, or British botanists, the odd anthropologist, or even some German Orientalists. Then the war happened.

'What's the Nuristan Intercontinental?' I asked.

Peter and Julian's description of the hotel fuelled my expectations. On their way into Afghanistan they had stayed there and found it a bit primitive, but really quite comfortable. There were two or three beds to a room, showers, views over the valley and a limited menu whose special feature was apple crumble. Otherwise, the food had been an unexciting selection of mutton dishes, omelettes and chicken stews. Apparently, the owner of the hotel was able to keep going by catering to the needs of the journalists and television crews who passed through, on the way in or out of Afghanistan. Such people were overcharged by two or three times,

sometimes by as much as ten times. Mujahedin, by contrast, paid
only a nominal amount.

We hoisted our packs and started down a winding pathway into a
bare, sunlit valley. But my attention was focused on the Nuristan
Intercontinental; I could think of nothing else. A shower! Then
mutton stew and rice, followed by apple crumble. Then tea, with
milk and sugar, a cigarette or two, then bed. I hardly noticed the
landscape altering as we descended the pass: the patches of scrub
dotted here and there among the rocks, the tussocks of withered
grass and stunted thornbushes. But at some point I woke from my
dreams of luxury to see, further down the valley, a thread of smoke
above a small mud- and stone-built house. It was the first building
we had seen for almost two days and the group's spirits rose.
Karim and Selim laughed and joked with one another and our pace
quickened.

As we came closer we saw that Hamid'allah had stopped beside
the house and was lying on the groud, propped comfortably against
a pile of our baggage while his horse grazed some distance away.
Raising himself on his elbow he greeted us with a welcoming cry.

'Ho! Have you been sleeping on the way, or eating some food?
I've been here for an hour at least!' He was smiling and boasted
gently of the speed and strength of his horse.

'The men of Nuristan are used to the mountains and their horses
understand the ways of rocks and snow. Men who live on the plains
or in the cities hurry but they cannot catch up with us. We travel
further because we are mountain people.'

We sat in a field down the hill from the house, the occupants
remained inside and we did not disturb them. I was beginning to
understand how the constant passage of groups of mujahedin
imposed a difficult burden on the Nuristani villages. Provided the
harvests were sufficient and the livestock were healthy, their
delicately balanced economies were more or less self-sufficient. But
the people travelling back and forth between Afghanistan and
Pakistan, the mujahedin taking supplies in or the men accompanying their wives and families out to the refugee camps on the border,
threatened the villages with too many mouths to feed.

We cooked a couple of the tins of Russian food, but only Peter,
Julian and I ate it; the rest of the group refused to touch it.

'More fool they,' said Peter. 'Some of them think it's poisoned, or
else there's pork in it.'

Muhammad interrupted him.

'Not only those reasons. The meat is not halal: the animals have
not been killed in the correct way according to our religion. That is

why we cannot eat from any tins that contain Russian meat.'

Karim unfolded a bundle from his saddle-bag, and poured a mass of dried mulberries and walnuts onto a strip of cloth. Everyone helped themselves except for Hamid'allah. Even when he was invited to share the nuts and dried mulberries he refused. Instead he took a piece of maize bread from somewhere inside his long, brown waistcoat and pulled a few pieces from it, which he ate with slow, meditative jaw movements. Whether he was embarrassed to take food from a stranger in his own part of the country, or whether there was some other ill-feeling between the Panjshiris and himself, I did not know. But I noticed a curious mixture of humility and pride in his face and in his bearing, which I had not seen before.

We rested for an hour or so before setting off again. The path descended steeply. The stream of melt-water at the bottom of the valley became a mountain torrent, and as we entered the treeline the boom of falling water echoed up from the river below us. The sky had clouded over. The sides of the valley were wooded with ever-greens standing vertically from the rocky cliffs and their dark colours added to the sombre spirit of the landscape.

We met a large company of several hundred mujahedin coming up the valley and we stood to one side of the path since it was easier for us to interrupt our pace than for them. Some barely raised their eyes from the path under their feet, others looked up to exchange greetings.

'*Manda nabashi*. May you not be tired.' '*Zenda bashi*. May you be living.'

With a cry of joy, one of the men suddenly broke from the procession of figures and stepped towards Muhammad with his arms outstretched and a smile of recognition on his face. They put their hands on each other's shoulders and embraced, but their lips did not touch, and when they turned their heads to embrace again, only their beards grazed one another. The manner of their greeting reminded me of the ritual movements of birds, and their formality revealed a people close to the current of their hearts who knew the way to temper passion with reserve.

The man had known Muhammad in Peshawar. Now he was on his way to Baghlan. Muhammad told him that it would take them eight or nine hours at least to reach the top of the pass, and another three hours before the group came to any sort of shelter. His friend was unconcerned: a petou was enough and if it got too cold during the night he would continue walking by moonlight. But his expression grew solemn when Muhammad described the bombing of the Panjshir and he asked detailed questions about the positions of Soviet troops in the valley. Then they shook hands and, commending each other to the protection of God with the words '*Khoda hafiz*', they parted.

It was twilight by the time we arrived at Papruk. Julian pointed towards the Nuristan Intercontinental. A two-storey, wooden building jutted out over the edge of a cliff, suspended by a simple scaffolding of timbers hammered into the rock. Neighbouring houses had been built in equally precarious positions, so that the village looked as if it had grown out of the side of the mountain.

The owners of the Nuristan Intercontinental gave us a tepid welcome and directed us to a dim, low-ceilinged room with bare floorboards. There was a table in the middle of the room, surrounded by half a dozen dilapidated *charpoys* of different sizes, packed in tightly beside each other so that moving between them was almost impossible.

We then spent the next half an hour groping around in the deepening shadows, tying together the remaining strings of our *charpoys* so that they would support our weight. The standard of accommodation was lower than I had expected and I complained bitterly to Peter and Julian, who were unsympathetic.

'Can't think why there aren't any clean sheets – the laundry must be on strike.'

'We could go for a swim except the swimming pool's been closed for the winter.'

'They hope to have an indoor pool ready by next summer, though.'

'They might still have some apple crumble on the menu – what do you think, Peter?'

The room had grown quite dark. At last a lamp appeared at the doorway, held by a sullen-looking man who studied us for several seconds without saying anything, then entered the room and placed the lamp on the table. We clamoured impatiently for the chai which we had ordered long ago and the man nodded irritably, returning a few minutes later with a teapot and a collection of chipped tea-bowls and glasses.

The Nuristan Intercontinental was spartan, but it was more comfortable than many other places we had spent the night. Later, as I cautiously spread my weight over the cat's cradle of string and cord that was my *charpoy*, I realised that it was the first time I had lain on a bed since Ishkamesh. A bed. The luxury of a bed. Soon we would be in a world in which there were beds and tables, and chairs, and refrigerators, and televisions, and video cassette recorders, and cars, and compact discs, and swimming pools . . .

15

Peshawarak

The next morning we made a late start. The weather had cleared and the sun was already above the mountains. The air was still cool in the depths of the valley, and the light shone through the branches of the trees, stencilling their shadows on the mists. I soon lost touch with the others and for several hours I walked alone.

The path, which had been twisting and turning downhill continuously, began to level out and some way further on it emerged by the side of a dirt track. I was unsure which direction to take and for some time I looked around in vain for a familiar bootmark. At last I found an arrow drawn in the dust pointing to the left and a little later I caught up with Peter and Julian, sunning themselves by the side of the road. For some reason the sight of them annoyed me intensely so that I could barely manage to say hello as I slumped down beside them.

The river glittered in front of us. On the other side some boys were shaking the branches of a tree; others unwound their turbans and filled them with the fallen fruit. One of them called out to us across the rushing waters: the next moment a missile flashed out of the sun, hitting the cliff above our heads and an apricot landed on the pebbles beside us. The skin of the fruit was dusty and the flesh was broken, exposing the almond-shaped stone. A bombardment of apricots followed, and we dodged to and fro trying to catch them before they hit the ground. In all, we had three or four apricots apiece. The ones we caught were warm with the sun; others fell in the dust and after we had washed them in the river, they were chilled by the icy water.

We shouted and waved our thanks to the figures on the other bank and continued on our way.

We passed fields bordered by irrigation channels and further on we came to a village. Outside one of the buildings, a group of men were sitting at tables, drinking chai in the shade of a walnut tree; horses were tethered among some bushes on the edge of a field. The others had arrived before us and were talking to members of a band of mujahedin who were on their way into Afghanistan. There was not enough room for us all to sit down at the same table, so I joined Peter and Julian at a table nearby.

A man brought a tray of chai and Julian filled our glasses. The sight triggered the image of another table, dappled with sunlight, somewhere in Switzerland. Then I noticed how the tables and chairs had separated us into different groups: Englishmen and Afghans, Afghans and foreigners. A gulf was opening within me: between one world where men were reckoned by their piety and devotion to God and another world where men were valued like cattle and paid for with pieces of paper. Here a company of men, twenty or thirty strong, might kneel on the ground at sunset and pray towards Mecca; there men and women might sit at darkened tables and avoid each other's eyes across the candlelight.

Leaving a country is like dying: we leave a world for an indefinite future. But as the recollection of all that I had left behind in England faded, I realised how much I would be leaving in Afghanistan.

We remained at the chaikhane for an hour or two. The men who were going into Afghanistan had already heard of the offensive in the Panjshir, but they were eager for more detailed news. They had been in Pakistan since the late spring and as they listened to Muhammad's replies their faces changed. I saw how they had almost forgotten the reality of the war and were only now again awakening to its dream-like horror.

While they talked I smoked a cigarette and read the remaining chapters of the Le Carré novel. Then we bought some extra loaves of nan and a wedge of goat's cheese, and set off.

As the afternoon wore on, the sky dulled to a colourless glow suspended over the mountains. On the way a large group of Badakhshanis caught up with us: they were travelling faster than we were and one by one began to overtake us. The path was narrow and I could sense the frustration of the men behind me as their pace shortened, waiting for an opportunity to get past. They grew impatient, and when the pull of their collective momentum grew too strong, they scrambled over the rocks on either side of the path to catch up with the rest of their number. I left the path and watched them go by: many had faces that were almost Mongolian and some of them looked barely seventeen years old.

We stopped at the outskirts of Doulat. Here we had to be careful. We were about to enter the capital of the country of Nuristan. The government of Nuristan, the government of Ruritania, the government of never-never land: the thought-association was almost irresistible. But Peter was cautious about entering the town.

'One of the government's main activities has been setting up

check-points. Sometimes they ask for taxes. If the mujahedin don't
have any money the Nuristanis make them pay in kind: guns, for
example. They get weapons which they don't have any real use for:
anti-aircraft guns, even anti-tank rockets – as if you could get a tank
in here. The weapons are more like status symbols. The problem is
they're not going where they're most needed.

'If they find out we're foreigners it might give them an excuse to
search the baggage and take whatever they want.'

Luckily, the group of Badakhshanis had overloaded the bureau-
cratic resources of Doulat: an authoritative hand waved us on from
a window and we sauntered past, leaving a long line of Badakhshanis sitting glumly outside the Nuristani government tax office.

An hour later, we came to a river, just as dusk was falling. There
was a rudimentary sentry box before the bridge but there were no
guards and we walked across unchallenged. At last we arrived at a
place where we were able to spend the night. The floor of the room
was packed earth covered with straw and a couple of tattered
blankets; the walls were bare except for a small, shuttered window
which opened on to the twilit river. While we waited for supper to
be prepared Muhammad, Selim and Karim asked us what we
thought of the mujahedin.

'They need training,' said Peter. 'It's ridiculous sending them
weapons they don't know how to use. A complete waste. I've seen
men shoot half a dozen mortars at a target without even adjusting
the range finder.'

'But from what I can see the mujahedin are getting more organised,' added Julian. 'There's a bit more communication between
the commanders now.'

'They're lazy though. Some of them don't bother to harvest food
when they have the opportunity: they just walk around showing off
their guns and pistols to one another, and talking a lot of nonsense.
They've got to realise it's not just a *jehad* where they all pull a trigger
for the sake of Allah and go to heaven when they step on a mine. It's
a war: they've got to act more like soldiers.'

'It takes time,' replied Muhammad. 'Already many commanders
know what you say. But men do not become soldiers in a day.
Besides, there are other things which are more important for them:
din (religion), *azadi* (freedom). It is difficult to walk together in lines
counting numbers when you want to fight the enemy.'

'What do you think of the Russians?' I asked.

Selim entered the conversation: 'They are our enemies and we
must kill them. But we know that there are Russians who do believe
in God: their war is not with us and our war is not with them. We are

fighting against the traitors who wish to give our country into the hands of Russia. We are fighting against men who forget their God for the sake of the things of this world.'

A man appeared with a tray of rice and nan loaves. The talk subsided as we squeezed the rice between our fingers and pushed it conscientiously into our mouths, only stopping to brush a stray grain of rice from our beards, or to drink a mouthful of cold water from a communal cup. But when the meal was over and a pot of chai had arrived, we resumed the conversation.

'It is very difficult for foreigners to understand this war,' said Karim. 'They see it through their eyes; they cannot see it through our eyes. Americans want to make difficulties for Russia more than they want to help men who are making the *jehad*. The people of the West think politics are more important than religion. They do not understand Islam.'

Peter and Julian were silent and I considered the effect of his words. Belief can unite; it can also divide. Saddened, I saw how that the strength of Karim's belief in some way excluded us from his universe – we were denied the full status of brotherhood, we were unrelated: like creatures of a distant star receding into the past or the future. I wanted to preserve the link between us so I asked him why we, as Westerners, could not understand Islam.

'Because you believe God had a son and that man was God. For us, such thoughts are *kofr* – irreligious. But because you believe in one God we respect your faith. Muslims, Christians and Jews all honour the prophet Ibrahim; Muslims and Christians honour the prophet Hazerat Issah; but only Muslims honour Muhammad, blessed be his name.'

I translated a line of a song I remembered: 'One light, light that is one though the lamps be many', and Karim asked whether it was a verse from the book of my religion. Then he asked to see my Bible and turned the pages carefully until he came to a bookmark. It was a photograph of the crucifix which spoke to St Francis of Assisi.

'Is this your God?' asked Karim, pointing to the photograph. I said that it was Hazerat Issah. Selim nodded and gently replaced the card between the pages of the Bible. Once again we were united in the unknowability of each other's God.

We laid out our blankets and bedding for the night. Selim and Karim talked while the rest of us lay down to sleep. Then they too wrapped themselves in their blankets and Selim extinguished the lamp. Later, we heard the sounds of men arriving in the darkness and their voices calling to one another as the owner of the house directed them to another part of the building. Then there was only the sound of the river outside the window, interrupted once or twice by a soft curse and a rustling of blankets as one or other of us discovered another fleabite.

We woke early the next morning and loaded the animals under a sky of clouded stars. Then we took a path along the river which we had crossed the night before and did not stop to rest until an hour or so after sunrise. Mist still lay over the closely cropped fields and our footsteps rustled in the swathes of fallen leaves under the walnut trees. We stopped under one of the trees and hurled rocks into the branches to dislodge the walnuts, several times almost braining one or other of us as the rocks bounced back down to earth again.

At midday we stopped at the mouth of the valley which led up to the Peshawarak Pass, and ate the remaining nan loaves and cheese. As we finished the meal two men came up the path behind us. They did not stop to talk for long, but told us that they were the first in a group of over a thousand men from Badakhshan, who were on their way to Pakistan. While we prepared the horses, a steady flow of men passed us. Some carried rifles or Kalashnikovs, others had staffs and many were empty-handed. We did not want to be caught behind the Badakhshanis' pack animals, which we knew would be bringing up the rear, so one by one we hurried into the line of men walking past. Their pace hardly altered as relentlessly they strode up the zig-zagging paths of stone and shale. The sun was shining on our backs and our shadows went in front of us up the mountain. My mouth was dry and when I tried to spit out some naswar from under my tongue the spittle stuck to my lips and caught in my beard. I was sweating and knew I had to rest. The Badakhshani who had been following me stopped too. His forehead was a fiery bronze colour and beads of sweat trickled from the sides of his turban. He thrust his hand into one of the pockets of his waistcoat and pulled out a handful of boiled sweets which he gave to me: they were wrapped in clear paper, made in Pakistan and traded across the border. We each unwrapped a sweet and stood sucking them in silence. Then he pulled an aluminium bangle from his wrist and gave it to me. It was engraved with the names of the Prophet, Ali, Fatimah, Hosein and other saints. We set off again.

Clouds rolled across the sun and our shadows disappeared. At first it was a relief not to feel the burden of the sun's heat on our shoulders, but soon our sweat began to chill and we wrapped our petous tightly around us. The light was fading but it was not yet dark and mists and vapour were drifting down off the top of the pass. There was a flurry of snowflakes and a sharp spattering of sleet. I looked up at the slopes above us. Hundreds of men were moving in an uneven line across the contours of the mountain towards the mists, like a doom-painting come to life with the souls of mankind passing one by one into the clouds of eternity. The sight was like a great stone placed in my arms and my strength seemed suddenly to leave my body. I was on the brink of another existence, watching the workings of an unknown universe: life in a constant state of war with creation, life against rock, life against mountain, life against darkness, life against life. Hamid'allah's voice called my name out of the twilight.

'Abdul Baz, Abdul Baz. *Manda nabashi!*'

He was standing by the side of the road, with a thin petou hanging from his shoulders and his hands folded into the insides of his waistcoat. He looked cold and miserable and when we shook hands his fingers felt icy.

'It is too late to cross the pass. Where are the others, Abdul?' he asked, 'Have you seen them?' His face lengthened when I told him that I had not seen any of them for several hours.

'We must find some shelter before it is too dark.' He frowned. 'It will snow tonight.'

We set off up the path again: my knees stiffened and I had to stamp my legs to keep up with Hamid'allah's slow, effortless stride.

We came over a ridge and saw the lights of fires and columns of smoke rising in pale shapes against the shadow of a huge cliff. Here and there among the boulders on the scree at the base of the cliff were roofless stone shelters with groups of men crouching inside. We walked among them for a while until we came to a shelter which was so decrepit that no one had laid claim to it. Three angular rocks had been propped together and the gaps between them had been loosely filled with stones. In front of them, a shallow ditch had been scratched among the pebbles as added protection from the wind.

'Let us be here,' said Hamid'allah. 'It is a good place.'

While he unsaddled the pony, I wandered over to where the lights of fires were flickering in the darkness. A man called out to me from one of the shelters and, shielding my eyes against the glare of the flames, I recognised the face of the man who had given me the bracelet. He beckoned me in to join the circle of men gathered round the fire and made a space for me to sit beside him. They had collected a supply of branches and withered roots of dead thorn-bushes to make a cheerful blaze, and the flames leapt wildly to and fro as the wind blew at the walls of the shelter. My neighbours were all from the same town in Badakhshan. There were about a dozen altogether; most of them were young, hardly into their twenties, and they laughed and joked and mocked each other's shyness or stupidity as we talked. The man next to me was slightly older than the rest. His name was Muhammad; he was twenty-eight years old and the year before had completed his studies at the madreseh to become a mullah.

While we were three foreigners travelling together, Peter, Julian and I had made a separate world which was almost impervious to the spirit of friendship which greeted a single traveller. Now that I was alone again communication was more direct. What we lacked in language we made up in friendship. Muhammad brought out a parcel of raisins and walnuts and I handed round the contents of my naswar pouch. Someone asked whether I had a pot: they had chai, but nothing to boil it in. I remembered the clanking black metal teapot attached to Hamid'allah's saddle. Reluctantly I left the warmth of the fire and trudged back to find Hamid'allah hunkered down in the ditch with his horse tethered to the rocks. He was so cold that it took several attempts before I finally succeeded in making myself understood. He bent over the saddle-bags and, after fumbling for a while, produced the teapot, a handful of sugar wrapped in paper, and the last remaining tin of Russian food.

Hamid'allah and I returned to the welcoming ring of firelit faces. At Muhammad's request, one of the youths fetched some water from a nearby stream and then we waited for the pot to boil. Someone produced some hashish and several smouldering cigarettes were passed around. Muhammad looked on at the proceedings with a tolerant eye.

'Too much *charas* is not good, but sometimes a little is good. It makes men happy and they forget the cold.'

One of the youths started singing and the others clapped in time to the rhythm, sustaining the beat when he was unable to improvise the words quickly enough, and chanting enthusiastically whenever the song returned to the chorus. I could not understand the words of the song, but Muhammad told me it was a description of their journey from their homes in Badakhshan to where we were now, on the last pass before Pakistan. In return I sang a couple of verses of 'the British Grenadiers' and Muhammad asked me whether it was a song of love or war. Then I sang a Bob Dylan song and when I had finished Muhammad nodded his head as if in agreement. 'That I know is a love song,' he said, and we were both silent.

The wind had dropped and the sky had begun to clear: stars shone through torn skeins of cloud, silent and luminous in the light of the crescent moon.

I looked from the hot red blaze of flames to the cool brilliance in the sky and realised that I did not know the name of the moon in its first quarter. Muhammad was drowsy from the heat of the fire but as he gazed at the bright crescent he remembered: '*Helal e nou*,' he said, 'when the moon is growing.'

Some of the men got up from the fire and lay down to sleep on the frozen ground. Others fell asleep where they were, pillowing their heads on each others' shoulders. Muhammad and I talked but we were both tired, our thoughts were slow and our sentences ended in longer and longer silences. It was my last night in Afghanistan; the journey was almost over.

I thought of the Professor sitting in the vineyard, and I knew I would remember his kindness and friendship. Other memories followed: a line of hills at sunset; a man praying; a bowl of rice in the twilight of a mosque; Rahim; bodies stretched out in the rubble of a garden; a bright river; a little girl stepping across a scree of rocks and ice; a smoke-blackened wall; a man carefully rubbing the bony flanks of his horse with a ragged cloth; Mustapha Khan; a handful of dried apricots on a dusty carpet; a young man lying on a bed in the light of a window; a grey mountain pass; the firelit forms of sleeping men.

The silence of the moon and stars above us, and the stillness of the night were like the height and depth of that hidden world where truth may pierce the heart and change the nature of the traveller to pilgrim. The tops of the mountains were just visible with a light covering of snow gleaming on their peaks. Muhammad was asleep.

The fire was out but the moon was still high in the sky as we prepared for the climb to the top of the pass. Scores of men and pack animals were already on the move and I soon lost contact with Hamid'allah and the others in the darkness. We climbed higher and as the sky grew pale I could see the final step of the mountain.

A massive cliff of rock stood over a barren plateau of frost-covered boulders. A thread of moving figures stretched from the base of the cliff up an invisible pathway towards a cleft between the peaks. I followed slowly in their footsteps.

The path was in shadow all the way up. Near the summit I stopped to look back at the mountains behind me. The snow-covered peaks were glowing in the early dawn. For the first time I saw their beauty; they seemed almost feminine and I remembered the company of women.

At the top of the pass I leaned against a rock. A shadow stretched diagonally across the path: it seemed as good a frontier as any, and I stepped forwards, under a sickle moon, towards the rising sun.

Epilogue

The rest of the party with whom I had been travelling crossed safely into Pakistan and, after a brief period of detention by the Pakistan border police, we made our way together as far as Chitral. From there, Peter, Julian and I went on to Peshawar where we parted company.

In mid-October I flew back to England. Within a week I entered hospital with hepatitis and was unable to complete the article on the people's war as I had originally planned. Three months later I began to write this book.

Glossary

AFGHANI a unit of currency. There are approximately 100 afghanis to one pound sterling

AHL E KETAB People of the Book. The phrase is used to describe those who adhere to the monotheistic religions of Islam, Christianity, Judaism and Zoroastrianism

ALLAH. AKBAR God is great. The initial sentence of the *azan*, the call to prayer

ALOU a plum

AYATOLLAH leading religious figure; the title of a mullah who has attained
the degree of authority to rule on matters of theology

AZADI freedom, liberty

AZIZ beloved

BARADAR brother, often used as a term of friendship or affection

BATEN what is within. Sometimes used to refer to the mind or the heart and thus, the inner meaning

BAZ falcon

BEHESHT Paradise, Heaven

BEKHOR eat (imperative)

BIADAB impolite (*bi* – without, *adab* – courtesy)

BISMILLAH in the name of God. The word is often used by pious Muslims when they begin or complete an action or prayer

BIZHRA coward (literally without heart)

BOROU BEKHEIR go with a blessing. A joyous shout at the beginning of a journey

BURACH name of the wonderful creature on which the Prophet Muhammad ascended to the Seventh Heaven on the night of the *miraj*

BUT-PERAST idol worshipper. *But* derives from the word Buddha. During the early years of Islam, Buddhist sculptures and figurines were to be found in the north-eastern part of Afghanistan. Later the word *but* acquired another meaning in Persian poetry and was used to describe the object of the poet's desire and affections. This in turn became one of the many words used by Sufi poets to refer to the Beloved

CARAVAN group of travellers or merchants who journey together for safety

CARAVANSERAI inn at which travellers or caravans lodge for the night

CHADOR veil worn by many Muslim women. When a woman wears the chador it is supposed to spare her the discomfort of being looked at by men as a sexual object. However, it is more unfavourably perceived in the West as a means by which men can protect what they consider 'their property' from others

CHAI tea, drunk without milk, but often taken with a mound of sugar at the bottom of the glass

CHAIKHANE tea-house or tea-stall

CHAPAN silk robe, often presented as a token of respect

CHARAS hashish, a substance derived from the hemp plant. Among Afghans who have had dealings with Westerners the word 'hashish' is also used

CHARPOY wooden framed bed with a network of cords strung together, acting as a support

DEIWANEH mad or foolish. Philologically the word is related to the word 'divine'. In Sufi terminology it is sometimes used to refer to one who is intoxicated with divine love

DIN religion, faith

DUSHMAN enemy

ENSANIAT mankind, humanity

FÁNA dying-to-self, passing away into God, annihilation in God. A Sufi term which, according to some authorities represents the final stage of the soul's journey towards God

FAZ'L excellent, virtuous

HAFIZ protector. Used in the phrase *khoda hafiz* – God protect (you): *hafiz* is also an honorific given, to one who has learned the Qur'an by heart; the name of a Persian poet, 1325–1390

HAJ the pilgrimage to Mecca, one of the duties of all pious Muslims

HAJI a pilgrim to Mecca: the word *haji* is also used as an honorific for one who has made the pilgrimage to Mecca

HALAL lawful, permitted according to religious law

HAMMAM bath-house, usually a series of interconnecting rooms of varying temperatures. Occasionally the *hammam* is used as a metaphor by poets to describe the various stages of existence

HARAKAT movement; name of one of the mujahedin factions

HARAM forbidden by the precepts of Islam

HAZERAT highness, excellency: term of respect preceding the name of a king or prophet

HELAL E NOU the moon in its first quarter

HESB ISLAMI Hesb-faction: one of the Mujahedin factions

IBLIS the Devil, Satan

INJIL Gospels, the New Testament

INSHA'ALLAH if God wills; may it please God

ISSAH Jesus

ISLAM submission to the will of Allah; the name of the Muslim religion

JAMIAT ISLAMI Jamiat — community: name of one of the mujahedin factions

JAN soul. Often used in conversation as a term of special affection

JAN E JOUR a greeting

JANG war

JAVANMARDI manliness, chivalry

JEHAD exertion in the way of God, holy war

JOUR HASTI a greeting

KA 'ABA structure of blue grey stone in Mecca. In one corner is set the black stone, the *qibleh*. It is towards the *qibleh* that all Muslims turn when they perform their prayers

KAFIR unbeliever, a pagan, an infidel. A term which refers to any atheist or
polytheist

KOFR irreligion, blasphemy

KARGAH work place; mujahedin base

KEBAB portions of roasted meat

KETAB book

KHAD name of the Afghan State Police or agents

KHATARNAK dangerous

KHERAB destruction, ruin, desolation

KHEZR A prophet. According to some traditions Khezr discovered the Water of Life, of which he drank and thereby became immortal. Other traditions assert that his soul has known many forms. Recognisable by his green robes, he appears to Sufis and other seekers after Truth, to whom he reveals the secrets of the hidden world

Note: the account of Khezr in Chapter 10 is as I understood at the time and afterwards recorded. It was only much later that I recognised the story as a version of Sura 18 of the Qur'an. Variations between the two may be ascribed to the story-teller in the cave, (who was narrating the story in Dari, rather than the Arabic of the Qur'an), my own imperfect understanding of the language, and the period of time which elapsed before I wrote the account

KHODA HAFIZ *Khoda* – God, *hafiz* – protector: said when bidding goodbye

KOWK small, quail-like bird

KOJAH where?

KOHL powdered antimony used by both men and women for darkening the eyelids. It serves a twofold purpose: as a cosmetic, and to protect the eyes from the glare of the sun

KUN FA YAKUN Be and it was; become! and so it became (Sura 36 of the Qur'an)

LA ILAHA ILLA LAHU There is no God but God

LAKH One hundred thousand

MADRASEH theological college

MANDA NABASHI May you not be tired: a greeting

MARIZ sick

MAULAWI an honorific meaning lord or master, often used among Sufis

MECCAH birthplace of the Prophet Muhammad, in which there is the Ka'aba. The holiest city in the world of Islam

MEHMAN guest

MEHRAB prayer niche in the mosque, oriented towards Mecca

MOHAJER refugee, fugitive

MOSA FER traveller

MUEZZIN one who calls the people to prayer

MUJAHED one who strives in the way of God, a champion of liberty, one who fights for his religion in the *jehad*

MUJAHEDIN plural of mujahed

MULLAH scholar or teacher of theology

MUSLIM one who submits to the will of God, thus, one whose religion is Islam

NAN circle of unleavened bread, usually baked on hot stones

NASWAR tobacco-based substance, cut with other spices resembling snuff; it is held under the tongue or behind the lower lip

NEMAZ prayer

PETOU wool blanket, carried or worn by almost all mujahedin and Afghans living in the country. Usually a dull brown colour, the border is picked out with brighter colours of green, yellow, pink and blue so that the effect is rather like a stylised representation of the landscape of Afghanistan. Petous have many uses: knapsack, tent, fan, stretcher, burnoos, filter for water, saddlebag and cummerbund

QISMET part, portion, share, thus the portion of fate or destiny allotted to a person by God

QU'RUT very hard, dry, salty cheese taken by the mujahedin when travelling through the mountains

RUHANI a spiritual man (*ruh*–spirit); also a term describing some Muslim clergy

RUMI Rumi, a man of Greece or Rome and, by extension, Byzantium. The name is most often applied to the great mystical poet Jalal Uddin Balkhi Rumi, 1207–1273, who spent many years in Konya, Turkey, thereby acquiring the title Rumi

SA'ADI Persian poet, c.1215–1292

SABR KU have patience, fortitude (imperative)

SHAHID martyr, one killed in a holy war, a witness

SHISH KEBAB portions of meat skewered on a spit and roasted

SHURAVI the Soviet forces

STAMBOUL small dried melon with a pleasing fragrance, which serves as a pomander

SUFI a number of suggestions have been made to explain the origins of the word: i) the Arabic word for wool—*suf:* in the eighth Century a number of Muslim devotees wore wool, allegedly in imitation of Jesus, for which they were roundly criticised by Ibu Sirin, d. 728; ii) *safé*—a bench. Those who came to listen to the discourses of the Prophet Muhammad, if they were fortunate, sat on benches close to the Prophet; iii) *safa*—purity, thus a man of purity; iv) *sophia* (Greek)—wisdom

SURA chapter of the Qur'an

SUSAN lily

TAMAM SHOD it is completed, it has come to an end

TAQDIR destiny, fate

UMMAH the congregation of all Muslims, in some ways analogous to the concept of Christendom

YAQIN direct, intuitive knowledge: a central concept of the great philosopher and Sufi, Al Ghazali, 1058–1111

ZAHER apparent, manifest, external, thus, the outer meaning

ZELZELEH earthquake

ZENDE BASHI a greeting (literally 'may you live')

ZIKHR remembrance, a form of meditation, to have God constantly in mind and heart, a central element of Sufi ritual

ZOLM oppression

Index

ABOUT THE AUTHOR

PEREGRINE HODSON read Oriental Studies at Merton College, Oxford. After working in banking in Tokyo, he returned to England and became a barrister. He now lives in London, where he works in investment banking. Mr. Hodson is a Fellow of the Royal Asiatic Society.